HITMAKER

HIT

MAKER

The Man and His Music

TOMMY MOTTOLA

with

CAL FUSSMAN

GRAND CENTRAL
PUBLISHING

NEW YORK   BOSTON

Grand Central Publishing
Hachette Book Group
237 Park Avenue
New York, NY 10017

www.HachetteBookGroup.com

Printed in the United States of America

RRD-C

First Edition: January 2013

10 9 8 7 6 5 4 3 2 1

Grand Central Publishing is a division of Hachette Book Group, Inc. The Grand Central Publishing name and logo is a trademark of Hachette Book Group, Inc.

The Hachette Speakers Bureau provides a wide range of authors for speaking events. To find out more, go to www.hachettespeakersbureau.com or call (866) 376-6591.

The publisher is not responsible for websites (or their content) that are not owned by the publisher.

Library of Congress Cataloging-in-Publication Data

Mottola, Tommy.
Hitmaker: the man and his music / Tommy Mottola with Cal Fussman.—1st ed.
p. cm.
Includes index.
ISBN 978-0-446-58518-7
1. Mottola, Tommy.   2. Sound recording executives and producers—United States—Biography.   I. Fussman, Cal.   II. Title.
ML429.M787A3 2012
781.64092—dc23
[B]
2011047069

*For Thalia, the angel who dropped into my arms
from the sky. Your eternal love and commitment,
and my long journey to find you, has changed
my life forever. Te amo mucho por siempre.*

*For Sabrina, whose beautiful sparkle makes me believe
that dreams really do come true. When you wake in
the morning and I hear you say, "I love you, Popi,"
it's like hearing music for the first time.*

*For Matthew, whose huge smile and enthusiasm to spread
it make me stop and count my blessings twenty times a day.*

*For Sarah, my precious princess, who has taught
me more than she'll ever realize, and who I love
more than she'll ever know.*

*For Michael, who has the kindest heart and the strength
that comes with it, and who makes me proud as a
father simply to see him as a brother.*

*For Mom and Dad, who were there for me every
step of the way, who filled my days with love, music,
great food, and the most festive Christmases ever,
who made me everything I am, and who I miss every day.*

*For my dear sisters, the twins, Jean and Joan,
and Mary Ann, to whom I apologize for terrorizing
for the first five years of my life, but also thank for
giving me a complete sense of family, and for
that radio blasting out of their bedroom every day.*

Contents

Introduction

When you see the songs set at the beginning of each chapter, you'll be looking at a snapshot of the music that helped inspire and define me. Though they're not set in chronological order, these songs became the fabric and sound track of my life.

These are just *some* of the songs, melodies, and lyrics—as simple as they were sometimes—that helped me do what I did and become who I am.

By the end of this book, you will have gone through a library of music that had an overwhelming and profound influence on my life—all the way from Elvis to the iPod. It was without a doubt the most golden age of music in history, and the voices at the end of various chapters will offer other takes on what was happening during this amazing time.

I know you're curious about my involvement with Mariah and Michael and Bruce and Billy Joel and so many other great artists from this dazzling period that will never be duplicated. I'll get into all that.

Maybe you're interested in knowing what the star-making development process was like before it became releasing a song and going viral on YouTube. Or how the Latin Explosion got started. Or what it was like when Napster came along and music was ripped away from the artists and the companies

that were producing it. I felt the earthquake coming. We had many plans to restructure at the time, including trying to have Sony work in tandem with Apple at the cutting edge of the digital era, and maybe you'll be interested to know why that didn't happen. I'll get to all of that, too.

Eight billion units of CDs and cassettes were sold during my fifteen-year tenure as chairman of Sony Music. It will take some explaining to cover the strategies we used during that time to reach $65 billion in sales.

But nothing I say will have perspective unless you take a walk with me in the place where I first heard the music: the Bronx. So we'll start at the intersection of 187th Street and Arthur Avenue.

HITMAKER

The Platters

(Gonna) Rock around
ock" • Bill Haley and
His Comets

erely" • The McGuire
Sisters

erry Pink and Apple
n White" • Perez Prado

ellene" • Chuck Berry

)iddley" • Bo Diddley

Frutti" • Little Richard

h Angel (Will You Be
ne)" • The Penguins

som Prison Blues" •
Johnny Cash

d Dog" • Elvis Presley

n't Be Cruel" • Elvis
Presley

rtbreak Hotel" • Elvis
Presley

e Me Tender" • Elvis
Presley

Great Pretender" • The
Platters

emories Are Made of
is" • Dean Martin

Do Fools Fall in Love" •
nkie Lymon and the
Teenagers

ueberry Hill" • Fats
Domino

Prayer" • The Platters

alk the Line" • Johnny
Cash

ase, Please, Please" •
Brown and the Famous
Flames

he Still of the Night" •
The Five Satins

I'm Not a Juvenile
uent" • Frankie Lymon
and the Teenagers

Vhat a Night" • The Dells

Loved" • Jackie Wilson

ue Christmas" • Elvis
Presley

nook Up" • Elvis Presley

ilhouse Rock" • Elvis
Presley

Send Me" • Sam Cooke

e Up Little Susie" • The
Everly Brothers

e Bye Love" • Everly
Brothers

"Whole Lot of Shakin' Goin'
On" • Jerry Lee Lewis

"Great Balls of Fire" • Jerry
Lee Lewis

"Searchin'" • The Coasters

"Peggy Sue" • Buddy Holly

"Silhouettes" • The Rays

"Come Go With Me" • The
Dell-Vikings

"I'm Walkin'" • Fats Domino

"Rock & Roll Music" • Chuck
Berry

"That'll Be the Day" • Buddy
Holly and the Crickets

"I Wonder Why" • Dion and
the Belmonts

"Johnny B. Goode" • Chuck
Berry

"At the Hop" • Danny & the
Juniors

"Get a Job" • The Silhouettes

"Sweet Little Sixteen" •
Chuck Berry

"A Lover's Question" • Clyde
McPhatter

"Rockin' Robin" • Bobby Day

"Tears on My Pillow" •
Little Anthony and the
Imperials

"Tequila" • The Champs

"It's Only Make Believe" •
Conway Twitty

"All I Have to Do Is Dream" •
The Everly Brothers

"Twilight Time" •
The Platters

"One Night" • Elvis Presley

"You Are My Destiny" • Paul
Anka

"Yakety Yak" • The Coasters

"Splish Splash" • Bobby
Darin

"Fever" • Peggy Lee

"Little Star" • The Elegants

"Lonely Teardrops" • Jackie
Wilson

"Good Golly Miss Molly" •
Little Richard

"16 Candles" • The Crests

"One Summer Night" • The
Danleers

"Stagger Lee" • Lloyd Price

"Smoke Gets in Your Eyes" •

Darin

"Maybe Baby" • Buddy Holly
and the Crickets

"Witchcraft" • Frank Sinatra

"Wear My Ring around Your
Neck" • Elvis Presley

"Put Your Head on My
Shoulder" • Paul Anka

"It's Just a Matter of Time" •
Brook Benton

"What'd I Say" • Ray Charles

"Charlie Brown" • The
Coasters

"Poison Ivy" • The Coasters

"Dream Lover" • Bobby Darin

"A Teenager in Love" • Dion
and the Belmonts

"There Goes My Baby" • The
Drifters

"Sorry (I Ran All the Way
Home)" • The Impalas

"Personality" • Lloyd Price

"Don't You Know?" • Della
Reese

"Since I Don't Have You" •
The Skyliners

"Lavender Blue" • Sammy
Turner

"What a Diff'rence a Day
Makes!" • Dinah Washington

"I'm Sorry" • Brenda Lee

"It's Now or Never" • Elvis
Presley

"The Twist" • Chubby
Checker

"Only the Lonely (Know the
Way I Feel)" • Roy Orbison

"Where or When" • Dion and
the Belmonts

"Walk—Don't Run" • The
Ventures

"Chain Gang" • Sam Cooke

"Let It Be Me" • The Everly
Brothers

"Beyond the Sea" • Bobby
Darin

"Please Help Me, I'm
Falling" • Hank Locklin

"Harbor Lights" • The
Platters

"Let the Little Girl Dance" •
Billy Bland

"Georgia on My Mind" • Ray
Charles

Wilson

"Money (That's What I
Want)" • Barrett Strong

"Short Fat Fannie" • Larry
Williams

"So Fine" • The Fiestas

"Will You Love Me
Tomorrow" • The Shirelles

"Save the Last Dance for
Me" • The Drifters

"Shop Around" • The
Miracles

"At Last" • Etta James

"He Will Break Your Heart" •
Jerry Butler

"Stay" • Maurice Williams
& the Zodiacs

"Finger Poppin' Time" • Hank
Ballard and the Midnighters

"This Magic Moment" • The
Drifters

"Are You Lonesome
Tonight" • Elvis Presley

"A Fool in Love" • Lke and
Tina Turner

"Angel Baby" • Rosie and the
Originals

"Tonight's the Night" • The
Shirelles

"Bye Bye Baby" • Mary Wells

"Lonely Teenager" • Dion

"Alley Oop" • The Hollywood
Argyles

"Stand by Me" • Ben E. King

"Crazy" • Patsy Cline

"The Wanderer" • Dion

"Runaround Sue" • Dion

"Crying" • Roy Orbison

"Hit the Road Jack" • Ray
Charles

"Quarter to Three" • Gary
U. S. Bonds

"Running Scared" • Roy
Orbison

"Please Mr. Postman" • The
Marvelettes

"Can't Help Falling in Love" •
Elvis Presley

"Blue Moon" • The Marcels

"Duke of Earl" • Gene
Chandler

"Mother-in-Law" • Ernie
K-Doe

1

The 'Hood

The beauty of going to Arthur Avenue is that it always opens its arms and takes you back even if you've never been there before.

There are no longer teenagers singing doo-wop on the corners, and there are now flatscreen TVs in all the restaurants and bars. But outside of that, Arthur Avenue doesn't look much different than it did when I was a kid.

The butcher. The fish market. The bakery. The pasta store. The fruit stands at the huge indoor market. The old-school espresso machine at DeLillo's pastry shop. There aren't many other places in America where you can find lettering over a restaurant's doorway that says Five Generations. Hey, you want some clams? We can have them fresh, right on the street, they're over there on ice in front of Cosenza's. Let's get a dozen. Here, try it with a little cocktail sauce with horse-radish, a touch of vinegar, a squeeze of lemon, and a drop of Tabasco. What did I tell you? The best!

You get your mozzarella fresh out of the water at Casa Della Mozzarella. And your onion bread at Madonia Brothers—but remember, they only make it on weekends. Look, there's Full Moon Pizzeria. It was the first stop to feel better after every funeral when I was a kid. In this neighborhood, there's a pizzeria on almost every block. But each one does it a little differently, which gives you its own particular reason to come through the door. It's like music.

Arthur Avenue was one of my first tastemakers. It taught me what is good.

We all went to church at Our Lady of Mount Carmel. The people who got married there when I was a kid didn't get divorced.

My parents were married for seventy years. It's important that you know that because family framed my youth. Music has taken me around the world, and I was fortunate enough to meet and work with some of the biggest stars and most influential people in business. But my successes were accompanied by personal mistakes—some very public. In so many ways, I've spent much of my life trying to become the man that my father was.

My father, Thomas Mottola Sr., was a quiet man whose sole mission in life was to take care of his family. I couldn't imagine having a better dad. It was no secret what drove his complete devotion to his children, and to me in particular. My father never knew *his* father. The only image he had was a framed photo of his dad in an Italian army uniform. I don't think he ever found out how his father died. My father was born on Bleecker Street in Manhattan, as the nation was struggling through some hard financial times. His brother

and a sister were taken in by a kind woman who owned a farm in the Bronx and could better care for them. That was how it was done back then.

As a teenager, my father went to Roosevelt High School on Fordham Road in the Bronx at night so that he could work during the day downtown as a runner for a customs brokerage firm. He ran entry forms to the Customs House for approval, enabling the importers' goods to enter the country. After scraping together $750, he left the company he was working for and started his own business. It was called Atlas Shipping. His office was the definition of paperwork and drudgery. Every case of liquor brought in by Seagram's and every crate of furnishings made in India had to be meticulously documented. While it didn't elicit passion, this work took care of his family, and very well. I watched my father go off every morning like clockwork, and I often went with my mother to the train station in the evening to pick him up. He steadily moved us up from a small apartment only a few blocks from Arthur Avenue. First, to a home connected side by side with another only a few miles away on Pelham Parkway. And then, eight years later, to a comfortable suburban house about thirty minutes north in New Rochelle that might have been *his* father's idea of the American Dream.

My father wasted little time when it came to starting a family. He met my mother—Lena Bonetti, whom everyone knew as Peggy—when she was fifteen in the Fordham neighborhood of the Bronx. My mother had wanted to be a singer. But her father was very strict and traditional. He did not believe it respectful for a young woman to go into show business. When she told him of her career aspirations, he made his point by smacking her across the face.

I remember how my mother loved to sing, but she did so only in church as a child, or in our home in the company of

family and friends. My father played the piano and the ukulele, and my uncles joined in on the guitar. On weekends, the
family room in my house was filled with food, guests, food,
music, food, laughter, and more food. The foundation of my
parents' marriage couldn't have been more solid or clear.
They had a common ancestry—her family came from Naples
and Bari, and his came from Naples and Avellino. They had
their church and religious traditions. They shared an unrelenting devotion to their kids. And underneath all that and
the personal chemistry, Thomas and Peggy Mottola were connected by a love of family meals and music.

My parents had three daughters long before I was born:
Jean and Joan, the twins; and Mary Ann. But they'd always
wanted a boy, so my arrival made me the Christ child. The
godfather they chose for me bore little resemblance to Marlon Brando or Al Pacino. His name was Victor Campione and,
early on in his life, he'd worked for the FBI. So much for ste-
reotypes.

After he left law enforcement, my godfather decided to go
into local politics, and he eventually evolved into the Democratic district leader of the Bronx. Uncle Vic was one of those
guys who wielded tremendous power behind the scenes in the
age of Tammany Hall, a kingmaker, who helped people like Abe
Beame get elected mayor of New York City. He was a stern and
direct man, and you paid attention to his every word. All I had
to do was look at Uncle Vic to know that it was my duty in life to
become a prominent professional and make my parents proud.

My three older sisters had grown and moved out of the
house by the time I was five. That gave me 1,000 percent of
my parents' time. My mother took me to school. She picked
me up from school. She worked with me on my homework.
She rubbed me down with alcohol when I had a fever. She was

also the disciplinarian. She had to be. I could do no wrong in my father's eyes. Once, when I was very young, maybe three or four years old, I was in the basement playing with a hammer and hit one of my older sisters in the head. When she complained, my father asked: "Who left the hammer out?"

I was bursting with a boundless energy that today would probably be diagnosed as ADD. It sure came in handy much later on when I became chairman of Sony Music, because that kind of energy and personality was perfectly suited to the constantly shifting demands of the job. But it got me into some trouble when I was young, even though I wasn't a bad kid, because I was incredibly restless and always sticking my nose into something new. My oldest friend, Ronny Parlato, remembers a day when I turned the ignition key that had been left in a bulldozer and drove it around the empty lot behind my home on Pelham Parkway. He swears I was only three years old at the time. My endless supply of energy often took me where I wasn't supposed to be, and I rarely met a wall that I didn't want to smash through.

The Christian Brothers of Ireland at Iona Grammar School in New Rochelle had ways of dealing with kids who deviated from their rigid expectations. The brothers used to walk around with cat's-paw straps under the sleeves of their habits and whack you if you got out of line. Once, I stuck my tongue out at the principal and another kid snitched. The principal took me into his office and beat the crap out of me. That night, when I was getting into the bathtub, my mother noticed bruises and welts on my behind. She immediately told my father. My father was the kindest and sweetest man you could imagine. But you'd never want to threaten or harm his children because that sweet man would turn ferocious in a way that you didn't want to imagine. My father didn't say a

word—he just put on his coat, left the house, and went directly to see the principal. I was never told what was said or what transpired. But I can tell you that the Christian Brothers of Ireland never touched me again.

C'mon, let's go to Dominick's and get a quick bite to eat.

Oh, boy, we're only on page 6 and I'm already in trouble. I just know the hard time I'm going to get from my friends at Roberto's and a few other restaurants for not choosing their place. Listen, before you die you've got to go to Roberto's for the cavatelli with sausage and broccoli rabe sautéed in garlic and oil because it's to die for. But that's another meal for another day.

By the way, there are no menus at Dominick's. Either you tell the waiter what you want and you get it, or he tells you what you want and you get it. There are long tables. Everyone sits together. If there's one place you want to eat in your life with your best friend, it's Dominick's.

And right now I want to talk about my oldest and dearest friend. My connection with Ronny Parlato will explain a few things that may surprise you. For instance, you probably didn't know that I once converted to Judaism. It's a long story, and we'll get there in time. But it all starts with Ronny and the neighborhood I grew up in.

The Pelham Parkway neighborhood where I first started to hang around with Ronny was a mixture of Italian and Jewish families, and Ronny was a mixture himself. His mother was Jewish and his father was Italian.

My mother and Ronny's mother, Libby, were like sisters. No, they were *closer* than sisters—almost joined together at the hip. As soon as we moved from the Bronx to New Rochelle,

Ronny's mother and father moved from the Bronx to New Rochelle. Every day Peggy and Libby would go out together.

When Ronny celebrated Chanukah there was always a present for me as we lit the candles of the menorah. My parents sent me to an all-Jewish camp for a couple of summers that included Friday night services. So I knew what it was like to put on a yarmulke, light candles, follow the prayers in Hebrew, and drink Manischewitz. I thought it was fun to say *baruch*. I always liked the *khhhhhhhh* sound.

Likewise, there was always a present under my family's Christmas tree for Ronny. Every year my mother would prepare almost thirty different seafood dishes to celebrate the holiday, and over the years Ronny probably tasted every one of them. I can't remember a better time than my childhood Christmases. But from early on I was comfortable at any holiday. Religion seemed and felt seamless to me. The only walls I didn't have to smash through in life were religious and cultural walls. They didn't exist for me. That was a gift from the streets of the Bronx.

I soon was putting a towel around my shoulders in the school bathroom so it would look like a cape when I tried to mimic the dance moves of James Brown singing "Please, Please, Please." When I was about fourteen my parents allowed me on many occasions to take the train to Harlem with my friends to watch Stevie Wonder, Wilson Pickett, and Joe Tex sing at the Apollo Theater. When I met Gloria and Emilio Estefan nearly twenty-five years later, they were immediately like family because their Cuban culture made me feel like I was back in the Bronx. This openness to all cultures became a real strength as I became the head of a multinational corporation, and it also was reflected in my personal life. My first wife was Jewish; my second was part Irish, part black, and part

Venezuelan; and the beautiful woman I now wake up to every morning, Thalia, was born and raised in Mexico City. So, years later, when Michael Jackson staged a press conference to call me a racist and a devil, it had nothing to do with race, heaven, or hell. It had to do with an artist who was starting to melt down because he couldn't adjust to his shrinking album sales. Michael was lashing out at authority and simply looking for a way to get out of his contract with Sony.

The attack was sad and pathetic. As the head of the company, I remained above the fray and most certainly did not comment on it. Now that Michael has passed there's little benefit to me in bringing the incident back up. But if you know me, you know that I'm not the kind of guy to avoid it. This is the story of my life, and it's important to get it straight for the record. So I'll tell you what really happened. You just have to be patient. It'll be a little while before we get there.

You want some wine?

One of the things that writing a book about your life forces you to do is to think back on the earliest moments that helped turn you into what you have become.

For me, timing and growing up in the Bronx were key elements. On the day I was born I had fifteen-year-old twin sisters and a thirteen-year-old sister. From the first day I woke up in the tiny apartment that was our home, my ears were listening to pop hits blasting from the radio in their room. As soon as I could walk, I would stop in my tracks when I heard different sounds that attracted me—and my mother was keenly aware of this. She'd be holding me by the hand as we walked to Alexander's department store on the Grand Concourse and Fordham Road when I'd just stop, stand still, and listen to

the sound of music coming out of the many storefronts up and down the street. When that happened, she didn't impatiently tug me along. She'd stop and even sing the melody to me.

There were so many diverse sounds booming out of those stores—doo-wop, salsa, rock, Sinatra—or if you were shopping late on a Thursday night, you might even hear Tito Puente's band playing on the Concourse. Back in my home I would hear my mother sing and my sisters harmonize every single day, and on weekends I would watch my father on ukulele and my uncle Ray on guitar. Music was around me from morning till night. From the time I was two years old I would climb on the stool and bang on the keys of our family's piano.

But there *was* one single defining moment that ran through me like a bolt of electricity when I was eight years old: that was the first time I heard "Don't Be Cruel" blasting through my sisters' AM radio. The beat and the rhythm of that song branded me forever and was everything that motivated and inspired me to become what I became. Elvis Presley, the King.

I pestered my mother relentlessly to take me to the record store on Fordham Road, and I reached into the bin with two hands for my very first album. That first album was Elvis's first album. I loved everything about it. I loved the photo of Elvis in action on the cover with his mouth wide open, his eyes closed, and the guitar in his hands. *Elvis* was spelled in pink vertically down the left side of the album and *Presley* came horizontally across the bottom in green. I loved looking at the RCA label in the upper right-hand corner with the dog listening to the gramophone. I loved taking off the plastic shrink-wrap. I loved smelling the vinyl as I slipped the album out of its thin paper sleeve. And I loved placing the record on the turntable, setting the hi-fi to 33 1/3, picking up the arm, and lowering the needle into the groove. In my mind and in my ears back

then, the clicks and pops on that vinyl actually enhanced the sound of the music.

I wasn't really conscious of the sexuality in Elvis's gyrations at first, or the controversy that his dance movements caused. There was no negativity toward Elvis in my home. Both my parents thought he was phenomenal. I was completely unaware that church leaders were writing to J. Edgar Hoover to warn the FBI that Elvis was a threat to morality and a danger to national security. Or that whites in the segregated South who didn't like what they called the "race music" coming out of Elvis's mouth were smashing his records to pieces in public. To me, at eight years old, it was simply about just how good music could make you feel.

I'd come home from Catholic school and change out of my uniform into black chinos and a leather jacket, take my sister's eyebrow pencil and draw sideburns over my temples, pump up my pompadour, and put on sunglasses to walk around the block. But there was one thing that I could never figure out. How did Elvis get that bluish tint in his black hair? To this day it's still a mystery to me.

There were only three major television networks—CBS, ABC, and NBC—at the time. That limited the opportunities we had to see Elvis and made each one even more special. Television shows were not just television shows when Elvis appeared. They were events that we waited for all week. Sixty million people crowded around black-and-white television sets with rabbit-ear antennae to watch Elvis on *The Ed Sullivan Show* in 1956. That's three times the number of people who now watch *American Idol*—and it came at a time when the country had roughly half the population it does now.

There was a lesson that Elvis ingrained in me from the very start, even though I didn't understand it as a lesson at

the time. I saw it as a succession of hits. "Heartbreak Hotel." "Blue Suede Shoes." "Hound Dog." "Don't Be Cruel." "Love Me Tender." All in the same year. Bam. Bam. Bam. Bam. Bam. Years later, when I was running Sony, I would seek to duplicate that whenever I could. Introducing that same strategy actually created friction between me and Mariah Carey, but that's for a few pages down the road.

It may seem odd that I started to play the trumpet around the time that Elvis exploded across America. But when you hear why, it'll make sense. My sister Mary Ann married a guy named Joe Valentino, who sort of became a mentor for me at that time. Sometimes I'd stay with Mary Ann and Joe on weekends. I tried to emulate my brother-in-law in many ways. He played the trumpet and told me about Harry James, so it seemed like the thing to do. Before I had a chance to think about playing the guitar, there was a trumpet against my lips. I got good at it, so I got stuck with it. I became first trumpeter in the school orchestra, played all the solos, and was given a music scholarship to Iona Grammar School after attracting the attention of the principal, who never stopped kissing my ass after my father paid him a visit and who, as it turns out, was a trumpet player himself.

The trumpet came easy to me even though I eventually considered it torture. I began to study *Arban's Complete Conservatory Method For Trumpet*, which has been in print since 1864 and, for a kid, is the definition of demanding. I had to learn all the notes and the signatures as well as music theory. It put me that far ahead of the game musically, even as I began to grow and realize that trumpet players didn't get the girls. Singers, guitar players, and actors got the girls. And if you could do all three like Elvis...

The concept of *cool* got closer still when Dion and the

Belmonts came out with "I Wonder Why" and "Teenager in Love." The band's name made a doo-wop monument out of Belmont Avenue in the Bronx. All our friends worshipped Dion and seemed to know him or somebody attached to the group. As Bruce Springsteen once said, Dion was definitely the link between Frank Sinatra and rock 'n' roll. Elvis was everybody's. But Dion was *ours*.

I continued to play the trumpet during grammar school. But I began running home every afternoon to watch Dick Clark and *American Bandstand*. I would watch that show intensely. The beauty of *American Bandstand* was that Dick Clark programmed it as if it were a radio station. He counted down the top hits like a DJ—only it was on television. The show was based in Philly. But it featured a huge cardboard cutout map of America that the camera zoomed in on to show cities and promote the call letters of television affiliates. Dick might read a letter from a kid in Akron and tell you she listened to WAKR. It was interactive TV long before the word *interactive* ever became famous, and it made every teenager who watched feel connected to something larger. When Buddy Holly sang, you knew you were getting a piece of Lubbock, Texas, and when Smokey Robinson came on, you understood what was going on in Detroit.

I can remember the stars that I saw on that show: the Big Bopper using a phone as a prop onstage to perform "Chantilly Lace." Jerry Lee Lewis banging the keys to "Great Balls of Fire." Chubby Checker doing "The Twist." Fats Domino, Frankie Lymon and the Teenagers, Chuck Berry, Sam Cooke, Bobby Darin, Jackie Wilson, the Temptations, the Marcels, the Duprees, the Coasters, the Drifters, the Shirelles (*sha-la-la la-la la-la*), and, of course, James Brown and the Fabulous Flames.

That's just a short list off the top of my head, and it doesn't nearly convey the world that show opened for me.

There were some really great weekly shows, too, like *Shindig*. But *American Bandstand* was so ahead of its time. I'd study the fashions of the teenage dancers. I knew every kid who was dancing off against every other kid. It was almost a model for shows like *Dancing with the Stars*. The music on *American Bandstand* not only opened a door in my mind, it evoked my dreams and pointed me toward where I wanted to go. And Motown, the music that was about to change the world, was not even in full bloom yet. Sometimes after the show ended I'd head out with my mother to pick my father up from work at the train station. Seeing him come home the way he did, same time, every day, day after day, made me start to question whether 1 ever wanted to follow him into his business. One thing was for sure: I no longer wanted to play the trumpet in the school orchestra.

After I left elementary school my brother in-law started taking guitar lessons, and, following his lead, I picked one up when I was about eleven.

I started with a cheap one—I think it was a Harmony—that you could get at Sears for about thirty bucks. As I began to get good, I asked my parents for Fenders—the solid-body electric guitars that were becoming the rage. I got a Telecaster, a Stratocaster, and then a Jazzmaster. I became obsessed. I knew everything about these guitars. Fender guitars were geared toward mass production, and I'd known how to take them apart and put them back together. But I wish I'd known enough to keep them, because the same $300 Fender Stratocaster and Telecaster that I was messing around with are each worth about $50,000 today.

I started playing in two or three different garage bands at other kids' houses. And as I began to meet more experienced musicians, word spread that I was pretty good. Out of the blue I got a call from somebody asking if I'd like to audition for the Exotics.

The Exotics! Oh, my God! The Exotics! The hottest local band in New Rochelle. They played covers of the latest hits at school dances and at country clubs over the summer. You could not be a teenager in New Rochelle in the early sixties without knowing about the Exotics. When one of the members left the group, the audition fell in my lap.

I walked in nervous, anxious, cocky, and assured—if you could be all that at once. I was at least four years younger than the other guys in the band. But as I started playing along with them, I noticed them all looking at each other, as if to say, *Hey, check this guy out.*

After we finished playing, the leader said straight up: "Do you want to join the group?"

"Yeah," I said.

"You're in."

I was so excited I ran home to tell my parents. They were excited, too. They had no idea that I was going to age four years overnight. At least it seemed that way to them.

My first stop with the Exotics was the tailor, to be outfitted for my new group jacket. If you were an Exotic, you had to look like an Exotic. Even though the other band members were only eighteen, they had the air of hardened professionals and they were very particular about their look: "Fit him like this..." I got collarless sport jackets in three different colors, which came down over white shirts, a skinny tie, tight black pants, and pointy Flagg Bros. shoes. I most remember the royal blue jacket. Once I put that jacket on, I felt official.

The Exotics began treating me as if they were my older brothers, but they were not the older brothers that my parents wanted for me. They were street kids living in apartments on the other side of the tracks. When they showed up at my suburban house to pick me up, the disparity was clear to my parents. These guys were mesmerized by the fact that I actually lived in a nice house.

It wasn't any particular band member that bothered my parents. It was the energy around all of them. My parents just didn't like where they were taking me. I had been raised to assume my father's business, or to become a doctor, or a lawyer. In their eyes, the Exotics seemed to be pulling me back toward everything on the other side of the tracks they had worked so hard to cross.

The guys in the Exotics had no curfew. Their parents let them do whatever they wanted. *You're playing music, that's great. So go make some money!* Soon I was making two hundred bucks for a Friday night gig. Hanging out with these guys, whether we were playing music or not, was fun and exciting for me. When my parents would go out I'd sneak off in my father's Caddy and drive it down to the College Diner to hang out with my friends from New Rochelle High. They were so much cooler than the guys I went to school with at Iona Prep. Also when my parents were out, I'd bring my girlfriend home and fumble around with her on the living room couch. Funny, the stuff that you remember. Just when you were trying to get from first base to second or, if you were really, really lucky, to third, you were always sliding off that couch because it had a plastic slipcover, and it would blow the mood.

Before long, I started to ask my parents to let me out of rigorous Iona Prep so that I could hang with all of my new friends at New Rochelle High. The Exotics' rehearsals and

gigs became more and more frequent and my arrivals at home later and later into the night. My parents did set a curfew, and when I started to break it they began to worry that I was headed into a world of danger, drugs, or whatever and wherever their imaginations took them. Looking back now, I certainly understand their concerns. I was only fourteen years old.

They tried to reel me back in, but I fought them. Over about a year, the conflict built to a crescendo that peaked at a high school gig.

We were performing our best show ever that night. As I was playing and singing, I could see the impact on the faces of some of the kids who were dancing. A few of the girls' heads were tucked on their boyfriends' shoulders, but their eyes were looking up at me. It was an unbelievable feeling. It reminded me of watching Elvis on TV when the girls were looking up at him—which, of course, like any teenage boy at that time, was all I wanted in life.

My parents showed up early to pick me up that night and watched this magnetism unfold from the side of the stage. When I first noticed them, I was happy. I thought they finally understood where I was at, and where I wanted to take my life. The performance ended, and a few girls started coming over to me on the bandstand. They wanted to know my name and were looking for a way to give me their phone numbers. My mother pushed straight through them.

"Get in the car!" she yelled.

"What do you mean?" I asked.

"Now!"

"But I want to hang around for a little while!"

"That's it, Tommy. Let's *go*!"

My mother practically dragged me out of the place by my royal blue jacket in front of all these girls and the other band

members. I couldn't have been more stunned and embarrassed. She marched me straight into the backseat of the car, while my father sat behind the wheel in silence. She got in the front, slammed the door, turned around, and said: "That's it. It's over. You're not going to hang out with those bums anymore. You're not going to play the guitar anymore."

My father drove us home. When I woke up the next morning, I couldn't believe it. All of my guitars were gone.

The loss of my guitars led to my first deal. Looking back, it was one of the hardest deals I ever made. You could even say that every deal that came after it was easier because of it.

I went through every closet in the house, searched up in the attic and down in the basement. But I couldn't find those guitars.

Over and over I asked my parents when I could get them back.

The only answer I got was: "We'll see."

Then one day toward the end of summer the house became quiet—conspicuously quiet. Almost everybody had left, and I was alone with my father.

"I'd like to talk to you," he said.

He was solemn and his eyes were teary. I knew something was about to happen. Whatever it was, it was not going to be easy for him.

We went to the living room. He took his special chair, the large recliner. I sat on the couch. There was no reclining for him. And there was no slipping on the plastic for me.

My father started to speak. He was very firm, but gentle and calm. I don't remember his exact words. But he started by saying something to the effect of: *This is going to hurt me more*

than it's going to hurt you. And he knew it was going to hurt me plenty.

You know how in a movie you see a scene from a character's point of view, and then something happens so that the character can still see everything around him but suddenly the sound is gone. That's just the way it felt—like the blood was rushing out of me.

My father and mother had enrolled me at a military boarding school in New Jersey.

When the sound came back I was shouting, "No, no, no! I'm not gonna go!"

But my father was prepared. It was sort of like an intervention. Everything had been arranged.

Tell him.

Pack him up.

Then drive him to the institution.

I ran up to my room. I was infuriated. No, I was beyond infuriated. I was apoplectic. That's the word. Apoplectic! A lot of that day is blocked out of my memory, but I do recall phoning my sister Mary Ann and her husband, Joe, for help. There was no getting out of it. They were behind my mother and father.

"It's gonna give you some boundaries," Joe said, "and the academics are really going to help you."

Looking back now, I can understand how my parents were thinking. I was fourteen going on twenty, hanging out on the wrong side of the tracks with greasers who were a lot older than me and had no curfew. All of my parents' giant aspirations for me were dissolving right before their eyes. I seemed to be going headstrong in the other direction, even trying to squirm out of Iona Prep, my private school, and into nearby New Rochelle High because that was where my friends went.

In their eyes, I was on the road to becoming some kind of show business bum.

So they'd asked around and been assured that the discipline at Admiral Farragut Academy would set me back on the right course. It wasn't long before I was being guided into the backseat of my dad's Cadillac. The very same Caddy that my friends and I used to fill with laughter on our way to the College Diner now felt like a hearse.

My dad drove to Toms River in New Jersey, and through the gates of what looked like a miniature Annapolis. If you ever dreamed of becoming an astronaut and going to the moon like Alan Shepard, this was a great place to be. But for a guy like me, Farragut Academy was Mars with prison gates.

From the moment I stepped on campus I was stripped of everything I cared about. With words, I'll never be able to make you feel in your belly what I felt in mine the moment I stepped into the campus barbershop with some of the other newcomers. The best I can do is a scene from the movie *Saturday Night Fever*. Remember when John Travolta is eating dinner with his family, and his father is angry and takes a swing at him from across the table. Travolta says something like: "Don't hit my haih!" Like, you can hit me in the face, but *don't touch my hair*. Your hair was your signature—more than that, it was everything that made you *you*. Which was probably why it was the first thing Farragut Academy wanted to take away. I heard the buzz, looked down, and saw the black strands that I had Brylcreemed to perfection for twenty minutes at a time every single day lying in thick clumps on the floor. It felt like my heart and soul had been cut out of me all at once.

Every turn I took on that campus was a reminder of something else lost. Meeting my three new bunkmates let me know just how far away I was from my buddies and my girlfriend.

And just when I thought things couldn't possibly get worse, they did. I remember going to the dining hall for the first time. My mother's home-cooked meals were replaced by some sort of bread, with some sort of fried ham and cream on top that the cadets called SOS—shit on a shingle. As an underclassman, you couldn't even eat until you were told. We'd have to sit in the cafeteria with our arms crossed—shoulder to the elbow straight out, then arms folded in front of the chest, one overlapping the other. The arms were supposed to be six inches apart to make it more difficult. You didn't get to eat until it hurt. Then when you did it was shit on a shingle.

Late nights of music were replaced by nine o'clock curfew. And at five in the morning, the damn bugle was outside the door—

Duh, duh, teh-deh-duh

Duh, duh, teh-deh-duh . . .

Those notes ripped us out of bed, a bed that had to be made so crisply that a tossed quarter would bounce off it, and if the quarter didn't, the inspecting officer would strip the bed, throw it on the floor, and have you make it up in front of him until it was perfect.

If the usual rituals of military school weren't maddening enough, there was one upperclassman from Staten Island who delighted in constantly looking for new ways to make my life miserable.

Chest out!

Stomach in!

No matter how rigid I was standing at brace position, the guy would always have a frown or a comment. The worst part was I always seemed to give him an opening. In those first few weeks, I could never figure out how to spit-shine my shoes to a high gloss.

Get back and shine those shoes!

Forget fun and fries after school at the diner. Now, there were hours of marching drills.

I had only a few fleeting moments of comfort at Farragut Academy. There was a music class where I learned to play the upright bass. There was the sight of my name on envelopes in the handwriting of my girlfriend—and the reading and rereading of the aching love letters inside. And there was the sound of seagulls coming through the little transistor radio hidden under my pillow at night, telling me the Tymes were about to sing "So Much in Love," one of the great love songs of all time—but more than that, those seagulls meant freedom. No matter where on earth you were, that song could magically put you and your sweetheart barefoot on the beach. As the last notes faded away there'd be tears in my eyes—and cold reality in front of me. I was miles from my girlfriend, and marching drills were only a few hours away.

After only a month at Farragut, I couldn't take it anymore. "I'm getting out of here," I told another student. "You wanna come with me?" He said he was in. It wasn't like the campus was barbed-wired, but the escape took on big-time proportions. It felt a little like *The Shawshank Redemption*. We left with the lights out. But the other guy got scared along the way and turned back. "See you later, man," I said, and just kept running. I didn't stop for miles until I was in town.

I went to the Greyhound Station and got on a bus to New York City, then I called Mary Ann and took a train to Westchester. She and Joe picked me up, spent hours convincing me to return, then drove me to the academy in the middle of the night. I was back by six in the morning. I don't remember being caught or getting in any trouble. Didn't matter, when the bugle sounded that morning the upperclassman from

Staten Island woke up smiling with the thought that the sun had come up shining on another day to bust my balls.

Some of the more experienced guys taught me the secret to making my shoes shine like they were patent leather, so after a while the upperclassman could no longer complain about that. Didn't matter. When he didn't have a reason to torment me, he invented one.

One day he ordered all the underclassmen at my cafeteria table to cross their arms six inches apart. After a while, he said: "Everybody put his arms down except Mottola."

I kept my arms up for about five more minutes and then one of them got tired and sagged just a little. The son of a bitch took a spoon and smashed it into my elbow—right into my funny bone. The force went through me like a shock and I totally snapped. I leaped out of my seat, got behind him, grabbed him by the throat, and pulled him back so hard that his chair flipped out from under him and over as he went down. I jumped on him and whaled away, just beat the shit out of him until the other cadets stepped in and pulled me off.

I'll bet nobody in the history of Farragut Academy was ever so happy to do hours of extra marching drills. My punishment was totally worth it. That guy never stopped hating and resenting me. But he never bothered me again.

It was time to get the hell out of there. I escaped again at the beginning of December. I got to Mary Ann's house and my parents came over.

"I don't care what you do," I told them. "I'm not going back. I will *not* go back there."

That was how I learned to make a deal. Basically, I just said no. If you can say no, you control the negotiation.

Okay, my parents said, we'll let you come home. But you

have to finish high school at Iona Prep. No more talk about going to New Rochelle High.

Oh, man, I felt like I had just parted the waters. "Fine," I said, "just take me back home." I didn't get everything I wanted, but it was a good deal. It taught me that both parties have to walk away feeling like they got something.

I came home to another great Christmas. Not long after that my parents gave me my guitars back.

VOICES

RONNY PARLATO

Longtime friend and builder

There I was, five years old, maybe five and a half. And Tommy is three, maybe three and a half. And he told me to climb over the fence because he was going to show me how to start up that bulldozer.

We went over there, and he knew where the key was and everything. He started it up and began to drive. I got so scared, I jumped off and ran home. That was the start of our relationship—the younger guy being in charge of the older guy.

Tommy knows how to draw people in. He knows whom to hire. He knows how to delegate what he wants them to do. And that was his masterful dynamic at Sony that turned a company that was purchased for $2 billion into a company that at one point was worth $14 billion.

JOE PESCI

In the case of Tommy, and even somebody like myself, growing up in the neighborhood you get a great street sense and you learn how to manipulate. You know how to talk to people. And you know where people are coming from when they talk to you. You know what's on the guy's mind

right away. You know where to go, how to approach them, things like that.

Tommy knows how to treat people really well. I mean, he moved into a whole area of Spanish-speaking people. How do you account for that? You have to be some kind of smooth talker and operator to get in there.

"...ertips, Part 2" • *Little Stevie Wonder*

"...oyfriend's Back" • *The Angels*

"...k Like a Man" • *The 4 Seasons*

"...ay Will Come" • *Ruby ...nd the Romantics*

"...Louie" • *The Kingsmen*

"...y Baby" • *The Ronettes*

"...uby Baby" • *Dion*

"...oo Ron Ron (When He ...ed Me Home)" • *The Crystals*

"...h Street" • *The Orlons*

"...You're) Devil in ...guise" • *Elvis Presley*

"...I Fell For You" • *Lenny Welch*

"...Wave" • *Martha and the Vandellas*

"...aby" • *Garnet Mimms ...nd the Enchanters*

"...t's All Right" • *The Impressions*

"...olish Little Girl" • *The Shirelles*

"...Him" • *The Exciters*

"...usted" • *Ray Charles*

"...mphis" • *Lonnie Mack*

"...oy Workout" • *Jackie Wilson*

"...One Fine Day" • *The Chiffons*

"...na the Prima Donna" • *Dion*

"...nderful! Wonderful!" • *The Tymes*

"...of Fire" • *Johnny Cash*

"...ase Please Me" • *The Beatles*

"...nt to Hold Your Hand" • *The Beatles*

"...My Room" • *The Beach Boys*

"...e Bayou" • *Roy Orbison*

"...in America" • *Jay & the Americans*

"...u Need Me" • *Solomon Burke*

"...he Price" • *Solomon Burke*

"...ristmas (Baby, Please ...me Home)" • *Darlene*

Gonna Marry • *Darlene Love*

"She Loves You" • *The Beatles*

"Pretty Woman" • *Roy Orbison*

"I Get Around" • *The Beach Boys*

"Everybody Loves Somebody" • *Dean Martin*

"My Guy" • *Mary Wells*

"Where Did Our Love Go" • *The Supremes*

"People" • *Barbra Streisand*

"A Hard Day's Night" • *The Beatles*

"Do Wah Diddy Diddy" • *Manfred Mann*

"Dancing in the Street" • *Martha and the Vandellas*

"Under the Boardwalk" • *The Drifters*

"Chapel of Love" • *The Dixie Cups*

"Suspicion" • *Terry Stafford*

"Glad All Over" • *The Dave Clark Five*

"Rag Doll" • *The 4 Seasons*

"Dawn (Go Away)" • *The 4 Seasons*

"Come a Little Bit Closer" • *Jay & the Americans*

"Baby Love" • *The Supremes*

"Let It Be Me" • *Betty Everett and Jerry Butler*

"Walk On By" • *Dionne Warwick*

"The House of the Rising Sun" • *The Animals*

"The Shoop Shoop Song (It's in His Kiss)" • *Betty Everett*

"Bits and Pieces" • *The Dave Clark Five*

"Can't Buy Me Love" • *The Beatles*

"Remember (Walking in the Sand)" • *The Shangri-Las*

"Keep On Pushing" • *The Impressions*

"Baby, I Need Your Loving" • *The Four Tops*

"Leader of the Pack" • *The Shangri-Las*

"The Way You Do the Thing You Do" • *The...*

Dionne Warwick

"It's Over" • *Roy Orbison*

"Ronnie" • *The 4 Seasons*

"I'm So Proud" • *The Impressions*

"Money" • *The Kingsmen*

"Cotton Candy" • *Al Hirt*

"I Saw Her Standing There" • *The Beatles*

"Needles and Pins" • *The Searchers*

"Fun, Fun, Fun" • *The Beach Boys*

"No Particular Place to Go" • *Chuck Berry*

"You're a Wonderful One" • *Marvin Gaye*

"Goin' Out of My Head" • *Little Anthony and the Imperials*

"I Only Want to Be With You" • *Dusty Springfield*

"Come See About Me" • *The Supremes*

I Walk the Line • *Johnny Cash*

"Wooly Bully" • *Sam the Sham & the Pharaohs*

"I Can't Help Myself" • *The Four Tops*

"(I Can't Get No) Satisfaction" • *The Rolling Stones*

"You've Lost That Lovin' Feelin'" • *The Righteous Brothers*

"Help!" • *The Beatles*

"Crying in the Chapel" • *Elvis Presley*

"My Girl" • *The Temptations*

"Help Me, Rhonda" • *The Beach Boys*

"Shotgun" • *Jr. Walker and the All Stars*

"I Got You Babe" • *Sonny and Cher*

"Stop! In the Name of Love" • *The Supremes*

"Unchained Melody" • *The Righteous Brothers*

"What's New Pussycat?" • *Tom Jones*

"Ticket to Ride" • *The Beatles*

"Papa's Got a Brand New Bag" • *James Brown and the...*

"Baby, I'm Yours" • *Barbara Lewis*

"Like a Rolling Stone" • *Bob Dylan*

"Goldfinger" • *Shirley Bassey*

"Eight Days a Week" • *The Beatles*

"I'll Be Doggone" • *Marvin Gaye*

"Tired of Waiting For You" • *The Kinks*

"What the World Needs Now Is Love" • *Jackie DeShannon*

"It's Not Unusual" • *Tom Jones*

"Nowhere to Run" • *Martha and the Vandellas*

"Tell Her No" • *The Zombies*

"The Tracks of My Tears" • *The Miracles*

"It's the Same Old Song" • *The Four Tops*

"Hold What You've Got" • *Joe Tex*

"We Gotta Get Out of This Place" • *The Animals*

"The Last Time" • *The Rolling Stones*

"Ooo Baby Baby" • *The Miracles*

"How Sweet It Is (To Be Loved by You)" • *Marvin Gaye*

"Turn! Turn! Turn! (To Everything There Is a Season)" • *The Byrds*

"Get Off of My Cloud" • *The Rolling Stones*

"Hang On Sloopy" • *The McCoys*

"Tonight's the Night" • *Solomon Burke*

"Positively 4th Street" • *Bob Dylan*

"(You're My) Soul and Inspiration" • *The Righteous Brothers*

"Reach Out I'll Be There" • *The Four Tops*

"Monday, Monday" • *The Mamas & The Papas*

"You Can't Hurry Love" • *The Supremes*

"Summer in the City" • *The...*

2

The Dream

Nobody likes looking at scars. I have one that I couldn't bear to look at for years. But when I look at it now I realize it changed my life.

During my senior year of high school, I felt a pain in my stomach. My life could've been very different if I'd never felt that pain. You know how it goes. Change one day, and there's a chance it'll change the dynamic of every day that follows.

If not for that pain, my career might've been delayed by a few years. Change the sequence of events, and maybe I'm not in an office at Chappell Music a few years later when Daryl Hall and John Oates first walk in. I was always driven to succeed. So maybe I would've gone on to run Sony Music in any case. We'll never know. All I know is what did happen.

The pain in my stomach was one of those turning points that lead to other turning points. It came in 1966, at a time when my life at home was balanced and beautiful. I was putting on my jacket and tie in the morning, going to Iona Prep,

and getting good grades. I was making plans to go to college at Hofstra University on Long Island. My parents were happy about that. I no longer had to sneak out in their Caddy. On my sixteenth birthday, they bought me a 1966 turquoise GTO with 389 cubes, triple carburetors, and a four-on-the-floor Hurst shifter. We're talking right out of *American Graffiti*. The only thing that car didn't have was air-conditioning. I specifically ordered the car without it, because air-conditioning makes the engine overheat more quickly, and I wanted all the heat in that engine focused on going fast. No matter how much I drove that GTO, the white leather interior stayed showroom clean.

As soon as my day at Iona ended, I headed home, took off the jacket and tie, changed into jeans, got behind the wheel of that GTO, and left skid marks for the College Diner. You'd find me at a booth by the window—in the spot closest to the miniature jukebox on the wall at the end of the table. Always. That seat wasn't even up for discussion. I was in control of that jukebox. My buddies would crowd in, we'd order our french fries and cherry Cokes, and check out the parking lot for the hot cars coming in and the girls that might be stepping out of them. There was a whole strategy to timing the mood in the diner to just the right song on the jukebox. My hands would flip through the metal-backed menu of selections and I'd make the call. Might be "Under the Boardwalk" by the Drifters. Or "Stand By Me" by Ben E. King. If I wanted to get the attention of a particular girl coming by the table, I could always reach for the Duprees' "You Belong to Me." Sometimes I and my buddies would join in on "Hold On, I'm Comin'" as if we were Sam & Dave. Our joy in that jukebox was boundless and infectious. The guys sitting in the booths around us would join in, and the next thing you knew half the diner would be

throwing their heads back and wailing "When a Man Loves a Woman" from the depths of their souls. Percy Sledge, man. Those were the days.

The nights were even better. Sometimes my buddies and I would start out at the Riviera Lounge in Yonkers just to hear Larry Chance and the Earls sing "I Believe" and "Remember Then." From there, we'd drive over to Mamaroneck to see one of the greatest guitar players of all time at the Canada Lounge. His name was Linc Chamberland and he was the leader of an R & B horn band called the Orchids. You won't find any mention of Linc when *Rolling Stone* magazine does a cover story listing their top hundred guitarists. Take it from me. In 1966, you never heard anything like Linc Chamberland.

Not many people knew of Linc outside the Northeast. The Orchids put out only one album, entitled *Twistin' at the Roundtable with the Orchids*, on a small label called Roulette Records. But if you pulled up to the Canada Lounge on a Friday or Saturday night, there was no disputing the uniqueness of his sound.

Nobody else could even play Linc's Fender Telecaster because of the way he tricked it out. I know because I took some guitar lessons with him and tried to emulate him any way I could. One of his techniques was to replace the E string, the bottom string, with a banjo A string that he bent to almost the top of the neck of his Telecaster. There was no way to bend a normal guitar string like that because the tension was too taut. But the banjo string was so thin that it allowed Linc to bend it and create his signature style of rhythm and blues. He pushed that sound out even further by hooking his guitar to an amplifier that was made for a bass, and, in fact, he used a double-stacked Fender Bassman amp. Going to hear Linc play rhythm and blues for the first time was like ordering a dish

that you loved, but then having it prepared with an amazing spice that you'd never tasted. Nobody, nobody, *nobody* in this universe had a sound like Linc Chamberland's.

The Canada Lounge had room for about 150 people. But 250 people who understood exactly what was going on packed the place on a Friday night. Linc was not out front. He was behind the Orchids' lead singer. The only way you can understand how much influence Linc Chamberland would soon have on the undercurrent of music was by knowing who was in the room.

When you hear Dr. John sing "Right Place Wrong Time" and when you hear Freda Payne's "Band of Gold," you're listening to the guitar of David Spinozza. David was at the Canada Lounge, listening and studying Linc, just like me. When you hear James Taylor's "Walking Man," the drums you hear are coming from Rick Marotta. When you hear Orleans' "Still the One," that's Rick's brother, Jerry, on drums. Listen to John Lennon and Yoko Ono's album *Double Fantasy*, and you're hearing the drums of Andy Newmark. All of us came to this little musical hot bed in Mamaroneck because of Linc and the Orchids. If you were lucky enough to be part of this brotherhood, you were connected and influenced by this music for the rest of your life.

What a scene it was. I'd be looking like Sal Mineo in *Rebel without a Cause* and ordering these horribly sweet Sloe Gin Fizzes from the bar with the little umbrella poking out the top of the glass. If I had one of those drinks today, I'd probably vomit. But back then it was part of the religious experience. The drinking age in New York was eighteen back then, and it was always cool to look old enough to drink when you weren't.

Linc would be dressed in a sharp suit with an open collar, and he'd have a great rhythm section and big band of horns

behind him. The Orchids were all about great musicianship rather than crazy gyrations. Linc stood tall and proud as a master of his craft, and when he started playing I'd be locked into his every lick. I know I'm going on and on, but I just can't convey how powerful this music was and, like Elvis, the influence it had on me. When Linc Chamberland was playing I didn't even notice the women around me.

And if you can believe it, sometimes life got even better. I might drive my GTO over to McDonald's on Boston Post Road in Mamaroneck, where the parking lot looked like a drive-thru for drag racing instead of hamburgers. All it took was a challenge and everyone would head over to a quarter-mile stretch of Mamaroneck Avenue. One guy would go down the road to the finish line to declare the winner, while another would stand between the two cars in the hole and raise his arms for the start. When the arms came down the tires squealed.

Nobody could ever beat this guy called Superman in his red 396 Chevelle with a single four-barrel carb. Nobody. So I went to this hot mechanic who bored and stroked my engine and then installed a Crane roller camshaft. I put on headers, which allowed the exhaust to flow more freely, and finished the job off with cheater slicks, racing tires that were modified to make them street legal. Took two weeks to get the job done. And when it was I pulled into McDonald's looking for Superman.

Superman had this big, confident smile on his face. You know, that look that said, *How many lessons do I have to teach you guys?* But everyone in the parking lot came to Mamaroneck Avenue to watch. In the hole, I could see Superman listening to my engine, and his face had a very different expression. This time it was *Something's going on here.*

The arms dropped. I popped the clutch, my slicks dug in, and there was so much power in my engine that the front

tires actually came off the ground a few inches and I popped a wheelie. Superman was ahead of me by second gear, but when I threw it into third I pulled two car lengths in front of him, and by fourth gear he was eating my dust.

Superman got out of his car. "Yo, man! What you got in there? What you got in there?"

I played it smug. "Just running some slicks, that's about it."

"Nobody beats me. Nobody!"

The word traveled faster than the GTO. "Mottola blew Superman's doors in!" People wanted to see the GTO; they'd come by just to listen to the engine and try to figure out what I'd done to it. I eventually told everyone . . . eventually.

Beautiful, beautiful days. The future seemed like a cloudless blue sky. Sometimes I'd get in that car and drive through Westchester's most exclusive neighborhoods and dream. There was this one beautiful brick mansion in Rye on the Westchester Country Club grounds that just kept tugging at me, just kept pulling me back. One day, I swore to myself, *One day I'm gonna own that house.* It was a dream, yeah, but it was as real to me as my seat next to the jukebox at the College Diner. Which meant that it, too, was not up for discussion.

When the world seems sweeter than a Sloe Gin Fizz, you'd better be careful. A sucker punch may be coming your way. I was completely blindsided by this strange pain that showed up in my stomach one afternoon during my senior year.

I figured I'd eaten something bad at lunch and paid no attention to it. But as time passed, there was no avoiding it. The pain became sharper and sharper. By six o'clock, it doubled me over.

My father drove me straight to New Rochelle Hospital. The next thing I knew I was on my back getting rushed through the corridors on a gurney to X-ray. The doctors' and nurses' expressions only made it worse. They looked like they didn't have a clue what was wrong. Then, all of a sudden, a doctor was talking to me. His words were all white noise blurred by pain. But I got the message: they were going to put me out, and then cut me open to figure out what the hell was going on.

I'm not sure if I replied. If I did, it must've been something like: "Hey, whatever you gotta do. Just get rid of this pain."

The next thing I remember is my mother standing over me with happy tears in her eyes. My whole family was hovering over my bed in the recovery room. They'd all been waiting for me to wake up. The surgeons had made a huge exploratory gash in my stomach. They figured out it was my appendix that had to go, and they cut it out just before it was about to explode.

The scar that it left behind freaked me out, and my parents were far more affected by it than I was. It wasn't hard to see what was rolling around in their minds. If my father hadn't gotten me to the hospital in time, they'd have been looking at me in a coffin.

After the operation, I remained in the hospital for a few days, and about a month later, once the doctors had gotten me stabilized and I was feeling okay, my parents took me to South Florida to fully recuperate.

Better medicine could not have been prescribed. We stayed at our old favorite, The Castaways, once the hottest place in North Miami Beach. It was built by Teamsters' pension funds, if you know what I mean, for the type of guys who wanted a taste of the exotic but would never think of making a trip

to Tahiti. There were waterfalls, tiki-style houses, lamps with flames. Just waking up and heading to the pool on the ocean was intoxicating. The air was filled with a blend of rum from the tiki bar, Coppertone suntan lotion, and salt air. Beautiful girls were all around in Capri pants, high heels, and Cross Your Heart bras. They were coming out of the pool in their bikinis on those little metal ladders—headlights first. A jukebox by the outdoor bar between the pool and the beach was loaded with incredible music. But everybody who put a quarter in seemed to punch in the same song: "Summer Wind" by Frank Sinatra.

I remember closing my eyes and seeing an image of Frank performing live just a few years before in the Boom Boom Room at the Fontainebleau Hotel. I saw him give a nod to the orchestra, and that command brought them in with a downbeat.

I opened my eyes, and to my right at the tiki bar was this stunning girl with dark hair, and I knew I was no longer in a trance. She was real. She was not a 10. She was a 20. Every guy was trying to catch her attention. I got up, walked over to her, and asked her out to dinner. She said yes. It was like a fantasy. At dinner, I leaned over and whispered in her ear: "Hey, it's so beautiful out. Why don't we get a blanket and sleep on the beach?" She smiled and nodded yes. The next morning I woke up completely bitten by sand fleas. Every single bite was worth it. I'd say it was a dream come true, but I couldn't have dreamed it up.

Being in Miami Beach was like vacationing in a live jukebox. Just walking down the street you'd stop to hear music pouring out of the hotels. I'd pass the Newport and know: they've got Steve Alaimo tonight. But some of the really amazing sounds came out of a place on the 79th Street Causeway called the Barn—especially when Wayne Cochran and the C.C. Riders were in town.

People called Wayne Cochran the white James Brown. He was this big redneck guy from Georgia with a two-foot-tall blond pompadour. That's no lie. If Madame de Pompadour—the mistress of Louis XV whom the hairdo is named after—ever saw Wayne Cochran, she'd have fucking fainted. And that's not all. Wayne came onstage wearing a cape and jumpsuit that would've made Elvis jealous. He looked like a perfectly coiffed villain out of professional wrestling, and he sang with the fervor of a Baptist minister. His white patent-leather dance shoes almost levitated off the floor as he blended rhythm and blues and gospel while beer bottles went flying. Let me tell you, when Wayne Cochran sang "Goin' Back to Miami" at the Barn, you didn't want to be anywhere else on earth.

I didn't even realize everything I was taking in at these performances. But I was making subconscious connections. Even though Linc Chamberland played behind a lead singer and was all about the craft and musicianship, and Wayne Cochran was out front and trying to tear the beams down from the roof, there was something very similar about them. They were both local superstars—almost gods. But neither had singles that made it to Top 40 radio. Both recorded on small independent labels that didn't have major distribution. A seed was being planted in my mind, an awareness of what separated a local superstar, a regional superstar, a national superstar, and a global superstar. I had no idea that it was even in my mind. All I knew was, I was having the time of my life.

And you know what made that trip even better? My parents finally got it; finally, they looked at me and understood. I could see the change in their eyes: *Life is short. You know what? We're not gonna fight him on this anymore. We're going to let him follow his dreams.* Our dinner conversations were no longer

about what courses I should take in college. They were about what I'd like to do in music. I'll never know if my mother was thinking back on the slap in the face she took from her father when she mentioned "show business." The fear of what might have happened if my appendix had burst was overwhelming enough.

By the time we headed back up north I was ready to follow in the footsteps of Dion and Elvis. The scar and everything it stood for had left an indelible mark on me, a mark that nobody saw more clearly than my parents. They were now behind me 100 percent.

I'll give it to you straight. If a demo from an eighteen-year-old kid named Tommy Mottola had come across my desk when I was running Sony Music, I never would've signed him. I would've known immediately that on a scale of 1 to 10, his voice was only a 5 or 6—even though his singing interpretation and intention were there.

Deep down inside, I'll bet I knew that it was a 5 or a 6, even when I was eighteen years old. I knew it because, thank God, I was blessed with a great set of ears. Those ears have always known what's good—even more than that, they've allowed me to hear the potential in unknown talent. That blessing, that gift, worked both ways because when I listened to myself playing the guitar I understood that my hands couldn't do what my ears wanted to hear.

But, hey, you're only eighteen once in life. Not only did I have ambition in overdrive, but I was rolling on an indestructible set of wheels because I was innocent and naïve. I didn't know what I didn't know about the music business. So it felt like there

wasn't any obstacle I couldn't run over. I'd seen Dion make it out of Belmont Avenue and Sal Mineo make it onto the big screen opposite James Dean in *Rebel without a Cause*. So it was the most natural feeling in the world for another Bronx guy with a pair of balls like mine to think: *Hey, if they can do it, why can't I?*

The quickest way to the top, I figured, would be to have a singing and acting career at the same time. My father helped pay for my acting lessons in the city at the Wynn Handman Studio. That was big-time. Wynn is the artistic director of the American Place Theatre. If you've never heard of Wynn before, you've probably heard of some of the people who worked with him. To name a few: Robert De Niro, Robert Duvall, Lee Marvin, and Denzel Washington.

My parents were not only behind me financially. They were behind me emotionally. That meant I also had the benefit of all my father's connections. He asked a cousin who knew Sinatra about a singing coach. This led to lessons in Carnegie Hall with a big-time voice coach named Carlo Menotti.

I felt like a made man. I'd drive my GTO from my dorm room at Hofstra into the city for my lessons, have a bite at the Carnegie Deli, and stroll through the lobby of the Americana Hotel at night to see if I could run into any famous celebrities. Then I'd walk down Broadway past the Brill Building—which housed the offices of the big music companies—in the hope that some of the magic dust in the air would sprinkle down on me. Dreamer...dreamer...dreamer...I actually believed I was on my way.

I got a part in *No Way to Treat a Lady* with Rod Steiger. Didn't matter that it was a bit part walking by Rod on the street. Didn't matter that I was a $75-a-day extra. I was acting with Charley from *On the Waterfront*. I was going to be seen on

the same big screens around America as Sal Mineo and Elvis. I did work as an extra on about eight films. I was like a sponge soaking up every detail—studying the moves of the directors, the actors, and the lighting crews. There was no better student on those sets. I was where I wanted to be. I dropped out of Hofstra with my parents' blessing.

My father had a childhood friend from the Bronx who knew people in the nightclub business. That friend introduced me to Pete Bennett. This was huge, the next big step. Pete Bennett was the number one radio promotion man in the country. When it came to getting a record played on the radio, there was nobody more powerful in 1968. I'm telling you, Pete Bennett was wired like Con Edison. At one point, he was working simultaneously with the Beatles, the Rolling Stones, Bob Dylan, and Sinatra. I may have been unknown, but it was said that Pete made "unknowns into stars and stars into superstars." And it was said in *Billboard*.

Pete was a short, chubby guy with a cherubic face, but he spoke and acted like he was connected to the mob. While he may have come off as a "dem, dese, and dose" guy, he was a street fox. He could take the money out of your pocket without you even knowing, then smile at you and walk away. He could also give off the aura that he'd shoot you if he needed to. Nobody crosses a baby-faced killer. Moral of the Pete Bennett story is, if he walked into the offices of WMCA in New York with a record, it got played—period. End of story. And WMCA was the breakout radio station at that time.

Pete listened to some demos I'd created with my buddy David Spinozza and talked it over with my father. I don't know the details of the deal they made. But it wasn't long before I was walking behind Pete into the offices at Epic Records. There I was, nineteen years old, being ushered in to see the

vice president. The vice president was David Kapralik. David Kapralik had good ears, too. He'd signed Sly & the Family Stone.

"Dis," Pete Bennett said, nodding to me, "is my nex protégé."

"Okay," Kapralik said. "No problem."

Yes, it was the Bronx School of Business. There were no papers to sign. When Pete Bennett said, "Dis is my nex protégé," the papers came later.

First, we needed a producer. Kapralik picked up his phone, and soon Ted Cooper came through the door. Cooper was the guiding hand behind hits for Bobby Goldsboro and B. J. Thomas. You wanna talk about a contrast in extremes. Cooper had produced records that sold millions of copies. I had never done a single original song in my life.

"You're producing this kid's single," Kapralik said. There was no *Do you want to?* There was no *What do you think?* There was only "You're producing this kid's single."

Cooper clearly understood the rules. Pete's new protégé needed a couple of songs to record. So Ted went looking for a couple of songs to record.

The songs he chose were country and blues. "Women without Love" and "Evil Woman." I wasn't too thrilled with these choices at first, because I wasn't a big fan of country music at the time. But I didn't write my own songs, and I had nothing in hand. So this wasn't the time and place to argue. Hey, man, I was on Epic Records. I'd hit the big time.

Cooper's strategy for me was very common at the time. Make an old song sound new by crossing it over to a different genre. He hired an arranger to make these songs contemporary. Not just any arranger. He hired the hottest arranger in the business. He hired Charlie Calello. For a short time,

Charlie filled in as a member of the 4 Seasons. But his true talent was in putting together the entire musical package. Charlie would arrange for Sinatra, for Ray Charles, for Barry Manilow, for Neil Diamond and, because of Pete Bennett, for a kid named Tommy Mottola.

The next thing I knew I was in the living room of Charlie's house in Riverdale. I was sitting next to him trying to be cool, but my mouth was probably wide open. The guy who'd worked out the arrangements for Neil Diamond's "Sweet Caroline" was doing the arrangements for *my songs*!

Charlie was this short, little Italian guy with big, thick Coke-bottle glasses that covered half his face. He was completely into his work, and he operated with the power of confidence. He'd hit the keys on the piano and listen to the notes, write all the horn parts, the string parts, and the rhythm section parts, and blend it all into one cohesive piece of music. It was unbelievable. *Unfathomable.* I'd question him, and he would explain everything he did. I felt like an intern watching open-heart surgery for the first time. There is no way to explain the exhilaration, inspiration, and invaluable experience I got from watching and listening to him. I couldn't have been a better student. Charlie made me love every note of those songs. I was ready to make them my own.

We went to the studio on Valentine's Day. Epic was part of CBS Records. Everybody who was anybody had recorded in the CBS studio. Bob Dylan might have sung into the same microphone. I've always had a pair of elephant balls. But I really needed them that day. There I was in front of that microphone with twenty-five musicians around me, a rhythm section, bass, drums, horns, strings, and background singers, with the number one arranger in the country conducting. For-

get about it! Once we started it was like being in the movie in your mind that you pray you might one day get to live. I can go on and on. But what's the point? There just aren't any words.

I was so happy I didn't even care when Cooper said to me: "You know, Mottola...Mottola...that's really not the right name for you."

"What do you mean?"

"It's too ethnic. What are your first two initials?"

"T.D."

"Okay. T.D....T.D....T.D...." He was quiet for a while. "Look," he said, "today's Valentine's Day. You're gonna become T. D. Valentine. Yeah. T. D. Valentine. That's your name."

I was so eager to make it, the words *Hold on a second* never even came to mind. "Okay, great," I said. If you say so.

Not long afterward I went to the office of Epic Records and was handed my 45. That's another feeling that can't be described. You look at it. You smell the fresh vinyl. You love it so much you almost want to have sex with it. That's how you feel about your first record. You try to get as many boxes as you can so you can pass them out to your family and friends.

Things only kept getting better. I got a call from Pete Bennett telling me to make sure my radio was tuned to WMCA at 3:09 that afternoon. I got everyone in my family around the radio—and there it was. My voice was in the air, just like Dion and the Belmonts'.

When it ended, everyone around me went crazy.

"And that," the announcer said, "is 'Women without Love' by T. D. Valentine."

I remember my whole family turning toward me with squinty eyes, and joking: *T.D. T.D.! Is that you?*

"Hey," I said, "they wanted something cool."

I actually began to introduce myself to people as T. D. Valentine.

Thank God, nobody calls me T. D. Valentine anymore. It's not hard to see where the next chapter in the story is headed. But here's the point: if you're going to hire somebody to dig a ditch, it's good to know how to dig a ditch yourself.

Years later, these early experiences separated me from the pack. Most of the other music execs usually came over from the legal department or some other corporate corridor. Many of them had never even played an instrument. But when I had my very first conversations with Daryl Hall and John Oates, or later with Billy Joel, they knew I was coming from a different place than the guys in suits, a fluid, creative place they were very familiar with, a place they could trust musically.

My singing voice may have been a 5 out of 10. But at least I had that chance to stand in front of an orchestra at CBS Recording Studios like Frank, Tony, and Bob, and sing.

Everybody's got a right to dream, right? There are a lot of singers who became stars with voices that are only 5 out of 10. We all know who they are. So do they. All it takes is for someone with just the right smile to be on a surfboard when just the right wave comes in. Pete Bennett knew that. That's why he was willing to give me a shot...so long as my father was making it worth his while.

I'd follow Pete into the radio stations after my single came out. The idea was to schmooze with the program director, then be interviewed on the air about the music. Afterward came the moment when I'd leave the room and Pete would make some sort of deal. I wasn't allowed to be part of it, and

I didn't know exactly what was going on. All I knew was that when he came out of that room my record was added to the playlist of that radio station.

The entire promotional setup was a series of back rubs. After the stations played your records, they'd call for favors of their own. They'd ask Pete to send me to their record hops. These were dances that the radio stations used to promote themselves at places like Palisades Park, Rye Playland, or Coney Island. The station would put its banner up over a stage and use the singers or bands whose hits it was playing as attractions. The artists didn't get a cent, but they never refused to show. Even today, major artists like Lady Gaga and Beyoncé still show up at Z100's Jingle Ball. The only difference now is there is no guarantee of airplay with all the new rules and restrictions. But we all know they are certainly friends of the family.

Though there were no regulations back in the time when I was singing, the rules were very clear. If a radio station wasn't playing a record that Pete Bennett wanted them to play, Pete just showed up and immediately that record went on the format. And artists who didn't show up at the record hop were committing career suicide.

The record hop was magical for an unknown like me. It was like being knighted. DJs like Cousin Brucie, Murray the K, and Dandy Dan Daniel were local royalty. And when one gave you the big sell on the air—"Next, a huge hit from singing sensation T. D. Valentine!"—you were off to the races. From the first moment you walked onstage, the DJ's teenage fans became all yours. I'd come onstage in a sport jacket and a high-collared, very starched shirt, take my applause, and lip-synch the words to my two songs as they came through the

speakers. Anybody paying attention had to know that I wasn't really singing, but absolutely nobody seemed to care. When the DJ called you a sensation at Rye Playland, for that moment in time, and in your mind, that's what you were. I learned to make eye contact with one person in the crowd, then sing to her, then fix like a laser on another, then spread my focus around the entire audience. If you moved the wrong way, I learned, the crowd didn't react. Move another, and it did. I was experiencing a tiny taste of the exhilaration and infatuation a star feels—and what a rush and a high it is. I'd come offstage to applause and a long line of girls waiting for autographs. Believe me, that rush gets to your head pretty quick. You can only hope to have somebody nearby saying: "Be oh, so careful, do not drink the *Kool-Aid*!"

You made appearances at the record stores. I opened the magazine section of the *Sunday News* and saw my picture in the Strictly Youthsville column, and I started to feel intoxicated. You can only begin to imagine what it feels like when the whole world is pumping that kind of jet fuel into you. You'd probably think it could fly you to the moon. But if it ever stopped coming... There's a lot of evidence that going cold turkey could put you six feet under. These were invaluable experiences to draw from throughout the rest of my career.

I'd go into the offices of Epic Records on a Monday after the gigs all amped up to push for more promotion. "The people love it," I'd tell the guys in publicity. For me, that's the moment when the sugar turned bittersweet. Because the potion Pete Bennett sprinkled on a record could only last so long. "Yeah, that's great," the guys in publicity would say. They were as kind as they could possibly be at the start. "Problem is, when we get it on the radio the phones aren't ringing."

The phones. The phones. The phones. For any record company, it all came down to the phones lighting up at the radio stations. The more they lit up, the more the station played the record. The more the station played the record, the more copies flew out of the stores. Every radio station had five or ten key local record store accounts that they'd check every day to monitor the market. "This sold thirty pieces. Looks like it might be a hit." They'd bang it some more and it would sell eighty pieces. "Hey, I think we've got one." They'd bang it five or six times a day and it would start selling three hundred pieces. Soon, it would be formatted a half-dozen times into the daily playlist. Radio was the "be-all and end-all" tool. Radio was the cause and effect. Radio was everything. But the phones at the radio station were the truth.

Which meant that when those phones didn't ring, you had a problem. Pete Bennett could get the airplay. And he could make sure a bunch of teenage girls were lined up for you with autograph books in hand. He could work with a PR firm to get your smiling mug in the paper. But he could not make those phones ring. When my record played on the radio, the phones just didn't ring.

Not that I was going to let that stop me, by any means. I kept working it, doing appearances at record stores, hitting the record hops, walking down the promotion corridor at Epic Records to talk up new ideas. I was a real pain in the ass. But I was a polite and engaging pain in the ass. Besides, I was Pete Bennett's protégé. So I still had some muscle. I started nudging everyone at Epic to give me another shot in a more contemporary direction.

When the VP, Kapralik, agreed, I asked to work with a producer named Sandy Linzer. I'm not sure if it was Charlie

Calello who introduced me to Sandy. But it wouldn't surprise me, because Charlie and Sandy were close. Sandy was one of the writers on "Dawn (Go Away)" and "Working My Way Back to You" for the 4 Seasons, and Charlie had done the arrangements. I felt I'd have a much better shot on my second record with the two of them behind it.

Sandy Linzer was a nice guy from New Jersey, only a few years older than me, very easy to get along with, and we hit it off immediately. Both Sandy and Charlie knew I wasn't a great singer. But I had style and passion and they liked me. Their attitude was: hey, let's try to help him make it.

Sandy came on as the director and producer, and chose a song called "Love Trap," written by a guy named Al Kooper, who was one of the original members of Blood, Sweat & Tears. Then he wrote a song for me called "Allison Took Me Away." That felt great. It was very cool to have my own voice covering an original song. Sandy was not only engaged, he was able to sing me the lines and help me with phrasing. I felt much more confident working on the second record. That was helpful, because there was tremendous pressure.

Like every other performer at that time, I had only one day to get it right. It didn't matter if your voice felt good or if it felt sore. The musicians were booked. The studio was booked. You had to come through. I also sensed that I might be coming to the end of the road if this record didn't hit. I didn't know exactly what that meant. But that feeling walked into CBS Studios with me.

Sandy was in the control room. Charlie was conducting the orchestra. Once again I stepped up to the mic and threw my soul into it. I could tell I'd done much better than the first time. But my ears also knew that "Allison" had come out much better than "Love Trap." "Love Trap" had some really high

parts that were hard for me to nail. Sandy and Charlie came over afterward with compliments. But the bullshit detector in me could tell that they weren't thrilled with the results. They were satisfied, yeah, but I knew what was underneath: *This is the best we're going to get out of this guy. Let's finish up and fix it in the mix.*

The 45 came out, and T. D. Valentine went through another round of whirlwind promotion. Again, the phones did not ring. I began to notice a distinct change when I walked down the corridor toward the promotion offices at Epic Records. Doors started to close ten steps in front of me.

That experience taught me a great deal. I learned you could push the gas pedal too hard. The promotion department was like the transmission on my GTO. I'd pushed that engine too far so many times that it just burned out.

It was clear that Epic might not go for a third record. But I didn't want to give up. That left me with Plan B: get on the road and play clubs. I figured it would be a good alternative to making records in the studio and just relying on radio. The idea was to better develop my voice and stage presence on the road. Made sense. But that was me talking to me.

I don't know what my father really thought about Plan B. I was the sun, stars, and moon in his eyes, and I'm sure he wanted to give me every chance at success. But he was realistic, and he saw that it wasn't working for me as a singer, or as an actor, either. I could get nontalking parts as an extra. But I never made the leap to a role with a speaking part in the script, and I certainly did not have the patience to wait for one. The way my father played it cut both ways. He decided to go all in on Plan B. He'd give the nightclub route his best shot. If it didn't pan out, well, there'd be no regrets.

So I went to the tailor and got measured for a custom-made

tuxedo, and we hired Bobby Kroll to write me a nightclub act. Bobby Kroll was pretty famous at the time for rearranging big standards and tying them together with a little shtick.

The act felt good. I rehearsed, then hit the road. Upstate New York. New Jersey. Pennsylvania. Massachusetts. Towns with names you can't remember. Clubs that you'd pass if you drove too quickly because your only clue might be a winking neon sign with half the bulbs burned out. Inside were horrible smells mixing cigarette butts and stale beer. If you ever went into one of these places during the light of day, you'd run out, head for the hills, and immediately jump into a shower. Darkness gave you only temporary cover. We're talking stages with squeaky mics. Audiences that made you sing over the drone of conversation and the clatter of silverware on plates. And those were the good nights.

There was one night I'll never forget, even though I'm trying hard to right now. I step out of my car with a garment bag on my shoulder like I'm about to play the Copa. Only I'm at a run-down joint somewhere in the wilds of New York. I get directed to a dingy dressing room, about ten by fifteen, the size of a prison cell, with a fat stripper sitting inside like she's serving thirty to life.

I want to avert my eyes. But there's no place for them to go. I have to wedge myself behind a curtain in this same room to change into my tux. When I step out, I can't help but notice that this woman has little white objects sticking out from between each of her toes.

"What's that?" I asked.

"Oh, I put garlic between my toes," she said. "Stops you from getting sick."

Here I am, in my custom tux, trying to look like Frank Sinatra, standing backstage in Bumfuck Upstate New York in

a snowstorm with a half-naked barrel-bellied stripper who's got garlic between her toes—and that's not the worst of it. I now have to go out and warm up the audience *for her.*

Good luck! If the music business goes any lower, I don't want to know about it.

"...rican Woman" • The Guess Who

"...ops Keep Fallin' on my ...ad" • B. J. Thomas

"...ar" • Edwin Starr

"...t No Mountain High ...ugh" • Diana Ross

"...There" • The Jackson 5

"...Ready" • Rare Earth

"...t Be" • The Beatles

"...nd of Gold" • Freda Payne

"...ma Told Me (Not to ...)" • Three Dog Night

"...thing Is Beautiful" • Ray Stevens

"...It With You" • Bread

"...C" • The Jackson 5

"...Love You Save" • The Jackson 5

"...andida" • Dawn

"...body Is a Star" • Sly & the Family Stone

"...ill the Wine" • Eric Burdon and War

"...o-h Child" • The Five Stairsteps

"...Down (Candles in the ...)" • Melanie with the ...vin Hawkins Singers

"...of Confusion (That's the World Is Today)" • The Temptations

"...ove on a Two-Way ...eet" • The Moments

"...Right Now" • Free

"...ant You Back" • The Jackson 5

"...d, Sealed, Delivered I'm ...rs" • Stevie Wonder

"...nus" • The Shocking Blue

"...stant Karma! (We All ...ne On)" • John Ono Lennon

"...nes" • Clarence Carter

"...ookin' Out My Back ...oor" • Creedence Clearwater Revival

"...y Night in Georgia" • Brook Benton

"...Me Just a Little More

"Hey There Lonely Girl" • Eddie Holman

"The Rapper" • The Jaggerz

"He Ain't Heavy, He's My Brother" • The Hollies

"Tighter, Tighter" • Alive and Kicking

"Cecelia" • Simon & Garfunkel

"Turn Back the Hands of Time" • Tyrone Davis

"Ziggy Stardust" • David Bowie

"Lola" • The Kinks

"Express Yourself" • Charlie Wright and the Watts 103rd Street Rhythm Band

"Still Water (Love)" • The Four Tops

"25 or 6 to 4" • Chicago

"Fire and Rain" • James Taylor

"Evil Ways" • Santana

"Didn't I (Blow Your Mind This Time)" • The Delfonics

"(If You Let Me Make Love to You Then) Why Can't I Touch You" • Ronnie Dyson

"I Just Can't Help Believing" • B. J. Thomas

"Who'll Stop the Rain" • Creedence Clearwater Revival

"Without Love (There Is Nothing)" • Tom Jones

"Thank You (Falettinme Be Mice Elf Agin)" • Sly & the Family Stone

"Walk on the Wild Side" • Lou Reed

"Whole Lotta Love" • Led Zeppelin

"Joy to the World" • Three Dog Night

"Maggie May" / "Reason to Believe" • Rod Stewart

"It's Too Late" / "I Feel the Earth Move" • Carole King

"How Can You Mend a Broken Heart" • The Bee Gees

"Just My Imagination (Running Away with Me)" • The Temptations

"Knock Three Times" •

"Tired of Being Alone" • Al Green

"Want Ads" • The Honey Cone

"You've Got a Friend" • James Taylor

"Mr. Big Stuff" • Jean Knight

"Brown Sugar" • The Rolling Stones

"Do You Know What I Mean" • Lee Michaels

"What's Going On" • Marvin Gaye

"Ain't No Sunshine" • Bill Withers

"She's a Lady" • Tom Jones

"Temptation Eyes" • The Grass Roots

"My Sweet Lord" • George Harrison

"If You Could Read My Mind" • Gordon Lightfoot

"Gypsys, Tramps & Thieves" • Cher

"Never Can Say Goodbye" • The Jackson 5

"Mr. Bojangles" • Nitty Gritty Dirt Band

"That's the Way I've Always Heard It Should Be" • Carly Simon

"If You Really Love Me" • Stevie Wonder

"Spanish Harlem" • Aretha Franklin

"Draggin' the Line" • Tommy James

"Proud Mary" • Lke and Tina Turner

"Mercy Mercy Me (The Ecology)" • Marvin Gaye

"I Just Want to Celebrate" • Rare Earth

"Wild World" • Cat Stevens

"Funky Nassau" • The Beginning of the End

"I Hear You Knocking" • Dave Edmunds

"Lonely Days" • The Bee Gees

"Won't Get Fooled Again" • The Who

"Theme from Shaft" • Lsaac Hayes

"...

"Love Her Madly" • He Doors

"Here Comes the Sun" • Richie Havens

"Right on the Tip of My Tongue" • Brenda and the Tabulations

"Riders on the Storm" • The Doors

"Stairway to Heaven" • Led Zeppelin

"The First Time Ever I Saw Your Face" • Roberta Flack

"American Pie" • Don McLean

"Without You" • Nilsson

"Lean on Me" • Bill Withers

"Let's Stay Together" • Al Green

"Brandy (You're a Fine Girl)" • Looking Glass

"Oh Girl" • The Chi-Lites

"(If Loving You Is Wrong) I Don't Want to Be Right" • Luther Ingram

"I'll Take You There" • Staple Singers

"Ben" • Michael Jackson

"The Lion Sleeps Tonight" • Robert John

"Slippin' into Darkness" • War

"Everybody Plays the Fool" • The Main Ingredient

"Nights in White Satin" • The Moody Blues

"Too Late to Turn Back Now" • The Cornelius Brothers and Sister Rose

"Back Stabbers" • The O'Jays

"Starting All Over Again" • Mel and Tim

"Day After Day" • Badfinger

"Rocket Man" • Elton John

"I Can See Clearly Now" • Johnny Nash

"Burning Love" • Elvis Presley

"Clean Up Woman" • Betty Wright

"Mother and Child Reunion" • Paul Simon

"Where Is the Love" • Roberta Flack & Donny Hathaway

3

Na, Na, Hey, Hey: The Beginning

Everything seemed to be exploding about three feet in front of me. I pushed my GTO too hard on a stretch of Long Island road created by God for drag racing, to impress a girl I'd been dating at Hofstra. For some reason, I thought going fast impressed girls, and for some stupider reason, the girls seemed to be impressed. But I went way too far this time, and heard crunching and crackling, like the sound of metal being thrown into a wood chipper, as the car limped to a halt. That was it. I'd blown a rod in the engine, and torn the transmission apart for what must've been the fifth time. I had the GTO towed home, but this time my father refused to fix it. "You want a car," he said, "go to work and buy a car."

It was almost shocking to hear those words—which I guess was his purpose. He never stopped supporting me, and he kept helping me out professionally. But otherwise, the money stopped flowing. It was time. He wanted me to see the reality of life as an opening act for Garlic Toes. He pulled my coat, no

doubt about it, but I also remember feeling disillusioned. He was about to sell his business. There was never an easier time for him to help me out, and he was being very generous with my sisters—even going as far as buying them homes. Mind you, a really nice house cost $20,000 at that time. But day after day I'd open the front door and see my GTO sitting out front as if it were on life support. Finally, I sold it.

I went to work parking cars at the beach clubs. I worked as a waiter. I drove a cab for Blue Bird Taxi in New Rochelle. The company still exists. When I go back there and see those cabs I get chills—and not good chills. But it was work, and at the end of the week I'd have a wad of cash in my pocket, which allowed me to go to all the clubs and hear music.

I scraped together about $1,200 and bought a 1962 Impala convertible. It was a broken-down piece of crap with a dent in the back, and I was ashamed to drive it into the parking lot at the College Diner. Early on, I was very conscious of the power in an image. Me pulling into the parking lot in that crappy Impala might as well have shouted out: *How did the guy who took down Superman lose all his powers?* I'd call my friend Ronny and ask him to pick me up so we could arrive at the diner in his car.

One night, Ronny and I went out and ended up on the other side of town at the Eastchester Diner. I'd eaten there a few times, but it was not my turf. Everyone knew it was the place where the nice Jewish girls from Scarsdale hung out. The tables had the same setup with the jukebox. But nobody ever sang to my selections at the Eastchester Diner. At the Eastchester Diner, I was just another customer.

I sat at a table with Ronny and noticed a beautiful girl with thick, shiny black hair at an adjacent table. She was sitting across from a really good-looking guy whom I knew. It was

more than her physical beauty that struck me. It was everything about her. She was meticulously dressed and polished down to the snap on her handbag—her Louis Vuitton handbag. I always had nice clothes. But hers were on another level.

I kept glancing over at her, and she must've caught the vibe because Ronny noticed her glancing back.

"Oh, that's Lisa Clark," Ronny said.

"Who's Lisa Clark?"

"I went to school with her. Her father is Sam Clark. He runs ABC."

"What do you mean?"

"ABC."

"What do you mean, *runs it?*"

"He's in charge of the music, the television, the films—all of that stuff."

It's hard for me to calculate the percentages of the two thoughts blowing through my mind at exactly that moment. One: that chick looks really great. And two: her old man was in show business.

"Ronny, I gotta meet her, man."

Ronny walked over to her and said, "Why don't you come over to our table for a second. I want you to meet my cousin Tommy."

Lisa got up and came over while the good-looking guy just sat there like a lox.

It started out as a "Hi, how you doing?" conversation. She was really nice, easy to talk with and sincere. "What do you do?" she asked.

"I'm a singer. An actor."

"Oh, really," she said. "My father's in the business."

"What does he do?"

"He started ABC Records. Now he runs ABC films and

53

theaters." She told us how her father had signed Ray Charles and Paul Anka. It soon became one of those "Wow, that's amazing" conversations, that ended: "Okay, cool. Here's my phone number. Give me yours and let's get together."

Then she went back to her table. About twenty minutes later the four of us got up from our tables to leave almost simultaneously. In the parking lot, I watched her step toward the driver's door of a midnight-blue Thunderbird convertible with a white top.

I just turned and looked at Ronny.

I called Lisa about two days after our meeting at the diner and we started to go out. We didn't go to the Canada Lounge to hear Linc Chamberland and the Orchids. Instead, she wanted to go to upscale restaurants. Lisa was a very different type of girl from the ones I was accustomed to going out with. There was a freshness to her, a newness, that made me feel like I was traveling for the first time. I was Italian, but she knew the streets of Rome. Lisa loved Italy. She'd been there many times with her parents.

Lisa was refined—not the type of girl you'd try to impress by whipping all the horses under your hood as fast as they could possibly go. There was a formality to her, a seriousness that asked me to lift my game, a uniqueness that brought us together quickly. After about a month, we were boyfriend and girlfriend. That was when she invited me over to meet her parents.

I was kind of anxious as I pulled up to the Clark home in my crappy Chevy Impala and parked near Lisa's Thunderbird. Sam Clark drove a *Mercedes*, at a time when nobody I knew drove a Mercedes. A simple shot of the three cars gives you a pretty good cinematic lead-in to what was coming.

I wanted to make a good impression, some kind of connection. At the bottom of it all, hey, I was meeting my girlfriend's father for the first time. I'd brought along one of my 45s. I was not only introducing myself. I was introducing everything I wanted to be. "Love Trap" may not have sold well, but I was proud of it, and I still believed in myself big-time. I wanted to show Sam Clark that I was good.

Sam was sitting in his usual chair in the den—a recliner—watching the news on television. He was always meticulously dressed. He went to work every day in a suit and tie, of course, but even around the house he'd wear custom-made pants, a nice sport shirt, and Gucci loafers. He did not get up out of his recliner to greet me. So I walked over to him to shake hands.

I'll never know what was in his mind. I'm sure he knew I was Lisa's boyfriend. But he probably figured it was some passing fancy, and if it wasn't, he'd have to deal with it down the road. Sam Clark and his wife had raised their daughters to keep the faith. That meant Jewish husbands. By the way, it wasn't a religious rule—the Clarks were not ultraorthodox. It was cultural. Central casting was simply not supposed to send an Italian from the Bronx over to the Clark home in Scarsdale to audition for the role of son-in-law.

Sam Clark was a self-made man. He'd started delivering records to stores in Boston when he was young and had become the top record distributor in town. That gave him a lot of power. There were many components to the music business back in the fifties and sixties: the artists, the songs, the producers, the record companies, the radio. But if you look at the mix of power as it pertained to the success of a music star, distribution was 50 percent of the pie. Distribution was the backbone and spine of the business.

Sam Clark caught the attention of two of the big bosses

at ABC corporate, one of them being Leonard Goldenson, who brought him in to start a music division in 1955. There was no label at ABC when Sam Clark arrived. Sam Clark created ABC-Paramount Records, and in doing so he became one of the pioneers of the music industry. I don't know how much Sam Clark knew about music. But he was close to Alan Freed, the disc jockey who broke all boundaries and coined the phrase rock 'n' roll, and he was an extremely smart businessman. He would've been successful distributing apparel to major retailers. He would've been successful in just about any business because he was a hustler and he made smart moves. It didn't take much of an ear to know that Ray Charles could sing. But it was Sam Clark who signed Ray Charles when he left Ahmet Ertegun and Atlantic Records. Sam had big hits with Ray, like "Hit the Road Jack," "Georgia on My Mind," and "I Can't Stop Loving You." They even portrayed Sam Clark in the movie *Ray*, starring Jamie Foxx.

Sam kept building. He acquired Dunhill Records with Jay Lasker, another great record man, and lifted that division into one of the most important record companies of that era. He'd done so well that by the time I met him he'd been given the responsibility of running ABC's film and theater divisions. When we first shook hands, I was looking into the eyes of a serious business executive with a monster job. Sam Clark looked at me as if trying to understand what his daughter was doing with T. D. Valentine.

I'll never know if Sam Clark thought that I was using his daughter simply to get to him. Even if he didn't feel that way, Lisa was in a difficult position. When Sam Clark walked into a room in front of Lisa it was as if God had suddenly materialized before her eyes. But she had brought home the forbidden fruit, and she knew it as well as he did. Lisa's parents made a

point of introducing her to the sons of affluent Jewish families from the country club in the hope that some sort of passion could be sparked. I can really understand, looking back now, that Sam Clark knew what would work best for his daughter over the long haul. But back then I was nineteen years old and unable to grasp the big picture. Neither could Lisa. All I knew at that moment in time was I really liked Sam Clark's daughter and wanted his respect.

"How do you do?" he said. He had a very formal Brookline, Massachusetts, way of speaking. Out of his mouth, Scarsdale sounded the way a Kennedy might say it: *Scaaaaaaaahhhhsdale.*

"What do you do?" he asked.

"Well, I'm a singer."

Lisa jumped right in. "Oh, Daddy, he's a singer, and he brought his record! Can you listen and see what you think?"

Sam reluctantly got up from his easy chair, crossed the foyer, and stepped down into the living room toward a credenza that held the family's stereo. It was a large piece of furniture containing a record player, a radio, and a shelf filled with LPs. Sam clipped my 45 over a round spindle on the turntable that allowed it to be played like an album, and soon the stereo's arm was hovering over it and the needle came down. Sam listened at the start, but I could tell after a little while that his mind was elsewhere.

I don't know if he knew that my voice was a 5 out of 10. Charlie Calello and Sandy Linzer had elevated it to a 7 in the studio, and even though nothing happened in the U.S., the record became a big cult hit in England. In any case, before the song ended he lifted the needle off the record.

"That's very nice, very nice," he said. He was trying to be polite, but his tone gave me the feeling that it was uncomfortable for him to have my Chevy Impala in his driveway. He

asked who did the arrangements and kept it civil. But then he said something that I cannot recall word for word because it hit me like a wrecking ball right between the eyes.

"Good luck. But if you want to come around here, you'd better forget about singing."

Looking back on those words now, I can see that maybe he was simply offering brutally sound advice. But between those lines there was no mistaking his other message: *Hey, look, kid, you're not Jewish—forget it.*

Three words were surging through me as I walked past the Mercedes and the Thunderbird to get to my Chevy and go home. Three words that would never allow me to ask Sam Clark for a job, nor take one from him if it were ever offered.

I'll show you!

I must've mentioned something about Sam Clark's comment to my parents, because they saw an opening. Not long afterward, my father came to me and said: "Your uncle Vic wants to have a talk with you."

That got my attention big-time. In some ways, going to see my godfather was like an event. Uncle Vic was a very important guy. So you had to feel good about it. Hey, Uncle Vic is paying attention to *me.* At the same time a meeting with Uncle Vic made me nervous. I might be getting called in for a sit-down. Maybe my parents figured Uncle Vic was the only figure I was sort of fearful of, and fear lasts longer than love. That line was from the movie *A Bronx Tale,* written by my buddy Chazz Palminteri, but I'm gonna steal it because it's a good one and he won't mind.

I went down to the Democratic Social Club on Fordham Road and the Grand Concourse, where Uncle Vic had an

office and all the big fish met. There was a huge hall in this club where the politicians spoke to crowds. But nobody was around on the morning I came by.

Everything about Uncle Vic's office was solid and made of wood. Wood door with a piece of glass in the middle. Wood desk. Paneled walls.

He greeted me with a hug. But then said: "Sit down." Just like that. "Sit down."

Uncle Vic was a big, strappy guy, six feet tall but broad and on the heavy side. His size was only one factor in his large presence. He was extremely authoritative, extremely opinionated, and extremely short on patience. There was no small talk at all. He was sharp as a tack.

"Look," he told me. "You gotta stop with this singing business. Nothing is gonna happen with it. You could continue to go on and on and waste your time. I'm telling you, you don't want any part of that business. I know lots of those guys. I've seen them all. And I've seen them all come and go. It's a rat business."

He pronounced that last line in a way that made you see a rat's whiskers right in front of your nose, in a way that made the line impossible to forget.

"You want to be a professional man," he continued. "You want to be in your father's business. You would make him so happy. He could teach you the business. Look at what it did for him. He was able to provide well for his family. You could make the business ten times bigger.

"And if you don't want that, become a doctor or a lawyer. But you gotta stop this singing now. This is a big opportunity for you, and you've got your parents behind you."

It was not supposed to be a conversation, and it was not supposed to be a long meeting. "Okay, thank you, Uncle Vic," I said, getting up. "Thank you very much."

"You understand?" he said. That was his way of saying good-bye. "You *understand?*"

I nodded, and walked out of his office with my head spinning. *You gotta do this. You gotta do that.*

But my brain and my body and my soul didn't want to do *this* or *that.* My brain and my body and my soul wanted to make music.

From out of nowhere Uncle Vic's voice resounded once more.

"You understand?"

There was a lot of bell ringing going on. I looked around and saw my friends going into their fathers' businesses, into construction, retail, the garment industry, and the financial markets. I saw my teenage friends becoming men. It got me to thinking: *Maybe I should listen to Uncle Vic. Maybe I should give up singing like Sam Clark says.* It didn't mean I'd have to remove myself from the world of show business. The more time I spent with Lisa, the more I began to hang around with the Clarks and their fancy friends. It was not odd for Sidney Poitier to come over for dinner. In a matter of months, I'd gone from opening for Garlic Toes to meeting Sophia Loren.

But there was an awkwardness to it for me. Sam Clark put an invisible wall between us. Not only was it invisible, but it was multiplatform. It was horizontal: *Don't come through here.* But it was also vertical: *Our Mercedes is up here, and your Chevy Impala is down there.* So I never felt legit when I walked into Lisa's house. I needed to make money. I needed a real path. If I couldn't drive over in a Mercedes, I needed to at least be on the road to doing something *that would become* successful.

Because success was everything in the eyes of the Clark family. That was all Lisa's parents talked about: success, people of success, and the benefits of success.

Which brought me back to my father. His dream always had been to pass on his business to me. Many times when I was young, he'd taken me to his office at the southern tip of Manhattan and tried to make the day appear fun and interesting so that in the future I'd want to make the business my own. I never took the bait. Now, he had just sold the company, but part of the deal called for him to stay on to oversee it. It was too late for me to take it over. But his idea was to teach me the business so that I could then start my own company. My only motivation when I took the job was to win over Lisa.

So I got on the train with my father every morning and headed downtown. That was the first jolt. Remember, this was the end of the sixties. There were no iPods back then. This was more than a decade before the Sony Walkman first made a splash. Nobody was listening to the radio on the train ride from Westchester into Grand Central Station at seven in the morning. I found myself sitting next to silent businessmen reading the *New York Times*. The trip was a succession of conductor's calls—"Mount Vernon, next!...One Hundred and Twenty-Fifth Street!...Last stop, Grand Central!" Then came the frenetic churning and steel braking of the subway downtown at Bowling Green.

I worked at a desk in a big open room right next to my father. There were no cubicles. Just lots of people around, all sectioned off, going about their duties. It was a brokerage house. So the entire job, unless you were the boss, meant filling out entry forms coming in from the importers that had to go to the customs house for clearance. It was a simple business.

But it was a boring business. It was all about pushing paper. Mastery of the simple diligent process was what had taken me on all those vacations to Miami Beach through my childhood. But I didn't hear "Summer Wind" playing at the tiki bar while I was doing it.

For about six months I worked through the minutiae of these tedious forms. During the monotony of this daily grind came a very unexpected moment. It must've happened on a weekend because I never took a day off. Lisa and I were walking on Fifth Avenue. It was damp and chilly out, and when it started to rain we stepped under an overhang for cover. I looked over at Lisa and saw tears on her cheeks.

"What's wrong?" I asked.

"I don't think I can continue seeing you," she said.

"What?"

There'd been absolutely no warning. Things had been going great between us—which was exactly why she was crying.

"What's the matter, Lisa? Don't you like me?"

"Of course I like you. It's not that. It's because...because you're not Jewish."

"Not Jewish? Of course I'm not Jewish. You knew that."

"You don't understand, Tommy. My parents will never accept you. They'll never accept me being with a boy who's not Jewish. It's hopeless."

So many conflicting feelings smashed inside me and knocked me off balance. I fired back in a finger snap with all of my heart and soul:

"Well, then, I'll convert."

It felt like I had seized the moment. Little did I know that those words would keep me off balance for almost thirty years.

Here's the thing: Those four words were not hard to say. They were easy to say. Remember, my best friend was raised Jewish by an Italian Catholic father and a Jewish mother. His Italian dad went to the temple with him, put on a tallith, and hummed along with the prayers. His Jewish mother learned how to cook rigatoni. I celebrated his bar mitzvah with him, and he came to Christmas Mass with me. Ronny Parlato was an example of how seamlessly it could work if two people were deeply in love. And make no mistake about it, I was definitely in love. At least I thought I was in love. I was nineteen years old, just a kid. What the hell did I know about love?

But there was more to my response than love. It was a way of finally smashing through the wall that Sam Clark had put up between us. I didn't fully understand all the reasons he put up the wall. What Sam Clark's ancestors had passed on to him alongside that one rule through more than five thousand years was self-preservation. When Sam Clark threw that rule out at me I took it as prejudice. So, in a strange way, me saying I would convert to Judaism was like telling him, *Hey, you can kiss my guinea ass.*

Again, this all happened in less than a finger snap. I didn't think it out. If Sam Clark were with us right now and standing in front of me, I'd tell him he was right. It was not fated to work out over the long haul. I feel terrible for any pain that moment caused Lisa down the line. But I can't apologize for what I did. I can't apologize because two beautiful kids who mean everything to me came into the world because of that moment. So if I had to do that moment over again, I'd make the same decision. I can only apologize to Sarah and Michael for the conflict that they grew up in, and tell them that I had the best of intentions when I said those words. My parents were married

for seventy years, and when I said I'd convert that was how I thought marriage would be for Lisa and me.

"You'd do that for me?" she said. It was as if the sunshine had just broken through the rain.

I can see now the depth in that moment for her. It was powerful for both of us. In some ways, in that moment, I became my own man. And a man never feels more powerful than when he's doing something for someone else.

The power in that moment would set me up for a marriage that was announced in the *New York Times* and an ugly divorce that was covered by all the newspapers. It would set me up to fall for a fairy-tale marriage to Mariah Carey that didn't end up like a fairy tale at all.

It would take me thirty years from that moment to gather my balance. When I look at that moment now, I see it as the first stop on the long road to Thalia.

Fate seemed to put the wind at my back. Within a couple of weeks, an unusual opportunity arrived on my desk. There was a problem with some wine that one of our importers was bringing into the country. I can't remember the details—maybe a couple of cases came in contaminated by bad corks. The point is, nearly all the wine was good. But because a couple of cases were bad, the importer wanted to play it safe. He didn't want to allow the lot out for distribution, and risk his reputation. So he made a suggestion.

"Look, I'll give it to you for a dollar a case. Do what you want with it. Keep it. Or just get rid of it."

So I opened a bottle and poured myself a glass. Tasted good to me. I didn't know shit about wine back then. Gallo

tasted good to me when I was nineteen. But I knew this wine *wasn't bad.*

What the hell. I rented a truck, got four of my friends, and we picked up hundreds of cases of this wine. I took the wine around to family and friends, gave them all a taste, and everybody liked it. I made everybody buy this wine.

I went to wine stores, asked for the owner or the manager, and said: "Listen, I got some great, great wine. I can sell it to you really cheaply. Why don't you taste it and see if you like it? If you like it, I'll sell you a case for twenty bucks."

Half these guys looked at me like I was nuts. But all those acting lessons really kicked in. They gave me a confidence and an assertiveness, a sense of how to carry myself and present myself to people who didn't know me. All those disastrous evenings on the nightclub circuit helped me, too. When you walk on a stage at a nightclub, you have to make people like you. All those lessons and experiences helped turn me into a great street salesman.

Most of the owners figured the wine was hot. But back then, people didn't have the same frame of mind that they do today. If there was a deal and a buck to be made, and nobody knew or cared, then that was the end of the story. Besides, nobody would have bought it if it didn't taste good.

I sold every case of that wine and pocketed about thirty grand. Back in the day, that was enough to buy a house. But I needed every cent of that money, and whatever else I had saved up, to buy the biggest possible diamond engagement ring I could afford for Lisa because I knew how status conscious her mother and father were. All I heard in that house were the words *Gucci, Bulgari,* and *Saks.* My offer to convert to Judaism had broken through Sam Clark's horizontal wall.

I figured a really big diamond could help me smash through his vertical wall.

I had no knowledge whatsoever about diamonds. But I figured, hey, I'm going to convert. Why not go down to the diamond district on Forty-Seventh Street and buy a ring from the Hasids like all the other Jewish boys? I looked in all the windows for the biggest, shiniest diamond that could be bought with the money I had.

There was a three-karat diamond that was long and flat, marquis shaped, and not a lot of depth, but this stone looked *big*. One of the salesmen with *peyes*, the beard, and the black hat really started pouring it on. "Look at the quality of this stone!" If he was taking me, I didn't give a shit. I walked out of that store with a big, shiny stone that I knew was impressive.

I put it in a candy wrapper and brought it over to the Clark home. I was sitting in the kitchen having tea with Lisa and her mother, and I said: "Open the bag. I got you some candy." Lisa opened the wrapper and went nuts. Her mother gasped and slapped a hand over her open mouth. If you were looking at her mother's expression without any reference, you wouldn't have been able to tell whether this was a happy event or if somebody had died. *Is this Italian guy really going to marry my Jewish princess?*

Lisa immediately ran with the ring into the den where her father was sitting, smoking a cigarette, and watching television. He took the ring from her hands, stood up and looked at it, then passed it back to her. He headed for the stairs. Halfway up, he turned back and said, "I hope you two are planning to elope."

*   *   *

66

If there had been springs in my head, it would've felt like I was being pulled to the point of bursting each day as I looked up from the paperwork in my father's office. *I am not cut out to do this. I am not made to do this. I do not want to do this!*

Everyone around me could see my disillusionment with the drudgery of the job. It was certainly no secret to my father. So he understood when I turned on a dime. I got his blessing to go back to what I loved. I pounded the pavement and got a job offer from Joel Diamond at MRC Music—the publishing arm of Mercury Records.

When I think of all the powerful connections I might've been able to access through Sam Clark, it's ironic how things turned out. Joel Diamond had been a life insurance salesman who wrote and sold songs on the side. Through a chance encounter on an airplane, he met an executive who quickly recognized his talent and enthusiasm, and chose him to run MRC Music over a lot of candidates with more experience. If anyone understood what it meant to give someone on the outside a chance, it was Joel Diamond. He started me at $125 a week. It was a bottom-of-the-barrel job in music. But for me, that paycheck was like getting a badge. I felt like a cop walking his first beat. I was a long, long way from detective, captain, and police commissioner. But I wore the badge. I was officially in the music business.

Just approaching that office on 110 West Fifty-Seventh Street was the most exhilarating feeling I'd known since stepping onstage with the Exotics. I exuded happiness as I swung through the door every day to greet the six-foot-seven-inch security guy with the face of a bulldog. Everyone called him Tiny. Tiny had the happy hello of a florist—which he was in his spare time. But cross him, and he'd take out your liver for lunch.

My formal job description was "professional manager." Which was a fancy industry term for "song plugger." There's nothing quite like it today. On the most basic level it was like being a cross between Simon Cowell and Dale Carnegie. Half of the job was about having good ears and taste, and the other half was about being able to communicate what you knew to influence people.

I'd walk from my office in a pair of jeans and a sweater about ten feet to a bank of writers' rooms. These rooms were essentially the same—no more than a piano and stool—but some looked different because the writers had decorated them. Not all the writers were permanent. Some would show up on a Tuesday or a Thursday. But the day-to-day crew hung art on the walls to make their space feel like it was home. It's important to understand how committed everyone was to their work. Some writers slept in these rooms overnight and woke to write.

It was in these rooms where I found myself, and the path that I would follow for the rest of my life. Having writers listening to my ideas and suggestions was an amazing new experience for me. These were the moments where the roles shifted and the course of my career turned. Musicians were now taking *my* advice.

And why did they take it? Because everything I said came from walking down 187th Street and hearing Dion and the Belmonts blare out of all the open windows and stores, and then walking a few blocks farther and hearing Tito Puente and all the Latin sounds and rhythms. Everything I said came from what Linc Chamberland and Charlie Calello had taught me. Those rooms gave me the first place to voice all of my musical experiences since that lightning bolt of hearing Elvis hit me at eight years old.

I'd walk into these rooms, sit with the writers next to the piano, listen to a song that they were working on, talk with them about it, and see if it was right musically and lyrically. I might even help them reconstruct it, or discuss how the lyrics might work best for a certain singer. Sometimes I'd listen to a finished song and know that it wasn't right for a certain artist, but that it might work for another. Other times I might think it was great. If I did, it was my job to know where to sell it. That meant I had to know which artists were in the process of making albums, and the stylistic themes of those albums. Matching the two ends took talent and creativity. Even though the job was technically called music publishing, it was still the process of music making.

I had found my niche. My forte, more than anything else, was being able to hear and to singularly focus songs and writers and artists and producers to help them create popular music just like the music I grew up with and loved as a kid.

Let me tell you, nobody ever worked harder for $125 a week. When the workday ended toward dinnertime it started up all over again with a trip over to the industry watering hole, a steak joint on Fifty-Fourth Street called Al & Dick's. There were a lot of familiar faces at the bar, and other people whom you didn't know but wanted to meet. After catching up on everything that had happened that day, I went out to the clubs to see what was going to be happening tomorrow.

This was back when clubs mattered. Max's Kansas City. The Bottom Line. The Bitter End. My Father's Place. These places were bursting with budding newcomers. If you found the right talent and if that artist didn't write many songs, you could hook them up with your songwriters. If you were impressed with a singer/songwriter, you could try to sign them to the publishing company. If you found a young talent

who might become a star, you could sign them to the publishing company, then make a production deal with them, and maybe even get them a deal with a record company, in which case you'd own the publishing. The job was all about discovering and developing talent.

The talent that rotated through that little bank of offices at MRC was something. Alan Bernstein wrote "This Girl Is a Woman Now," a huge hit for Gary Puckett and the Union Gap; and "After the Lovin'," which Engelbert Humperdinck made famous. Benny Mardones wrote "Into the Night." Phil Cody would go on to write "Laughter in the Rain," and "Bad Blood" with Neil Sedaka. Robert Flax put five songs on the *Billboard* charts and fifteen years later went on to become vice-chairman at EMI Music. Janis Siegel would develop into the lead singer for the Manhattan Transfer and win nine Grammys.

That little office on 110 West Fifty-Seventh Street was a magnet for creativity. Muhammad Ali showed up one day looking for the theme song to launch a product called Champburgers. A young singer-comedian named Joe Pesci, who had a nightclub act with his buddy Frank Vincent, hung out there and sang on many of our demos long before winning an Oscar for his performance in *Goodfellas*. The place was pure passion, a creative stew not only in music but in business development. I was listening, learning, watching, meeting, and doing. Tiny moments in that office changed my life. One of the writers walked around constantly saying he was going to Grub man's office. "I gotta call Grub-man." Grub-man. Grub-man. Grub-man... That was all he talked about, and that was how I met Allen Grubman, an up-and-coming attorney. This was long before Allen moved to Park Avenue and became Grewb-man. Fancy-shmancy. Our careers would become intertwined. I'll

never know if all that I accomplished over the years could've been done without him. As our friendship grew, we might call each other ten times a day.

The ultimate point here is, when you swung through the door past Tiny, you never knew whom you were going to meet, how it might change your life, or what was going to happen.

Late one afternoon, Joel Diamond came down the hall and sounded out a cattle call. "Hey, guys, we need some background voices. Doesn't matter if you can sing or not. We need five or ten guys."

A call for background vocals was commonplace and we paid no mind to it as we headed out to lend a hand. A bunch of us entered the recording studio to find Paul Leka, a jovial Wolfman with his full-face beard, who was a producer one floor up at Mercury Records. As Paul explained what he wanted, his tone was a little apologetic: "Guys, I know you're going to think this is silly. But I wrote this song and there's this one part I need you to sing like this: *Na, na, na, na . . . na, na, na, na . . . hey, hey, hey, goodbye.*"

We were all laughing from the get-go because the lyrics were so stupid. Anybody could sing them—which was Paul's point. He didn't want professional singers. He wanted this chorus to sound like a bunch of guys hanging out. We all put on headphones, got behind this one microphone, and let it rip. Then we went back to work as if nothing had happened.

Three months later, "Na Na Hey Hey Kiss Him Goodbye" was the Number One record all over America. You still hear it all the time when college bands and crowds at sporting events want to salt the wounds of an opposing team. And whenever I do I always listen hard for my voice buried somewhere in the background vocals.

The office of MRC Music was more than a place. It was a moment in music and time that will never happen again. When most people think back on 1969, they have images of long-haired kids rolling around in the mud and having sex in a haze of marijuana smoke while Jimi Hendrix played "The Star-Spangled Banner" at Woodstock. Or images of Neil Armstrong stepping out of a spacecraft onto the surface of the moon. Given the choice of walking in some crater in a space suit, rolling around in fields ridden with deer ticks, or walking the beat for MRC Music, there's no doubt I would've chosen to swing through the doors of 110 West Fifty-Seventh Street to say hello to Tiny. I was where I wanted to be.

One day I was in my office and heard a group of people jostling around. I got a call to go to Joel Diamond's office. Everybody who was around that day filled the room.

"I have some really bad news," Joel said. "You've all been fired. Including me."

There was an instant of stunned silence. Then, it was as if the entire room shouted out: "What the fuck are you talking about?"

"A big corporation called Philips-Siemens just acquired Mercury Records," he said, "including this publishing company. It also owns Chappell Music, and they're merging us together."

There was no severance. Certainly not for the writers who were paid by the songs they produced. We were told we had to clear out and vacate the offices by the end of the day. It was a bloodbath. Given the love that we all had for the place, it was cruel, like telling people without a moment's warning that they'd just lost their jobs *and* their homes. You can imagine the reaction. People were seriously pissed.

I don't recall who was in the office that day, and even if I do

I'm not naming names. But people decided to take their severance packages into their own hands. They started ripping the stereos out of the walls and rolling pianos down the hallway. "Let's get trucks!" someone shouted. The crew took turns distracting Tiny, inviting him out for a cup of coffee or other such nonsense, while the others carried stereos and speakers and wheeled pianos out the service entrance and into waiting trucks. It was a chaotic and funny, funny scene. If it were in a movie, it would surely be sound-tracked to "Na, na, na, na... na, na, na, na... hey, hey, hey, goodbye."

Because I haven't named any names, you'll never know most of the people in the office that day. But if you could ask anybody who was there, I'll bet they'd tell you that even after forty years, whenever they get close to 110 West Fifty-Seventh Street, they detour to the sidewalk on the north side of the street, because word swiftly spread that Tiny was looking for them.

It was the best corporate bloodbath I ever survived. I may have temporarily lost my badge and my beat, but the dismissal could not have turned out any better. A week later, Joel Diamond was talking to the vice president at Chappell Music about a job. There was nothing available at his level. But the vice president, Norm Weiser, mentioned that he was looking for a young song plugger, someone who knew the streets, and Joel recommended me.

A few days later I walked over to the Chappell Music offices on 609 Fifth Avenue for a meeting with the vice president. It was like stepping into a different style of shoe than I'd ever worn before and finding it to be a perfect fit.

Chappell Music dates back to 1811, and it was the largest music publishing company in the world when I walked into Weiser's office. Among the songs in its catalog is "Happy Birthday to You." Some of Chappell Music's writers included Irving Berlin, Stephen Sondheim, and Richard Rodgers and Oscar Hammerstein. But it was an old-fashioned music publishing company in dire need of fresh blood as it geared up for the 1970s.

I guess Norm checked around, because when I sat across from him there seemed to be no need to prove myself. "I hear you're the new young guy out there on the streets," he said, "a guy who knows how to get things done. How would you like to work here?"

"Are you kidding me?" I said. It almost came out as: *How about for free?*

A smile broke out on Norm's face. "I'll tell you what," he said, "I'll start you at $250 a week."

It was better than dying and going straight to heaven. That was double what I was getting at MRC. With $250 a week, I could move out of my parents' home and get my own apartment. That would put me another step closer to Lisa.

The meeting was coming to a happy conclusion when Norm said: "Oh, just one other thing...There have been reports that some equipment disappeared from the offices of MRC on the day it was closed down. You weren't part of that little mischief, were you?"

I never got even a small supporting role on the big screen. But Wynn Handman and his acting class would have been damn proud of me in that moment.

"You know, I heard something about that," I said in a tone that gave the appearance I'd been fishing off the coast of Peru at the time. "What exactly happened?"

"Never mind," Norm said. He was a wonderful, beautiful man who would become a mentor to me, and maybe he didn't really want to know. "I was just double-checking."

As I walked out of Weiser's office, not only did I feel like I'd gotten my badge back, it was like I'd miraculously been promoted to sergeant. No more showing up to work in jeans and a sweater. I arrived for my first day of work at Chappell in a suit and tie. There was a big office with a window overlooking Fifth Avenue waiting for me, and opposite my office was a glass-partitioned cubicle for my secretary.

I had access to the brass, and the brass had access to talent. I'd see Tony Bennett and a lot of other famous singers walking through the hallways for a conference with some of the songwriters. Little did I know that twenty-five years later I'd become part of a huge transition in Tony's career. Chappell was a place with such a tremendous history, and I felt proud to be part of it. Even better, it was a company with the intention of moving into the modern era, and I felt like I could be a force in making that happen.

I was hired to pound the streets, and pound the streets I did. I'd go to the office in the morning, get the latest songs from our writers, and walk to record companies and recording studios to play them for producers and A&R guys. The job at Chappell really broadened my contacts. While I was moving from studio to studio, I got a chance to listen to and talk about the music that was being recorded. I inhaled it all and developed a real understanding of what was going on in music. Not many people had ever gotten a chance to have this kind of experience at the start. You couldn't put a price on it.

The wall of my office started to fill with photos snapped of myself with famous artists. I even began to get the grudging respect of Sam Clark. He didn't know anybody at the pimple

of a company that was MRC. But Chappell Music, that was a whole different story.

I was doing everything I could to show him I was worthy of his daughter, including going to the Actors' Temple on West Forty-Seventh Street for conversion lessons with Rabbi Schoenfeld. The process took a couple of months. There was no graduation ceremony. But I remember getting a certificate that I took to the Clark home to show that it was official. *Hey, I got my license, I'm ready to drive.* Lisa and I did not elope. She and her parents began to plan the wedding she'd been raised for at, of course, the Plaza Hotel.

There was one hitch that should've told me something wasn't completely right. Yeah, I'd converted, and I was comfortable with it. Part of the reason I was able to feel comfortable with my decision was my parents. Not long after I'd told Lisa I'd convert in the Fifth Avenue rain, I sat down with my mother and father. I sat on the same plastic-covered couch where I'd found out I was being sent to Admiral Farragut Academy. This time, it was my turn to deliver some news.

"I think I'm gonna get married," I told them.

"You *think* you're gonna get married?" my father asked. "Or you *know* you're gonna get married?"

"Look, I know. I'm gonna marry Lisa Clark. But here's the deal. I have to become Jewish."

There was a moment of half shock and all silence. They both liked Lisa. But they loved me.

"Tommy, if that's what's going to make you happy," my mother said, "we want you to be happy."

My father was quick to back her up. "We're behind you a hundred percent."

We all hugged and kissed, and that was that. There was no

argument, or even a look at the pros and the cons. My mother's best friend had made it work. We'd all lived the experience with her and her family in the most natural way. And if my parents did have reservations about my conversion, by that stage in life they had to know that once I made up my mind to do something, there was no stopping me anyway.

Looking back now, I can see that part of the reason it was so easy for me to convert was I never really stopped to consider what it meant. I was moving at a thousand miles an hour, and the way my ADD looked at it, converting to Judaism was simply the quickest way to Lisa through Sam Clark's wall.

It has always worked for me in business because my instincts were more right than wrong, and it always got me to where I needed to go in the quickest way possible. But on a personal level, it worked against me. It hurt me because my emotions whipped me forward without allowing my mind the time to clearly think things through. I didn't think the conversion through. In the rare moments when I was forced to confront the reality of what I was doing, I started to feel little twinges of *Are you sure about this?*

I first felt a twinge when Lisa showed me the floor plan for the wedding. There was going to be a chuppah set up in the Terrace Room of the Plaza, and that, along with the old tradition of the crushing of the glass, was great by me. But the walk down the aisle...Something just didn't feel right about the walk down the aisle.

Talk about a scene from a movie. The right side of the aisle was going to be filled with upper-middle-class and wealthy Jews. The left side was mostly going to be my side of the family, Italian-Americans who were used to receptions at a place with big chandeliers under the Whitestone Bridge that looked

much more like a wedding in *Goodfellas*. Something just didn't feel right about me wearing a yarmulke as I walked between these two groups. It's hard to explain the twinge, because I thought it was cool putting on the yarmulke at the Jewish camp when I was a kid. Maybe it was something about walking between the two sides. It made me feel like I should somehow stay in the middle. But the yarmulke wouldn't allow that, and the yarmulke was an ironclad part of the deal. There seemed to be no way out of it. I couldn't go through the ceremony with my head uncovered. When I mentioned to Lisa that I was feeling a little awkward about the walk down the aisle, I got a slight sign that the wall Sam had put between us might finally be coming down. Someone in Lisa family's came up with a smart idea. It was to be a very formal wedding...that called for tails. Just put a top hat on his head. Perfect! Done! My head was covered. And my father looked great walking down the aisle in a top hat, too.

It was quite a sight to see. There was a reception and cocktail hour on one floor of the Plaza. The ceremony took place on another floor in front of 350 guests at the Terrace Room. Dinner and dancing were set up on another floor in the Grand Ballroom. I felt like I was king of the world, and the Sunday edition of the *New York Times* proved it. There I was: HIGH SOCIETY. DAUGHTER OF ABC BIGWIG SAM CLARK MARRIES TOMMY MOTTOLA.

Our honeymoon took us to Paris, Geneva, London, and Rome. It was the first time I'd been out of the United States. I was twenty-two; it was like watching a movie, and all of that experience became part of what I was to become professionally. We stayed in some of the places Lisa knew well, like the Excelsior Hotel in Rome. During meals, I watched how the Europeans handled their silverware differently than I did. I heard how

elegant and polished the Italian language sounded in relation to the slang that came off the streets of the Bronx. There was an elevated level of dress and culture all around me. My eyes were opened. I felt like I had a lot of catching up to do. So I couldn't wait to get back home and go straight to work...

VOICES

JANN WENNER

Publisher of *Rolling Stone*

When *Rolling Stone* was started in 1967, the leading edge of the postwar Baby Boom was just turning twenty-one. This was the biggest, best-educated, and wealthiest generation of young people in the history of the world.

They grew up with this new form of rock 'n' roll and became intellectually wedded to it. It was the way young people spoke to each other. It was the way they expressed their concerns, their values, and anxieties. But back then nobody could see where it was all going.

Nobody was saying: *This will be the most powerful music in the world. It will marry a generation and influence presidents.* That wasn't even in the back of my mind. But John Lennon saw something when he said: "We're more popular than Jesus."

JON LANDAU

Manager of Bruce Springsteen

The '60s leading into the '70s was all about invention. The music was being invented. The way to present the music was being invented. The way to manage the music was being invented.

We were stepping out of a world where the artist made records and did shows—that's it. There was no Internet. There were no video channels. If you made a video before then, there was no place to play it. Yeah, if you were the Beatles, you got to make a movie—a real movie that people would go to see in a movie theater. Short of that, there was little use for video. If a musician was lucky, he got to play on *The Ed Sullivan Show.* The amount of things open to—and demanded of—the artist was much smaller. The machinery was just not that elaborate.

It all began to open up in the time when guys like Tommy and me got started. Nobody really knew how to navigate this new terrain. It just came up in front of us. We were all in the trenches trying to find our path, making it up as we went. When a guy like Tommy solved a problem in a certain way, that way became a model.

- Roberta Flack
et It On" • Marvin Gaye
" • Paul McCartney and Wings
e Rock" • Elton John
So Vain" • Carly Simon
er Louie" • Stories
Mrs. Jones" • Billy Paul
nstein" • The Edgar Winter Group
way" • Dobie Gray
the Sunshine of My • Stevie Wonder
Lady" • The Isley Brothers
n American Band" • Grand Funk
lace Wrong Time" • Dr. John
erstition" • Stevie Wonder
Train" • The O'Jays
On Truckin'" • Eddie Kendricks
ng in the Moonlight" • King Harvest
er One of Us (Wants e the First to Say ye)" • Gladys Knight and the Pips
d It Be I'm Falling in e" • The Spinners
niel" • Elton John
ht Train to Georgia" • s Knight and the Pips
oke on the Water" • Deep Purple
ind Closed Doors" • Charlie Rich
e Cisco Kid" • War
and Let Die" • Wings
er Ground" • Stevie Wonder
I Am (Come and Take Me)" • Al Green
eling Banjos" • Eric erg and Steve Mandell
rfly" • Curtis Mayfield
eling in the Years" • Steely Dan

"Money" • Pink Floyd
"Yes We Can Can" • The Pointer Sisters
"Free Ride" • The Edgar Winter Group
"Space Oddity" • David Bowie
"Papa Was a Rollin' Stone" • The Temptations
"Just You 'n' Me" • Chicago
"Smokin' in the Boy's Room" • Brownsville Station
"Ramblin' Man" • The Allman Brothers Band
"The Way We Were" • Barbra Streisand
"Doo Doo Doo Doo Doo (Heartbreaker)" • The Rolling Stones
"Saturday Night's Alright for Fighting" • Elton John
"Never, Never Gonna Give Ya Up" • Barry White
"Living for the City" • Stevie Wonder
"Knockin' on Heaven's Door" • Bob Dylan
Dark Side of the Moon • Pink Floyd
"Dancing Machine" • The Jackson 5
"Until You Come Back to Me (That's What I'm Gonna Do)" • Aretha Franklin
"Best Thing That Ever Happened to Me" • Gladys Knight and the Pips
"I've Got to Use My Imagination" • Gladys Knight and the Pips
"Waterloo" • ABBA
"Mockingbird" • Carly Simon and James Taylor
"Tell Me Something Good" • Rufus featuring Chaka Khan
"Please Come to Boston" • Dave Loggins
"Goodbye Yellow Brick Road" • Elton John
"Don't Let the Sun Go Down on Me" • Elton John
"Tubular Bells" • Mike Oldfield
"Hello It's Me" • Todd Rundgren

"The Joker" • The Steve Miller Band
"Benny and the Jets" • Elton John
"Rock the Boat" • The Hues Corporation
"Rock Your Baby" • George McCrae
"I Shot the Sheriff" • Eric Clapton
"I Can Help" • Billy Swan
"Cat's in the Cradle" • Harry Chapin
"Philadelphia Freedom" • Elton John
"My Eyes Adored You" • Frankie Valli
"Shining Star" • Earth, Wind & Fire
"Fame" • David Bowie
"One of These Nights" • The Eagles
"Jive Talkin'" • The Bee Gees
"Best of My Love" • The Eagles
"At Seventeen" • Janis Ian
"Lady Marmalade" • Labelle
"Fire" • The Ohio Players
"Magic" • Pilot
"Mandy" • Barry Manilow
"Could It Be Magic" • Barry Manilow
"I'm Not in Love" • 10cc
"You're No Good" • Linda Ronstadt
"Get Down Tonight" • KC and the Sunshine Band
"You Are So Beautiful" • Joe Cocker
"Cut the Cake" • Average White Band
"Someone Saved My Life Tonight" • Elton John
"Lovin' You" • Minnie Ripperton
"Fly, Robin, Fly" • The Silver Convention
"That's the Way (I Like It)" • KC and the Sunshine Band
"Let's Do It Again" • The Staple Singers
"Let Me Wrap My Arms

"Love Is the Drug" • Roxy Music
"Born to Run" • Bruce Springsteen
"Don't Go Breaking My Heart" • Elton John and Kiki Dee
"December, 1963 (Oh, What a Night)" • The Four Seasons
"Sara Smile" • Daryl Hall and John Oates
"Bohemian Rhapsody" • Queen
"Take It to the Limit" • The Eagles
"(Shake, Shake, Shake) Shake Your Booty" • KC and the Sunshine Band
"Love Rollercoaster" • The Ohio Players
"You Should Be Dancing" • The Bee Gees
"You'll Never Find Another Love Like Mine" • Lou Rawls
"Dream Weaver" • Gary Wright
"Turn the Beat Around" • Vicki Sue Robinson
"All by Myself" • Eric Carmen
"Love to Love You Baby" • Donna Summer
"If You Leave Me Now" • Chicago
"Lowdown" • Boz Scaggs
"Show Me the Way" • Peter Frampton
"Dream On" • Aerosmith
"Say You Love Me" • Fleetwood Mac
"Fooled Around and Fell in Love" • Elvin Bishop
"Island Girl" • Elton John
"Evil Woman" • Electric Light Orchestra
"Rhiannon" • Fleetwood Mac
"Got to Get You into My Life" • The Beatles
"She's Gone" • Daryl Hall and John Oates
"Still the One" • Orleans
"Walk Away From Love" • David Ruffin
"Baby I Love Your Way" •

4

An Offer He Can't Refuse

One day during my first year at Chappell, I was told to make time to meet two young songwriters coming up from Philadelphia. Made sense. When you're the young, contemporary manager, you're the guy who gets called to meet the unknown young new writers and acts.

I was a little surprised when they showed up, because I had been told the two Philadelphia guys who were coming had worked with Gamble and Huff, so I expected a look, and music, along the same lines.

Kenny Gamble and Leon Huff were two of the biggest songwriters at that time. They collaborated on "I'm Gonna Make You Love Me," which was recorded as a joint single by Diana Ross and the Supremes and the Temptations. And they were about to start Philadelphia International Records as an alternative to (and competitor with) Motown. Songs they'd write for that label, like "Back Stabbers" and "Love Train" for the O'Jays, and "If You Don't Know Me By Now" for Harold

Melvin and the Blue Notes, would become identified as the sound of Philadelphia. That's sort of what I was expecting.

The two guys stepping into my office didn't look like the O'Jays. For one, they were white. So, it was a strange encounter for a moment, also because their looks were so striking.

One of them looked like David Bowie, about six feet three inches tall, with long blond hair that fell way past his shoulders. He was wearing a short green leather jacket, but it was his shoes that wouldn't let my eyes go. His shoes were made of patchwork-colored leather—like they should've been a quilt but somehow got confused and ended up in another factory.

His buddy was about five foot five, with long black curly hair down to his shoulders, and a mustache. If he'd been carrying a sword instead of a guitar, he would've looked like D'Artagnan from the Three Musketeers.

It was a very friendly meeting. The tall blond-haired guy was quiet and withdrawn. The short black-haired guy was a little more talkative.

They'd both gone to Temple University and were obviously well educated. They had a quasi manager who'd brought them looking for a publishing deal, or a record deal, or any kind of deal, something to get them established in any kind of way. It was easy to see that they were at that early stage where an artist latched on to whoever could take him forward.

After we finished talking, I said: "Okay, let's go to the studio." We had one on the floor, a large room with a piano, where demos could be made. The tall blond guy sat at the piano. The short black-haired guy got out his guitar.

As soon as they started playing, my mind started racing. *This is unbelievable! This could be the best music I've ever heard!*

It was a strange combination of folk music and R & B. What was unique about it was that I never really liked folk

music, but from these guys it came out as a brand-new kind of sound. They were not a copy of anything. They were absolutely original.

I was very quiet as this music came into me. I knew this would be big, and from that day forward I knew my life was changed forever.

That's how I met Daryl Hall and John Oates. Looking back, I can only wonder if they knew what I knew in that moment. They didn't play "She's Gone" for me that afternoon, or "Rich Girl." But it was as if I could hear the seeds of those songs in what they were playing.

Two stark questions came to me: *How can I make it happen? And how can I be part of it?* Those questions grabbed every cell in my body and just wouldn't let go.

I was a year younger than Daryl. That's important to understand. In some ways these guys were looking at me like: *Yeah, this kid's got balls, but what can he really do?*

There are many snapshots in my memory that show exactly where my head was around that time. Once, when I was in the Atlantic Records recording studio at 1841 Broadway, I came out of a session and saw an elegant bald-headed man, with brown tortoise-shell eyeglasses, and a 100 percent perfectly groomed goatee, wearing a perfectly fitted suit and tie, turning down the same hall. It was Ahmet Ertegun. It was the Rolling Stones; Wilson Pickett; the Young Rascals; Led Zeppelin; Crosby, Stills, Nash, and Young; Bette Midler; and Aretha Franklin all in one coming down the corridor toward me. Ahmet Ertegun was all of that and more. He was the chairman and a founder of Atlantic Records, the man who put jazz into R & B. He was one of the pioneers of the industry. He was a giant.

Thirty-five years earlier he'd been an eleven-year-old boy when he arrived in the United States as the son of the Turkish ambassador. But it was hard for me to envision him that way. In my eyes at that moment, he was the godfather of the music I loved. I don't want to overexaggerate my reaction in that hallway. But I stood against the wall and nodded with respect.

Suddenly, at twenty-two years old, I had to figure out a way to make Hall & Oates trust me enough to guide them, and after that I had to figure a way to guide them into Ahmet Ertegun's world.

I always knew to trust my instincts, and when I did I was usually very convincing and got a great result. So I kept calling and spending time with Daryl and John. I took them into the studio and produced about six demos of their latest material. I got them some small advances from Chappell Music so that they could get an apartment in New York City. We began to hang out night and day and soon became close. I gave one of their demo tapes to a guy whom I'd become very friendly with at Atlantic Records named Mark Meyerson. Mark was the director of A&R, and he fell head over heels in love with the music. Not long after that, when Daryl, John, and Ahmet were all on the West Coast, Meyerson set up a meeting between them.

The meeting was a dinner at the home of one of Ertegun's friends named Earl McGrath. The joke back then was that just about anybody could get their own label if they were friends with the head of the company, and that was definitely how McGrath got Clean Records. Over dinner and lots of wine, Ahmet told Daryl and John that they were welcome to become part of Clean.

Daryl and John were ecstatic. I was not as happy. Clean Records was not what I had in mind for them. I wanted them to be on our dream label, the *Atlantic* label, because I sensed

we would never be treated the same if we were on Clean. Yeah, I was inexperienced, but I knew one thing for sure: the closer you are to the people in power, the better your results are going to be. It was a difficult situation. Ahmet had already committed to his friend. But luckily, Mark Meyerson also thought that it would be better to have Hall & Oates on Atlantic. He enlisted a famous producer to tell Ahmet that the Atlantic label would be the best fit, and worked it out internally.

I ended up getting Hall & Oates a three-album deal, a deal that gave Atlantic the option to extend the contract by putting up additional money. It wasn't huge money—it was the kind of money that got a band started. I only realized that we'd hit the jackpot when I asked Meyerson about the famous producer who'd campaigned for us.

He told me that it was Arif Mardin, and that Arif wanted to talk to me about producing their first album.

You can imagine how I felt when I heard that name. No, you can't. If I listed all of Arif Mardin's great work, this book might be ten pages longer. Arif Mardin arranged "Respect" for Aretha Franklin. That's all you really need to hear. But let me give you just a few more examples: "Where Is the Love" for Donny Hathaway and Roberta Flack. "Pick Up the Pieces" by the Average White Band. "Jive Talkin'" for the Bee Gees. "Wind beneath My Wings" for Bette Midler. We're talking about a guy who won eleven Grammys. Only a few months earlier, I couldn't even have gotten in the same room with Arif Mardin. Hall & Oates had basically gone from zero to a thousand, from obscurity to working with one of the greatest musician-producers of all time—and, by the way, one of the nicest men God ever created.

There was a developmental process in the early seventies that no longer exists today. Now, it's either come out with a

hit or die. Back then, your first album could be sort of a place marker, an introduction. Our concept was simply to record a collection of songs that John and Daryl had already written. No gigantic aims, just get some music out, engage an audience, start to create a following, and see where it all leads. Of course, we would've loved to have a big hit. But back then, there was time. It took Bruce Springsteen three albums to get to *Born to Run*.

Hall & Oates' first record was much more of an acoustic album with undertones of their R&B roots. It was called *Whole Oats*, and it was linked to a cool piece of art on the cover, a box of Quaker Oats. The album didn't have any hits. But it was a critical success, and one song on it, "Fall in Philadelphia," backed by Arif's great string arrangements, became the blueprint for nearly every Hall & Oates hit that would follow.

The album put Daryl and John in a good place and gave me open access to all the departments of Atlantic Records. I found myself once again as the artist-student, soaking up everything and looking over the shoulders of the masters. The head of promotion, Jerry Greenberg, would later become the president of Atlantic Records at the age of thirty-two, making him the youngest president of any major record company in history. Next to his office in promotions was a woman named Margo Knesz, who worked the phones like a truck driver: "Listen, you motherfucker, you'd better fucking play these fucking records!" Barbara Carr, then head of publicity, would later go on to comanage Bruce Springsteen with Jon Landau. Dave Glew, the senior vice president, showed me the ropes of distribution, marketing, and sales. I never forgot a thing he taught me. When I took over at Sony fourteen years later, he was one of the first executives I brought in. I was seeing, listening, and learning the promotional strategies that were propelling all of

Atlantic's big stars, knowing that this was the same machinery that was going to carry my acts out to the radio and into the record stores.

No area was too small or trivial to be overlooked or studied. When Hall & Oates hit the road to play clubs around New York, sometimes I needed to drive the truck, sometimes I needed to carry guitars and amplifiers, and sometimes I needed to set up the lighting and sound because the budget couldn't pay anyone else to do it. So I learned how to do everything, and this was all after I'd pounded the pavement for Chappell Music during the day.

You can go to school for four years and graduate school for another couple, get some diplomas, and still not necessarily know anything about how the world works. When you go through the crash course, nobody in a cap and gown hands you a diploma to hang on your wall. That's okay. It's written all over you.

I first heard Oates play the chords on his guitar and sing the melody and lyrics to "She's Gone" in their New York City apartment. It was just the raw roots of a song, but then Daryl stepped in and put those magical vocals on it, as only he could. When they sang the lead in octaves, I could tell it was going to be a smash.

Daryl and John started working on their second album right after the first one came out. We'd gotten the message that *Whole Oats* was too acoustic, that Atlantic and Arif wanted to put together a strong rhythm section to enhance Hall & Oates' Philly soul and R & B. This time, Arif was bringing in the big guns. He put together a killer rhythm section with players like Bernard Purdie on drums, Gordon Edwards on

bass, and Hugh McCracken on guitar, to name a few. If you don't know anything about the world of studio musicians, you might not recognize those names, but you've heard their sound on over a hundred hits. These guys played on a lot of the hit records produced by Arif, Jerry Wexler, and Tom Dowd. It's impossible to overstate what they brought to the game. It was like adding Kobe Bryant, Dwyane Wade, and LeBron James to your pickup basketball team. With these guys and "She's Gone" in the mix, the second album seemed destined to break out.

"She's Gone" was inspired by two women. One had stood John up on New Year's Eve. The other was Daryl's first wife. Daryl and his wife were going through a painful split at the time. When I think back on that period, I'm reminded of a lot of conversations Daryl and I had about the similarities in our marriages. Daryl's wife at the time was also Jewish, and he was dealing with so many of the same religious and cultural issues that I was. His experience might've felt like: "She's Gone." But my experience was starting to feel like: *I'm gone.*

I was working the equivalent of two full-time jobs and then going out with Daryl and John at night. I'd drive back home to New Rochelle late, but the reality is I was more connected to Hall & Oates than I was to my marriage. I wanted to be a good husband. The more time passed, though, the more I saw what Sam Clark had seen from the beginning: there was little connection between us. It wasn't really about the long hours. Hard work and success had always been the ethic in the Clark home. So Lisa understood. And it didn't really have much to do with religion. It was more like we were from two different worlds.

What she grew up with was the ritual of Friday night candles, Saturday night dinners, and Sunday morning golf brunches at the country club. I wasn't at home on Friday

night, and I didn't really feel at home at the country club. At the same time, she didn't seem to be thrilled when I brought her into my world. I remember taking her to my first Rolling Stones concert. The buildup to that concert had gone on for years inside me, ever since driving with "(I Can't Get No) Satisfaction" blasting from the radio in my friend George's Corvette down the Major Deegan Expressway to a club in the Bronx called Cholly's. The Rolling Stones, man! I was finally going to see the Rolling Stones! Halfway through that concert I looked over at Lisa and got the impression that she'd rather be at the country club.

I never expected to be divorced. No matter how bad the fights were, most couples I saw growing up didn't get divorced. Whatever the problems were, they just dealt with them. My deepest influences were what I'd seen at home as a kid. I can't remember my parents spending a night apart. But I hadn't taken the time before I got married to consider the depth of the connections my parents had: Their Italian-American Catholic heritage. Christmas. Easter. The shared dreams they had for their children. And deep, deep, down underneath it all was a love for music. These were things I couldn't build on with Lisa at the time. The more time passed, the more I began to realize my marriage was going to be a long haul.

Daryl was able to adjust his life more quickly. He'd met a stewardess named Sara Allen, and eventually she moved in with him and John in the New York City apartment and became the inspiration for a song on that second album called "Las Vegas Turnaround (The Stewardess Song)." Singing that song with John helped turn Daryl's pain into a happy rebound. I was not writing any songs to confront what was rumbling around my gut. So I buried the feeling underneath twenty-hour workdays.

Arif and his boys pulled the best out of "She's Gone" and "Las Vegas Turnaround" with additional help from a truly talented guitar player/band member named Christopher Bond. We were ready to roll.

The second album was called *Abandoned Luncheonette*. On the cover was a photo of an abandoned diner sitting in weeds that John and Daryl used to drive past outside of Philly. The album cover became a piece of pop history. Fans and photographers would make treks to find it and find out about it. It turned out the diner was originally located in Pottstown, Pennsylvania, but went out of business and was dumped in a small wooded area outside of Philly, where it was eventually carted away to clear the land. Sad, too, that album covers like *Abandoned Luncheonette* are now gone, but we'll get to that later. Trust me, at the time that cover was a big deal.

We were shocked when "She's Gone" failed to become a hit as soon as it was released. But by no means was I disillusioned. I knew that "She's Gone" was a hit. I knew it was a smash. I knew that Atlantic had dropped the ball. I was determined to at some point make that song a hit. Anyway, the album became the pivotal point in John and Daryl's career. It had total clarity. It described exactly what they were. It showed their Philly rock and soul side, their acoustic side, their vocal harmonies. It branded them. Reviews were great—and back then not every idiot could blog whatever the hell he thought without having even sat down and listened to the record a few times. Back then, reviews really meant something. They could make or break an artist. The Atlantic executives saw Hall & Oates on the verge of becoming the company's next giant superstars. The album was not a commercial success. But stories began to trickle back that Led Zeppelin's lead guitar player, Jimmy Page, was seen carrying around the *Abandoned*

Luncheonette album while on tour. That made Daryl's day. It made his day more than if you'd told him that "She's Gone" was at the top of the single charts, because Jimmy Page was one of Daryl's idols, and that meant integrity and credibility.

We were poised to smash through on album number three. The developmental process in those days was almost like putting together a jigsaw puzzle. Only a few more pieces in just the right places and it would be complete.

Just at that point, Daryl said he had a different puzzle in mind.

As crazy as that might sound, it was completely understandable. "I don't want to do *Abandoned Luncheonette Junior*," Daryl said. He was like an actor scared of being typecast into a specific role that was making him famous but threatening to confine him for the rest of his life. Daryl was an explorer. He didn't want to be locked into the velvet coffin of pop music—and John didn't want to be locked away with him.

For their third album they wanted to do something totally different. Daryl was infatuated with David Bowie, and loved musicians from England like Brian Eno and Robert Fripp, who made incredible but totally noncommercial music. Daryl wanted his next album with John to be progressive rock 'n' roll.

I did not agree, and one night at Joe's restaurant on MacDougal Street after enough martinis, wine, Sambuca, and grappa had gone down, we got into it.

"Hey, man, getting to this point was hard work," I told him. "We've just built an audience of people who found *Abandoned Luncheonette* so compelling that they went out and bought it. They bought the music that they heard and loved. You don't

know how they're going to react to a completely different sound. We are trying to build a dedicated audience here. It takes time."

"Look," Daryl said, "we can always do commercial songs. But this will give us credibility and integrity. *Rock* credibility. We need that."

Abandoned Luncheonette had given them all the credibility and integrity they'd ever need. We ended up mired in the classic debate between commerce and art for the sake of art. Whenever I tried to take it back to the strength of the R & B sound, Daryl might hit me with an argument from Aldous Huxley's *Brave New World*. Yes, listening to those arguments was part of my job, too, as the manager, and at 2:30 a.m., no less, as the grappa went down.

At the end of the day, I had to go along with him. I had tremendous respect for both Daryl and John. It was their lives and their career, and it was my job to facilitate their music and get the most out of it.

"We don't want Arif Mardin working on our next album," Daryl said. "I want to hire Todd Rundgren to produce it."

I fought it for as long as I could, but after a lot of back and forth, we got together with Mark Meyerson and agreed to make an album with Todd Rundgren producing. Rundgren was well known for his hits "Hello It's Me" and "I Saw the Light." I tried to see this collaboration in the best possible light. Todd was from Philadelphia, so there was a commonality, a Philly brotherhood. The problem was there were two Todd Rundgrens. The "Hello It's Me" side that made a ton of money. And an acid-guitar-experimental-rock side with a band called Utopia that didn't. Utopia won out.

The album was called *War Babies*. The cover art appropriately reflected the title. I remember delivering it to the execu-

tives at Atlantic. As they were listening, they would pick their heads up for a moment, look at me, and then drop their eyes down. Ahmet Ertegun was in the room when I played it. When it was finished, there was complete silence. Nobody said, *This sucks.* Nobody said, *This album is not going to make it.* The only comment Ahmet made was, "I think the drums need to be louder." Whatever the hell that meant.

Everybody seemed to respond the same way—that is, by not responding at all. It was a completely different body of music on an album that everybody was hoping would be the next big success in the music industry. But people were not as judgmental in those days, nor quick to kill. There was a respect for the artist that translated into: *Let's see what happens...*

Sadly, nothing did happen. The album wasn't the right format for the FM rock stations that represented integrity to Daryl. And there certainly weren't any programmable singles for Top 40 AM radio. I don't know how many fans *War Babies* made or turned away, but it definitely confused a lot of people. One DJ at WMMR in Philadelphia played the record one night and commented on the air that it sounded like elephants fornicating!

War Babies put all of us in a difficult spot from a business perspective. First of all, Atlantic wasn't going to throw money and all of its promotional muscle behind this strange left turn. The album made every exec there nervous. Second, Hall & Oates' contract with the label was up, and that album couldn't have put me in a worse negotiating position. All of a sudden the execs were wondering just where the hell Hall & Oates were headed.

A newcomer just couldn't afford to take that kind of a left turn at a company that was rolling out Aretha one month and the Rolling Stones the next. It just didn't make sense for

Atlantic to put any energy into left turns when it could spend its time creating blockbusters. Putting out *War Babies* was like losing our number at the deli. We had to take a new ticket and get to the back of the line.

Atlantic had to decide whether or not to extend the contract by putting up an additional $30,000. I had a feeling that Jerry Greenberg, Atlantic's young new president, was going to waffle. Even if Jerry did want to go forward, he'd definitely want to protect his downside by putting up as little money as possible on any contract going forward. The cards in his hand were strong. We'd put out three straight albums that didn't make money.

I needed a backup plan. While I was a song plugger, I'd become very good friends with a man named Mike Berniker, who in his late twenties had produced Barbra Streisand's first three albums for Columbia and was now an exec at RCA. Mike was looking for talent. He had to be, because the company that he worked for was jokingly known in the business as the Recording Cemetery of America. I met with Mike and figured out a way to turn the perfect storm that *War Babies* had created into my best-case scenario. Mike was in love with Hall & Oates and desperately wanted to sign them. There weren't many talented artists waiting in line to go to RCA. He could see the potential in Hall & Oates, and he was willing to pay attention and a *huge* advance right away.

It was the best time to make the move. There was no doubt that we could get a much better contract from RCA than from disillusioned Atlantic. I just needed to play my cards right. Jerry could extend the contract simply by writing a $30,000 check. That was not what I wanted him to do when I stepped into his office. If he wrote one, fine, a deal is a deal. But I wasn't going to let him start waffling...

Jerry was an aggressive, cocky guy, and he had to be think-

ing he had the better hand when we began to talk. He was running a powerhouse, and he couldn't conceive of Daryl and John going anywhere else. *Who else would sign them after that failure?* Jerry started hemming and hawing about how Atlantic might do another album with Hall & Oates, but he didn't want to write the check. He kept on hedging. Maybe we can do this. Maybe we can do that...

I just looked straight into his eyes and said: "Either give us the $30,000, or let us off the label."

"Look, dammit, I'm not sure," he said. "I don't know."

"I don't care if you don't know. I'm not walking out this door without an answer!"

The discussion got heated, really heated. I was even prepared to burn the bridge because I knew I had a backup plan. He kept hedging and I stepped toward him, looking ominously at the window behind him, getting right in his face as our voices got even louder. I certainly knew that I wasn't going to be the one going out that window. But maybe the Bronx coming out in me made him feel like he was.

It was nothing personal. I really liked Jerry. We were friends. But it was business. I felt like the future was at stake. It's hard to explain the dichotomy. But maybe this will help.

Under pressure, Jerry released Hall & Oates from Atlantic Records.

Fourteen years later, when I began to run Sony Music, one of the first things I did was give Jerry Greenberg his own label.

The view outside Jerry's window opened up a whole new world for me. The release from Atlantic had a huge and unexpected impact on my career because it led to a phone call that I hadn't planned on making.

The release needed to be legally expedited. The new contract with RCA had to go through the legal formalities as well. I was working with a prominent lawyer at the time, Bob Casper, who represented the Beatles' music publishing catalog and Elton John. The new deal with RCA was bringing in close to a million dollars, and Casper estimated his fee would be around $80,000. I thought that was absurd. Then I remembered that songwriter walking the corridor of MRC. *"Grubman. Grub-man. Grub-man. I gotta go see Grub-man."*

I'd spoken with Allen Grubman a few times, but I'd never done business with him. The irony of Grubman was that he didn't care about music at all. He used to make a point of telling the artists that came through his office: "I don't listen to your music." That was his line. It worked because he was a *haimishe* guy who had a way of making people feel comfortable around him, and also because, as someone in the industry once observed, "With Grubman, it's not about the money, it's *only* about the money." Grubman protected the people who came through his door and took care of them legally and financially. He said he'd charge twenty grand to do the deals. Soon he was not only representing Hall & Oates, he was also representing me.

Grubman started out with the Village People, and his list of clients would eventually include Madonna, Billy Joel, Bruce Springsteen, Mariah Carey, Bono, Lady Gaga, and on and on. Not only did he develop a skill and style to attract the artists, but he also developed relationships with the record company execs and producers, and he began to represent them as well. So he was connected to all the components. He was representing so many people in the industry that he could ask for favors and, just as important, he knew everything that was going on. Grubman made deals work on everybody's behalf.

Each artist and executive that Allen added to his list of cli-

ents meant more leverage. Anyone who dealt with Grubman knew: *If I screw Allen on this deal, I'm going to get screwed down the road.* And believe me, Allen was not hesitant to remind people of this. As charming as he could be, he was also aggressive in a very direct way. "You think you're not gonna give me a big advance for Billy Joel, you're out of your fucking mind! Period!" He'd say stuff like that to Walter Yetnikoff, the mad genius running CBS Music.

Allen's firm seemed to represent everybody in the music industry, but it never represented two parties in the same transaction. It might represent the artist against the record company, and it might represent the record company in a different transaction. So there never really ever was a conflict of interest— though Allen liked to joke about it. "If there is no conflict," he'd say, "there is no interest." Bottom line is, everybody in the industry went to his firm because they knew they would be protected and they knew they'd get the best possible deal.

For me, connecting with Grubman was like a right hand suddenly finding its left. He used to say that he worked so hard because he didn't want to go back to sleeping on a couch in Brooklyn. And I used to say I worked so hard to make sure that I didn't have to go back to the Bronx. I soon had a partner without a partnership. Good cop. Bad cop. Bad cop. Good cop. Our two arms could play it any which way.

Grubman soon got along famously with Mike Berniker at RCA, and the new deal with Hall & Oates was quickly concluded. It was time to rock and roll.

Daryl was able to laugh when he heard that the DJ in Philadelphia had compared the music on *War Babies* to elephants fornicating. But he got the message. It was time to return to his R & B roots.

I'm sure both Daryl and John appreciated me even more

for the big RCA contract. That was evident in a song Daryl had written about me for their next album called "Gino (The Manager)." There was a joking reference to my Gucci-Pucci pointed shoes, but the core of what I was doing for them came through the chorus:

Remember hard work means something
Live fast, die laughing
No hurt in asking
Nothing for nothing

Another song planned for the next album was called "Grounds for Separation." Sylvester Stallone told me it became an inspiration when he was putting together the movie *Rocky.* He even used it for temp music. The chorus on "Grounds for Separation" went:

Gonna grow a new set of wings
And fly away

Anybody who's ever watched Rocky run up the steps of the Philadelphia Art Museum to the music of "Gonna Fly Now" will get the connection. A ballad called "Sara Smile" would become the B-side to the first single. The music was shaping up to become the classic Hall & Oates album that everybody in the world was hoping for after *Abandoned Luncheonette.* The songwriting, the vocals, and the musicianship were just brilliant.

Arif Mardin didn't produce it, because his contract was exclusive to Atlantic, and Daryl and John wanted to spread their wings anyway. So we brought in some major Los Angeles session players like Ed Greene on drums, who worked on

Steely Dan's *Aja*, and Leland Sklar, the world-renowned bass player. Christopher Bond helped Daryl and John produce the record, and they hit it out of the park.

But there couldn't be a Hall & Oates album without another twist. There needed to be an air of eccentricity to make Daryl happy. John and Daryl had never put their faces on a cover up to that point, and they felt that if they were going to do so, they should do it in a very different way. Daryl and John approached Pierre LaRoche, an art director whose work they loved. LaRoche was Mick Jagger's makeup artist, and he'd also designed some David Bowie covers. LaRoche told Daryl and John that he'd make them immortal. *Okay*, I thought, *hopefully he'll come up with a great vision.* I didn't know that his vision would be to turn Daryl and John into two embalmed transsexuals.

When the cover came in, everyone said: "Whoa!" Even Daryl, when he got over his shock, joked that he looked like the woman that he'd always wanted to go out with. John just looked like a guy with a mustache and a blotch of rouge on his cheek.

LaRoche didn't stop there. Back in the day, there were inserts inside the album. On the insert was a photo of Daryl and John inside a tunnel toned with magenta neon fluorescent light. John was naked. If the message somehow didn't come across on the cover, this certainly took it to the next level.

Everybody was freaked out about it. RCA had spent a fortune because of the unusual technique involved in creating the cover. Albums generally use four colors. This album came to be known as the Silver Album because there was a fifth color. The fifth color, silver, was almost like real silver, and very expensive in the first printings.

In the end, John and Daryl decided to run with it and I supported them. Nobody could argue that it wasn't a great piece of art. I just wondered if the music would be pushed to the side by the question that everyone was sure to ask: are Hall & Oates gay?

It really didn't matter. It didn't matter because people listened to the music before they decided to buy an album. That's why radio was so important. That album, called *Daryl Hall & John Oates*, took off as soon as it hit the airwaves. When an R & B station in Cleveland played the B-side "Sara Smile," the phones lit up like a firestorm. The local promotion man called the national promotion guy at RCA to tell him what had happened. That was when you knew you had a smash. That was when you had to grab the bull by the horns and flip it on its back. I'd watched the same thing happen after the recording of "Na Na Hey Hey (Kiss Him Goodbye)." Paul Leka had us create that song as a throwaway B-side. The moment you discover you might have underestimated a song, you have to be able to turn on a dime and put everything you own behind it. We did just that with "Sara Smile," and it became a runaway hit.

Of course, the brass at Atlantic saw that. Although Jerry Greenberg got royally chewed out by Jerry Wexler and Ahmet Ertegun for giving us that release, he was quick to grasp the moment and rerelease the *Abandoned Luncheonette* LP. As soon as he did, "She's Gone" shot up the charts. Now, we had two monster hits back-to-back and the promotional energy of two companies behind us.

The parties and relentless hard work didn't stop. It was party on top of party on top of party. More work on top of more work. When you have your first hit record, everything changes. Everybody starts calling you. Promoters. Radio sta-

tions. Record stores. And not only that, but *everybody* takes your call.

When you're the manager of a hit act with hit records, you become seen as the guy who can get things done. When you're the manager of a hit act that's writing songs about you, other artists start to sing about you, too.

VOICES

DARYL HALL

I wasn't looking for a father figure. I was looking for a brother figure, somebody who had the thing I lacked, which was an absolute aggression and determination.

I remember Tommy trying to impress me. He was like, "I can get you in anywhere." So he took me backstage at the Spectrum Theater in Philly, and I met Rod Stewart. That was when I said, "Tommy, you're my manager."

I'll always consider those beginning days as one of the most significant times in my life. It was a wild ride. That's all I can say. It was a wild ride. And I think everybody should have a wild ride at least once.

Tommy Mottola is relentless—and that is the key to his success and everything he's done. He doesn't take no for an answer, and he really cares about what he's doing. The one thing I never had any doubts about was that he was fighting full force for anything he wanted from us and wanted us to have.

When it comes down to art versus commerce, Tommy will invariably come out on the side of commerce. I had a million arguments with him, daily arguments, about what I thought we should be doing, and what I felt comfortable doing. I know myself as an artist and I know myself as a person, and I always took the long view. Whereas Tommy took the shorter view. That's because he had to pay attention to where the money was coming in from.

DAVE MARSH

Writer/historian

The fact is, nobody gets rich without trying. Nobody gets famous without trying. There was never a time when the music wasn't commercial.

Dion, of Dion and the Belmonts, once told me: "Hit records are addictive." It's true. They are addictive to the audience and to the artist. They make you a lot of money. They make you famous. They get you laid. They get you into places you wouldn't normally get into. People kiss your ass.

That has never been different. Things were never pure. The Grateful Dead made a lot of money. Yo-Yo Ma made a lot of money. It's what you do with your success that counts. You can be a slut for a nickel, you can be a slut for a dime. You are supposed to have your pink Cadillac and your integrity.

rls" • Donna Summer

e Freak" • Chic

a Think I'm Sexy?" • Rod Stewart

ll Survive" • Gloria Gaynor

uff" • Donna Summer

.C.A." • The Village People

My Bell" • Anita Ward

rthur Park" • Donna Summer

Much Heaven" • The Bee Gees

• The Pointer Sisters

edy" • The Bee Gees

ood Times" • Chic

ou Don't Bring Me s" • Barbra Streisand nd Neil Diamond

d Me On" • Maxine Nightingale

y Life" • Billy Joel

e Your Groove Thing" • Peaches and Herb

Never Love This Way n" • Dionne Warwick

nt You to Want Me" • Cheap Trick

the Love Has Gone" • Earth, Wind & Fire

ven Knows" • Donna mmer and Brooklyn Dreams

y 1's a Winner" • Hot Chocolate

Are Family" • Sister Sledge

ogie Wonderland" • Wind and Fire with the Emotions

tans of Swing" • Dire Straits

ant Your Love" • Chic

k E.'s In Love" • Rickie Lee Jones

t to Be Real" • Cheryl Lynn

tember" • Earth, Wind & Fire

n't Stop 'Til You Get gh" • Michael Jackson

art of Glass" • Blondie

"Hold the Line" • Toto

"You Took the Words Right Out of My Mouth" • Meat Loaf

"Honesty" • Billy Joel

"Soul Man" • The Blues Brothers

"What a Fool Believes" • The Doobie Brothers

"I Need a Lover" • John Cougar

"Hey Hey, My My (Into the Black)" • Neil Young and Crazy Horse

"Highway to Hell" • AC/DC

"She Blinded Me with Science" • Thomas Dolby

Off the Wall • Michael Jackson

The Wall • Pink Floyd

"You Shook Me All Night Long" • AC/DC

"New York, New York" • Frank Sinatra

"Another One Bites the Dust" • Queen

"On the Road Again" • Willie Nelson

"Another Brick in the Wall" • Pink Floyd

"Rapper's Delight" • Sugarhill Gang

"Fame" • Irene Cara

"Off the Wall" • Michael Jackson

"I Wanna Be Your Lover" • Prince

"Upside Down" • Diana Ross

"On the Radio" • Donna Summer

"Lady" • Kenny Rogers

"Whip It" • Devo

"Love Stinks" • The J. Geils Band

"Hit Me With Your Best Shot" • Pat Benatar

"Heartbreaker" • Pat Benatar

"You May Be Right" • Billy Joel

"The Long Run" • The Eagles

"Rock Lobster" • The B-52's

"Call Me" • Blondie

"Against the Wind" • Bob

"I'm Coming Out" • Diana Ross

"(Just Like) Starting Over" • John Lennon

"Crazy Little Thing Called Love" • Queen

"Hungry Heart" • Bruce Springsteen

"Brass in Pocket (I'm Special)" • The Pretenders

"It's Still Rock and Roll to Me" • Billy Joel

"I Got You" • Split Enz

"Into the Night" • Benny Mardones

"Cruisin'" • Smokey Robinson

Back in Black • AC/DC

"Don't Stop Believin'" • Journey

"Super Freak" • Rick James

"Give It to Me, Baby" • Rick James

"Jessie's Girl" • Rick Springfield

"Start Me Up" • The Rolling Stones

"Celebration" • Kool & the Gang

"Waiting for a Girl Like You" • Foreigner

"Endless Love" • Lionel Richie and Diana Ross

"In the Air Tonight" • Phil Collins

"De Do Do Do, De Da Da Da" • The Police

"Lady (You Bring Me Up)" • The Commodores

"Urgent" • Foreigner

"The Tide Is High" • Blondie

"The Stroke" • Billy Squier

"Don't Stand So Close to Me" • The Police

"Guilty" • Barbra Streisand and Barry Gibb

"Woman" • John Lennon

"Rapture" • Blondie

"9 to 5" • Dolly Parton

"Physical" • Olivia Newton-John

"Slow Hand" • The Pointer

"Private Eyes" • Daryl Hall and John Oates

"Boy from New York City" • Manhattan Transfer

"Stop Draggin' My Heart Around" • Stevie Nicks with Tom Petty and the Heartbreakers

"Kiss on My List" • Daryl Hall and John Oates

"Crazy Train" • Ozzy Osbourne

"You Make My Dreams" • Daryl Hall and John Oates

"Mickey" • Toni Basil

"Open Arms" • Journey

"Eye of the Tiger" • Survivor

"Chariots of Fire • Titles" • Vangelis

"I'm So Excited" • The Pointer Sisters

"Ribbon in the Sky" • Stevie Wonder

"We Got the Beat" • The Go-Go's

"She's Got a Way" • Billy Joel

"Up Where We Belong" • Joe Cocker and Jennifer Warnes

"Get Down on It" • Kool and the Gang

"Gloria" • Laura Branigan

"Everybody Wants You" • Billy Squier

"Always on My Mind" • Willie Nelson

"Don't You Want Me" • Human League

"Genius of Love" • The Tom Tom Club

"Goodbye to You" • Scandal

"Juke Box Hero" • Foreigner

"Jack & Diane" • John Cougar

"Hurts So Good" • John Cougar

"Maneater" • Daryl Hall and John Oates

"Centerfold" • The J. Geils Band

"I Can't Go for That (No Can Do)" • Daryl Hall and John Oates

5

The Silver Cloud

White dance suits, platform shoes, and strobe lights were next. I could feel disco coming the moment a studio owner in West Orange, New Jersey, turned me on to a group called Dr. Buzzard's Original Savannah Band.

It was more than a band, it was a carnival, almost a dozen kids from the streets of the Bronx who'd grown up taking in the sounds of their neighborhoods. They blended Latin, black, and pop into the most unique music and visuals I'd ever come across. The music was only half of it. Watching the Savannah Band was like watching one of those Busby Berkeley movies from the thirties.

The group's costumes were not costumes. Their costumes were their street clothes. One of the leads, August Darnell Browder, wore zoot suits every minute of every hour of every day. He probably slept in his zoot suit. Other guys in the band wore baggy pants and old newsboy caps. The lead singer, Cory Daye, wore antique dresses from the forties and fifties. They

all took on their own personas and lived them. They were 100 percent the genuine article. If these kids would've had their feet on the ground and not gotten drunk on their first sip of success, they could've become one of the biggest acts in the world. Not only that, they'd still be here today!

I first saw the band with Sandy Linzer, whom I'd become close to during the production of my second T. D. Valentine record. We were amazed to find out that the Savannah Band had been turned down by four or five labels, because the moment Sandy and I saw them, we turned toward each other with looks that said: *Can you believe this? If we can get this on a record the right way, we're going to have a monster act.*

I immediately called Mike Berniker at RCA and told him of my excitement. "Do it!" he said. Talk about trust. Just like that, without hearing a note, and sight unseen. I brought in Charlie Calello to help organize the group's rhythms and connect the musical dots. Charlie came through big-time, especially on a song called "Cherchez la Femme," which opened like this:

> *Tommy Mottola lives on the road*
> *He lost his lady two months ago*
> *Maybe he'll find her, maybe he won't*
> *Oh, no, never, no, no*
> *He sleeps in the back of his big gray Cadillac*
> *Oh, my honey*
> *Blowing his mind on cheap grass and wine*
> *Oh, ain't it crazy baby, yeah*
> *Guess you can say, hey, hey,*
> *That this man has learned his lesson,*
> *Oh, oh, hey, hey*
> *Now he's alone, he's got no woman and no home*
> *For misery, oh-ho, cherchez la femme*

When I played this song and the rest of the album for a roomful of execs at RCA, most of them looked up at me with expressions of dismay. They might as well have shouted: *What the hell is this?* But Mike Berniker understood. He stood up and started making the cranking motion of an old-fashioned movie camera as if he were filming a kaleidoscopic choreographed dance scene from a thirties classic.

If the other execs didn't understand the music, they understood something else. I'd brought them Hall & Oates and "Sara Smile." And another thing: I was being invited to the corporate dining room to lunch with the higher-ups. RCA really had no choice but to sign the Savannah Band. At the beginning of 1976, almost two years before anyone heard the Bee Gees sing "Stayin' Alive," and three years before Donna Summer released "Bad Girls," the Savannah Band's first album broke huge, quickly selling more than half a million copies.

You couldn't walk down a street in New York without hearing "Cherchez la Femme" blaring out of bodegas, boutiques, car radios, and nightclubs. There are certain songs that will always be unique to the people who did them, because they stand for a moment in time and the vocal phrasing just cannot be duplicated. A lot of great singers sang "Cherchez la Femme," but it will always be associated with Cory Daye's voice. Cory was probably one of the best stylists I ever worked with, and what I mean by that is she had a sound and a phrasing that created a totally unique style. So that when the music, the time period, and her voice came together, something phenomenal was created that forced anyone listening to stop in their tracks. Something totally original had been created.

Hearing my name in "Cherchez la Femme" five times a day on the radio was so strange—almost surreal. At that age and

at that time it became very intoxicating, even dangerous, *and* I was only their manager. You can imagine what it was doing to the Savannah Band.

A few months after this splash, Hall & Oates came out with their next album. It was called *Bigger Than Both of Us* and featured "Rich Girl." That was it. Anything I wanted from that point at RCA was at my fingertips.

Two hundred percent of my time was now occupied with Hall & Oates and the Savannah Band—but don't forget, I was still working days in my job at Chappell Music. I was supposed to be a song plugger, which didn't exactly jibe with the image of a guy driving around in a polished 1959 Silver Cloud Rolls-Royce, wearing fur coats when the winter called for it, and smoking the finest pre-Castro Cuban cigars.

It was a highly unusual situation. Chappell owned the copyrights to the music of Hall & Oates and the Savannah Band, and it was deriving financial benefits through my efforts. But I was refusing to accept promotions because that would have given me more responsibility and required more of my time. My fatherlike mentor, Norm Weiser, allowed me to use his larger office in the evening to do work on my acts. And I was introducing him to people who might not necessarily take his call. So we made it work for as long as we could. But it soon became apparent to everyone that it was time for me to move on. One day, while at lunch with Ken Glancy, the president of RCA, we had a conversation about it, and he offered up a solution.

"How about we give you a talent scout/production deal?" he said. It was a simple arrangement. *You know how to find the hits. Here's some money. Bring them to us.* That deal would allow me to leave Chappell and start my own company. Glancy was smart. He knew this would allow me to focus all of my

attention and help increase the sales of Hall & Oates and the Savannah Band.

I found a two-bedroom apartment at 105 West Fifty-Fifth Street, second floor, great space, with wood floors and a fireplace. I got a desk, some furniture, and in a way I was just where my mother and father had always wanted me to be. I was in my own business.

The birth of Champion Entertainment couldn't have been better timed. Hall & Oates were on fire. So was the Savannah Band. And in December 1977, the same month that John Travolta and *Saturday Night Fever* sent everybody running to the discos, we released a song on RCA called "Native New Yorker."

There's some irony in "Native New Yorker." That is, not one member of the group that sang it was a native New Yorker. Two of the three members of Odyssey were sisters—Lillian and Louise Lopez—who were originally from the Virgin Islands and living in Connecticut when Sandy Linzer found them. The sisters knew a Filipino backup bass player named Tony Reynolds, whose dream was to make enough money to move back home and open a gas station. It wouldn't surprise me if he now owns an entire chain based on the success of that one song.

Sandy Linzer had written "Native New Yorker" for Frankie Valli. But maybe it was destined for a female voice. When it was channeled through Lillian Lopez it became magic, like she owned it. We brought in Charlie Calello to arrange the song in a way that made it pure commercial disco. This time, when the execs at RCA heard the song there was no denying it was going to be a huge hit. The music had every necessary ingredient: great song, great arrangements, the star power of

New York, and a disco beat that could play in any hot club from here to Hong Kong. Mike Berniker went nuts when he heard it.

I used my connections to book Odyssey on a bunch of television shows. We took the three band members, put makeup on them, styled them, and quite often had them lip-synch, because outside the studio their voices were not that great. But Lillian's voice will be the way that "Native New Yorker" is remembered. It worked. Odyssey was a one-hit wonder, but I was able to hit one more monster out of the park for RCA.

Even Sam Clark couldn't help but take notice. When I was first trying to break John and Daryl, he used to ask me how "Hallz & Oates" were doing. As if they were somehow connected to the buffoonish comedy of Huntz Hall, the guy who played Sach in the old Bowery Boys movies. But he began to see the respect I was getting around the industry, and I started to wonder if he was even becoming a little jealous. I was no longer driving a banged-up Chevy into his driveway. I had a very early model of car phone installed in my Mercedes convertible, and I know that definitely pissed him off. There was friction in his voice when he asked Lisa: "Why does Tommy need a phone in his car?" A giant fight over the car phone ensued between Lisa and me. She moved back in with her parents for a few days, and I began to wonder what the hell this was all about.

I tried to bury it all under the workload. But I was also starting to encounter difficulties there, too. Few people were aware of what was going on behind the hits. When a bunch of street kids like the Savannah Band start drinking the Kool-Aid, your job as a manager begins to feel like you're a 911 receptionist working the late Saturday night shift. If instant success is a spark, the Savannah Band was a tank of gasoline.

We'd schedule interviews for them at hotels and they'd show up late, six or eight at a time, carrying bags of laundry to be washed and dry-cleaned, then each of them would order two of the most expensive meals on the room service menu, one to eat just then, and the other to take home. Two of the three key members, Cory Daye and Stony Browder, were boyfriend and girlfriend. I remember getting a call late one night after they'd gotten into a major fight at the Continental Hyatt House on Sunset Boulevard in Los Angeles. They didn't call it the Riot House for nothing. When Cory locked Stony out of her room, Stony opened up a window on a floor below and climbed up on the terraces like King Kong mounting the Empire State Building, then smashed through the sliding glass doors on Cory's terrace and broke into her room. The group hired a screwy business manager who questioned everything that I was doing. Even the coleader of the band, August Darnell, who had a master's degree and had taught English in high school, once pushed me to the point of a fistfight in my office. I needed to pour myself a scotch to calm down after that one.

It was a weird experience, a paradox. Because managing the Savannah Band was also an invaluable study for me in imaging, artwork, live performances, clubs, sound, lights, hair, makeup, styling, and clothing. All of this would help me fast-forward so many careers later on at Sony. So I put up with the craziness. Besides, there were so many good things happening simultaneously to divert my attention. No matter how much crap went down with the Savannah Band on one day, there was always something amazing that would happen with Hall & Oates on the next.

For instance, shortly after that tense night with August Darnell in my office, Hall & Oates and I went to an Eagles concert

at the L.A. Forum. This was 1977. The Eagles were about to sing their just-released Number One hit, "New Kid in Town," when Glenn Frey stepped up to the microphone and said: "We want to dedicate this to the new kids in town: Daryl Hall and John Oates." It was as if we had just become part of an elite club.

On another night, we had a funny incident with Sylvester Stallone. He attended a Hall & Oates concert in New York at the Palladium, and I managed to convince him to walk out onstage during the last song and put his hands up in the air like Rocky, then grab Daryl and John by the scruff of their necks and yank them off the stage to close the show. This was when the movie *Rocky* had just made Stallone the biggest star in the world. When Sly showed up out of nowhere there was a silent shock of disbelief that set up the place for a delayed reaction, and then a roar that shook the entire street.

We were on fire. Nights were not nights, they were memorable events. When the baked clams, the lobster oreganata, the pasta, and the veal came out to our table at Joe's on MacDougal Street, the motto was not: "Eat, drink, and be merry, for tomorrow you shall die." It was: "Tomorrow you shall live and have another great day like this."

It was like a fantasy. Who wanted to go home?

We never, ever considered the possibility that the hits would stop or that the glasses would no longer clink. There was no concept of that. How could that possibly happen?

Of course, I was in for a rude awakening. You can work like a dog, have lots of hits and credibility with a huge network of people who think you're smart and brilliant, but in the end, as I found out, you are only as good as your last hit record. Sure enough, by 1979, the hits stopped cold.

Odyssey had had their fifteen minutes of fame. There was so much disarray around the Savannah Band that I broke off management ties. I didn't need a crystal ball to see the collapse coming, and it was no great surprise when the band broke up after its third album failed to chart. August Darnell started another group called Kid Creole and the Coconuts, which had a great run in Europe, but it was a shadow of what the Savannah Band could've been. And, of course, after huge successes with "Sara Smile," "She's Gone," and "Rich Girl," it was only natural for Hall & Oates to want to stretch in a new direction.

Daryl and John could write R & B pop hits in their sleep. They could've snored hits. Which, to Daryl, was exactly the point. He didn't want to repeat himself. He wanted new dreams. He wanted different canvases. And why not? He was an artist.

There was much more freedom back then for artists. But the bottom line remains the bottom line. The record companies put up million-dollar advances and expected hits. It was my job, as the manager, to support Daryl's dreams. At the same time, it was my job to help bring hits to the company that was paying him. At certain points, that was not an easy tightrope to walk.

The best way I can explain it is through the first solo album Daryl recorded—*Sacred Songs*. Daryl created it over a few weeks in 1977 with a very talented, experimental English musician, Robert Fripp, who improvised the guitar solo to David Bowie's "Heroes" and whom most people know as a member of the progressive rock band King Crimson. Daryl was totally infatuated with musicians like Bowie, Fripp, and Brian Eno. He loved England. And his collaboration with Fripp took him a long way from the streets of Philadelphia. Both Daryl and

Fripp were really proud of *Sacred Songs*, and to this day Daryl points to it as an important building block in his trajectory.

The execs at RCA didn't look at it that way. They just didn't think the music was commercial and, on top of that, they feared the new sound would alienate Hall & Oates' core fans. So they postponed the release indefinitely. Daryl and Fripp got upset, and they passed around tapes of *Sacred Songs* to music insiders to prove their point and build an underground demand. Ultimately, Daryl prevailed. But it took three years before RCA released *Sacred Songs* to very moderate commercial success.

This experimentation period would have been so much easier if Daryl and John were simultaneously putting out the hits that everyone was expecting. But they seemed to be in either one mode or the other: experimenting or creating hits. I was constantly caught between my respect for them as artists and their commercial possibilities. Daryl will tell you that I always pushed toward the commercial, and he's right. "Why," I'd ask him, "are you afraid of hit records? Hits *are* the biggest part of your credibility." But he was a trailblazer, and he simply needed to go down new paths.

Daryl and John veered toward rock on *Beauty on a Back Street*, which came out in 1977. The album contained no hits. The following year, George Harrison, Todd Rundgren, and Fripp joined Daryl and John on another artistic journey that was entitled *Along the Red Ledge*. Again, no hits. Look, I got what they were trying to do. And I respected it. Bob Dylan showed up at the Newport Folk Festival in 1965 with an electric guitar and got booed. He knew where he was headed, and it ultimately became part of his personal folklore. An artist is no longer an artist when he stops going to new places. Daryl kept telling me: "You've got to see the long road, man."

My beautiful parents, Tom and Peggy...puttin' on the ritz.

Me on Santa's lap at Macy's Parkchester, Bronx, New York.

Me, five years old, at my sister Joan's wedding. Check out the plastic on the sofa and lamps—very Bronx Italian.

Me, in my Admiral Farragut Academy uniform (ugh!), with my dad.

My 8×10 glossy, which got handed around to all casting directors and record companies. What happened?

As a young wannabe actor in one of my first and last movie roles.

Out to dinner with (left to right) Penny Marshall, Paulie Herman, and Robert De Niro. That's artist Peter Max leaning in behind Penny.

Me, twenty years old, at Chappell Music, working with Tony Bennett.

Recently...in the studio with Tony doing his *Duets* album. *Credit: Ruben Martin*

Early '80s, backstage at Madison Square Garden after a Hall & Oates concert. Left to right: me, John Oates, Daryl Hall, Mick Jagger, Todd Rundgren.

At last, at last—my first Champion Entertainment office at 105 West Fifty-Fifth Street.

Classic photo! The great Jerry Wexler, Marc Meyerson, John Oates, Daryl Hall, Robin Gibb, Arif Mardin, and me, with young Atlantic Records president Jerry Greenberg.

Two young dreamers: me and Allen Grubman in Acapulco, when he was "thin."

Puffing a great Davidoff Dom Perignon Havana in the '70s.

Holding my then one-year-old son, Michael, at the farm in Hillsdale, New York.

My two loves, Michael and Sarah, as children on my boat *Dreamtime*, named after a Daryl Hall song that Dave Stewart produced.

Me and Sarah out at her riding lesson at Kentucky Stables in Mamaroneck, New York.

Music! Music!
The great '70s:
me, John Oates,
Carly Simon,
Daryl Hall.

Me with (left
to right)
Antonio "LA"
Reid (chubbier
and with hair,
pre *X-Factor*),
Babyface, and
Arsenio Hall.
Credit: Sony Music

Between two
industry greats,
Ahmet Ertegun
and Walter
Yetnikoff.
*Credit: Sony
Music*

I could see the long road. But those artistic risks also brought financial consequences. I hung with these guys day and night, and I was very aware that Daryl and John's previous successes had brought them a taste for the good life—for expensive cars, fine wine, and beautiful homes.

I was constantly trying to strike a balance with Daryl and John between the old hits and a new journey. I'd brought David Foster in to produce *Along the Red Ledge*. Foster has won sixteen Grammys. But you have to understand the timing. This was the late seventies. This was *before* David Foster had won *any* of those Grammys or worked with everyone from Whitney Houston to Michael Jackson. Back then, Foster was a hot session keyboard player in Los Angeles. He had never produced any records. Hall & Oates were his first big break. The only reason I knew about him was because he'd come recommended by a guy I considered to be a genius: the lead composer, writer, and arranger for Toto, David Paich. At the time, I saw Foster as a new talent who could help Hall & Oates explore.

One day when Daryl, John, and I were in the house that we rented in L.A., Foster came over and sat behind the piano. David has these big hands, and when he put them on the keys and played, his sound and his attack were mesmerizing. Foster started to play this incredible melody to "After the Love Has Gone," which, of course, everybody now knows so well. Even though he wasn't a great singer, you knew immediately that this was going to be a gigantic hit. It was undeniable. I'm telling you, if an alley cat had sung it, it still would've gone to Number One.

"Yeah, it's a good song," Daryl said, "but it's really not our style. We don't need that song. We want to write our own music."

What could I do? He wanted to make his own music. But at the same time it was really frustrating to me because it was like having a golden goose that refused to lay golden eggs. More than a year after David Foster played us that song, he stepped onstage to accept his first Grammy for it at the 1979 awards.

I could only shake my head as the airways filled with Earth, Wind & Fire's rendition of "After the Love Has Gone." Meanwhile, John and Daryl released an album called *X-Static* that Foster also produced. Even though there were some brilliant songs, like the classic "Wait for Me," the album didn't achieve the success that we were looking for and, quite frankly, needed. It began to become really confusing to their fans. Where is *Abandoned Luncheonette*? they wanted to know. Where is "Sara Smile"? Where is "Rich Girl" and more of the songs we love?

All those twists and turns and ups and downs became more knowledge that was invaluable to me years later when I started at Sony and had to navigate around similar bumps in the road. Working so closely with Daryl and John, and later on with Carly Simon, John Mellencamp, and Neil and Tim Finn of the New Zealand group Split Enz and, later on, Crowded House, allowed me to really understand what makes artists tick, where they live, how they breathe, and how their thought processes come about. You know when that knowledge is absolutely indispensable? When you wake up one morning and find yourself working with a roster of *four hundred* recording artists in every genre of music from country to R & B, to pop, to rock, to classical.

There just aren't any shortcuts to that sort of wisdom. You've got to go through the journey and make all of the mistakes to be able to know what works and what doesn't, and that journey always comes with moments that make you want to kick a hole in the wall. If this period was frustrating to me, you can imagine how it felt to the execs at RCA. No mat-

ter how I felt about the choices Hall & Oates made, I never stopped breaking through the doors of the promotion and marketing departments at ramming speed. RCA put up with it through the first album with no hits. On the second, they started to question. And by *X-Static*, they began to push aside my requests for more promotion with excuse after excuse.

Champion Entertainment had hit an ice-cold front. Lisa and I were expecting our first child, Michael, and my daughter, Sarah, would come not long after. Certainly there's never a good time for the hits to stop. But this definitely felt like the worst.

When you're putting out money and it ain't coming back, you start to see the world in a whole different way. You don't immediately reach for the check at dinner. You stop and look around, and start to notice how many people have tiny alligator arms as soon as dessert is done.

By no means were Daryl, John, and I ready to give up the Petrus and start drinking Gallo. Daryl certainly *wasn't* trading our pre-Castro Cubans in for White Owls. We needed to come up with a new plan. Immediately.

The reason you go to all those cocktail parties that you vaguely remember is that one might turn into the night that you never forget. It was at one of those cocktail parties that I met David Geffen.

The timing couldn't have been better. I was looking to reinvent myself—and he, himself, was doing just that.

Geffen is one of the smartest and shrewdest guys to ever leave Brooklyn and work his way up from the mailroom of the William Morris Agency. He started Asylum Records in 1970, and quickly became a force by signing Jackson Browne, the

Eagles, Joni Mitchell, and Bob Dylan. But he stepped aside for a time after being misdiagnosed with a severe illness. When he found out he was healthy, he came back to start Geffen Records in 1980, and by no means did he stop there. He branched out into the movie business and would soon have a huge hit with the film that launched Tom Cruise's career—*Risky Business*. Geffen would go on to become one of the most influential people in the media industry. If you were looking to emulate someone's success, you couldn't do much better than David Geffen. The title of a book written about him says it all: *The Rise and Rise of David Geffen*.

Our initial conversations centered around his desire to sign Hall & Oates to his record company after their contract with RCA expired. But soon we were sitting over marrowbone steaks at Trader Vic's in L.A., and I was getting an education on Hollywood, the financial markets, politics, and anything else David chose to talk about. He'd taught business studies at Yale, and he was a genius at both: business and teaching. David had the uncommon ability to be cunning and shrewd at the same time that he shared ideas and opened doors.

One night over dinner I told him I wanted to go into the movie business, and he cringed. "It's the worst business in the world!" he said. "It's absolutely crazy. Don't even think about it. Why would you want to do that to yourself?"

"I have some great ideas for films," I told him.

"Stick with the music business," he said. "You're going to be really successful, and it's so easy compared to the movie business."

"I don't want to leave the music business," I said. "I just want to grow."

He gave me one of those looks that said, *If you insist, but don't say I didn't warn you.* One phone call later, and I was step-

ping into the office of the man who shaped nearly every major deal that went down in the film industry at that time.

The office belonged to a former tax attorney who opened a full-service entertainment law firm that represented the likes of Barbra Streisand, Nick Nolte, Robert Redford, Sean Connery, and almost everyone who'd recently left their fingerprints in cement outside Grauman's Chinese Theatre. The man behind the desk was buttoned down and quiet. His name was Gary Hendler. "Why," he asked me, "do you want to get into this business?"

I told him a couple of my ideas for films. A few minutes later, he picked up his phone, and a few minutes after that, a budding superagent whose offices were three floors below came through the door. It was Mike Ovitz. That meeting set in motion a string of phone calls that would introduce me to Michael Eisner, Dawn Steel (the first woman to ever run a major Hollywood film studio), Jeffrey Katzenberg, and Barry Diller. It boggles the mind to think now that all those people were once under a single roof at Paramount. The connections that Geffen and Hendler supplied didn't stop there. In no time, I was linked to virtually every studio head and television executive in Hollywood.

I'd gotten the rights to two ideas and was eager to begin developing. One was a true story of a street priest whose parish was in the South Bronx. He cared deeply about his faith, serving Mass and taking confession, but he also used his Georgetown education to build low-income housing units for minorities and take care of the less fortunate in his community. His name was Father Louis Gigante. It was said that Father Gigante built the South Bronx up from the ashes. The contrast in this story was that the priest's brother was Vincent "Chin" Gigante.

The second idea was a book written by a friend named Philip Carlo. It was called *Stolen Flower*. It was about a private detective tracking down a ten-year-old girl who'd been kidnapped and ensnared by the underground sex world. I'd talked about it with my friend Joe Pesci, and he thought it would make a terrific film. Joe spoke to Robert De Niro, and the three of us decided to develop it.

We spent months doing research. But the nature of the material made this project tough to get off the ground.

Lesson One: Pedophilia isn't exactly a topic that warms the hearts of studio execs.

Lesson Two: A project like this takes time. I just spoke with Joe Pesci about *Stolen Flower*—we're talking thirty years later—and he's *still* trying to develop it.

The story of Father Gigante needed time, too, but it moved nicely from stage to stage. Through an agent at William Morris I befriended a director who cut his teeth by creating a television series called *Naked City*. Later on, he directed classics like *Cool Hand Luke*, *Brubaker*, and *The Pope of Greenwich Village*. His name was Stuart Rosenberg. Father Gigante came to love and trust him, which was important because he was sharing his most intimate stories. Eric Roth, the writer who'd later win an Academy Award for best-adapted screenplay for *Forrest Gump*, also came aboard. We had many meetings with Al Pacino, who wanted to star in the movie. We set up meetings with Alan Ladd at the Ladd Company, and Laddie greenlit the project.

But after all of these amazingly talented people had come together for this project, the movie came to a screeching halt when we fully realized that nobody, and I mean nobody, wanted to risk the possibility of offending anyone in that family.

Lesson Three: Just because a film is in development doesn't mean it will ever be developed.

I didn't give up. The sun began to shine as I moved through these setbacks when Hall & Oates released their next album, *Voices*, and we were back in business big-time, going forward with a run of hits over the next few albums that included "Private Eyes," "I Can't Go for That (No Can Do)," and "Maneater."

These hits gave me the resources to step up and option big books. I had read a great one called *Wise Guy* by Nicholas Pileggi, and I fell in love with it. I knew it could be a major film. The problem was a lot of other people knew it, too. Getting the rights was going to be expensive. But the sun was shining again, and I was prepared to write the check.

The bidding started, and I told Mike Ovitz I was willing to put up $250,000 for the option. I told him that this was really important, and he had to get it for me. But after about a week, I didn't hear anything.

Finally, a call came from Ovitz. "Listen," he said, "you've got to do me a favor."

"What?"

"You've got to let this one go."

"Really? Why?"

"This is really important to me. I'm working on signing a major new client, and delivering this book is pivotal to me making that deal."

What could I do? Even if I said, "No, you owe it to me," I would've lost anyway.

"Mike," I said, "consider it done." That new client was Marty Scorsese. The movie came out four years later, and it was called *Goodfellas*.

Lesson Four: David Geffen was right.

Lesson Five: It was easier for me to convince Mike Ovitz to get into the music business, which I did, than it was to get a film made.

The differences between the movie business and the music business had been made brutally clear to me. In the music business, I could get excited about a song, find the right musicians, put them in the studio, and have a single out a week later.

With a movie, I had to option the book, find a writer, get a script that moved through second and third drafts, and pretty soon three years had passed. Back then producer fees were not that great anyway. Sure, there was the back end, but whoever gets to see the back end? It turned out much easier to get big advances in the music business.

There was a lot of irony in my journey to Hollywood, especially if you were watching it through the eyes of Daryl Hall. Of course, I hadn't made any hit movies. Forget that, I hadn't even gotten one made! But, as Daryl said, you've got to look at the long road. My frustrations in Hollywood ended up being a blessing in disguise.

I'd gotten my hands into the mix. It was an opportunity to meet and get close to all the heads of the movie studios and the agents at all of the agencies. These experiences gave me a chance to look at things differently than if I were just another music guy. All of the contacts and relationships that were made during this period would become invaluable ten years down the road when I became chairman of the biggest record company in the world. I instantly understood exactly how Celine Dion could benefit from doing the *Beauty and the Beast* and *Titanic* sound tracks. In fact, later on at Sony, we became the only record company in the world to have an exclusive sound-track division. It became enormously successful.

Which brings us to Lesson Six: Success may look like a hit, but it's really about finding a way through the struggle.

While I was trying to find my way around Hollywood and making my bones in the music business in the late seventies, a man who would have a profound impact on my life was beginning to make his mark on the world. I'd even go as far as to say this man would become like a second godfather to me. I had no idea who he was at the end of the seventies. And it would have surprised me at the time to learn that one day I'd have a Japanese godfather. Now, looking back, it's hard to fathom my life without him. His name was Norio Ohga.

Ohga grew up in Numazu, a city eighty miles west of Tokyo, wanting to be an opera singer. Around the time he was about to enter college, one of the founders of the telecommunications and engineering company that would later change its name to Sony came to his neighbor's home looking for investors. Ohga was introduced, and from that point on in his life he would straddle two roads: music and engineering.

Ohga went on to study as a baritone at the Tokyo National University of Fine Arts. This was the early fifties, around the time that tape recorders were being introduced, and he immediately became convinced of their power. "The tape recorder is for a musician," he said, "what the mirror is for a ballerina." He persuaded the university to purchase some.

When the company that would eventually change its name to Sony sent its model over, Ohga evaluated it and sent back a note listing ten serious problems with the machine. His note concluded that the university would not make a purchase until the problems were resolved. This memo set off a furor in the factory. Nobody believed that a college kid could know

so much about tape recorders and new technology. But the company founders, Masaru Ibuka and Akio Morita, were not angry about it at all. On the day that Ohga graduated, they sent a car to pick him up and drive him to company headquarters, where they asked him to become a contract employee.

Ohga didn't want to take the offer. He wanted to sing opera, and he was headed to Germany to study music. But a deal was worked out. Ohga got a monthly stipend, and in return the company got occasional reports from Europe. Ohga would go on to sing baritone in many operas and marry the famous Japanese pianist Midori. He simultaneously began to work as an executive at Sony. One night, after a long and serious company negotiation that had exhausted him, he had to go onstage to perform *The Marriage of Figaro*. Toward the end of the opera, he briefly fell asleep backstage just as the moment called for him to go out and sing. Jolted awake, he pulled his part off, but from that point on, he turned his attention to Sony. Most importantly for the world, and certainly for me, his love and passion for music would forever remain one of the most important things in his life.

When one of Sony's founders, Ibuka, wanted to listen to music on airline flights, he asked Ohga to come up with a portable device that could play cassettes for him. That's how the model for the Sony Walkman was born.

Looking back on it now, it seems like a caveman's version of the iPod. It allowed you to hear only a dozen songs or so on a single cassette as opposed to the thousands of choices the iPod now provides. But, believe me, at that time, the Walkman was heaven. Everybody wanted it. Everybody had to have it. For the first time, music was portable. You could actually take the music you wanted to hear to the beach. The closest I'd gotten as a teenager was a transistor radio and the hope that the DJ would play the songs I liked.

The Walkman represented more than just a shift in configuration. It was a shift in control. The 33 1/3 long-playing record—and the smaller 45—was about the only way you could own music through the fifties. In those days, a big innovation was high-fidelity stereo. A record could be heard through two speakers instead of one—whoa! Even through the development of the clunky eight-track cartridge in the mid-sixties and the tape cassette players that were installed in cars in the seventies, we associated a musical release with an album cover and vinyl. The Walkman changed all of that.

It was the beginning of the rapid death of vinyl, but few people in the industry seemed to care because everyone was too busy celebrating. Not only did the Walkman allow you to listen to the music you wanted wherever you went. Not only did it give everybody in the industry the convenience of working on their projects while they took a walk around the block. But it enticed consumers to go out and buy the same music on cassette that they already owned on vinyl—and sales soared.

The world of music was changed forever—and Ohga was just getting started. A few years after the Walkman, Sony came out with the first compact disc. In the planning stages, the CD was only supposed to hold sixty minutes of music. When Ohga realized that Beethoven's Ninth Symphony was seventy-three minutes long—he knew that sixty minutes just wouldn't do. A study showed that 95 percent of classical performances could fit into seventy-five minutes. That's why the CD holds up to seventy-five minutes of music to this day. Around the time the CD was released, Ohga became president of the most powerful electronics company in the world, a company whose four branded letters were as powerful as the word *Coke*.

But even as a boss and a president, he still thought and acted like a musician. He was a performer on the opera stage,

and this was really reflected in his personality. He was outgoing, and he enjoyed being attached to music and artists. That energy and creativity gave Sony a totally special and unique vision.

There was absolutely nobody in the world better suited to understand what I was capable of doing than this man.

The first commercial CD released was Billy Joel's *52nd Street*. I remember putting it on, sitting back, and listening in total shock and amazement to the clarity, the definition, the isolation of the instruments, and the brilliance of the overall sound. It was stunning how meticulously you could hear Freddie Hubbard's trumpet on "Zanzibar."

Once the music stopped, the contrast was as stark as the difference between black and white. *Oh, my God*, I thought, *is this the end of vinyl?* Flashing in front of my mind was a thirty-second movie of snapshots from the first Elvis LP to my 45 collection. But at the end of that movie, a burst of light was saying, *Do you know how incredible this is going to be?*

It took time for people in the music industry to adjust. I would sit around with musicians and producers, listen to the CD, and ask, "What do you think?" Some of them would say, "It's too clean, man, it's too clean." They just loved the blend of an analog sound. But, of course, that didn't last very long. Even the hard-core audiophiles who loved their jazz and classical music on vinyl, and cherished their albums as if they were their children, were swept away by the superior sound quality on the CD. Classical performances were taken to a whole new level. The rap of the conductor's baton against the music stand could be heard cleanly and clearly in a way that made vinyl feel primitive.

Within months, all of us embraced the CD. I can remember going into a record store one day and loading up on CDs for every favorite record I ever owned. I spent thousands of bucks and came out of the store with bags and bags filled with CDs. Entire catalogs were being repurchased by almost everyone I knew.

The CD was probably, to this day, the biggest sales catalyst in the history of the music industry. It was smaller than vinyl, it was portable, it didn't scratch like vinyl. It was an absolute gold mine. Higher prices could be charged because of the superior sound quality—and there was a *global* conversion.

Nobody could see what was waiting behind the door that the CD had opened. How could we? Billy Joel's CD came out in 1982. The Internet was created around 1983, and the first Apple Macintosh was sold in 1984. Nobody could fast-forward to glimpse just how powerful the information superhighway would become. Or envision how entire libraries of songs could one day be digitally shared around the globe in a matter of seconds. And not only that: Nobody I knew could imagine that the people receiving those songs over the Internet would come to believe that music didn't have a price tag and, what's more, feel entitled to get it for free as if they were listening to it on the radio. The way we all saw it back then, it was fun to go to the record store, talk to the people behind the counter, and sample the music, especially if it was an incredible place like Tower Records. That whole experience was part of enjoying the musical journey. And when you walked out the door, the music you wanted was yours. It was cool to own your own music.

There's always a question of ownership when it comes to a product. I'm going to dwell on this point in the case of the CD because it's going to bring clarity to the obstacles that

surfaced when searching for solutions to the downloading that rocked the music industry at the end of the nineties. I'm convinced that one of the reasons Apple was able to ultimately get a grip on the music industry was that very issue of proprietary ownership on the part of Sony.

There's something essential to understand here. Sony did not create those CDs by itself in 1982, just as it did not put out compact cassette tape technology on its own before that. Both the cassette and the CD were based on a partnership between Sony and a Dutch company called Philips that owned Poly-Gram Records. It was a perfect marriage. Philips was a leader in optical video disc technology, while Sony was at the cutting edge of digital-processing technology.

Norio Ohga was influential in putting together a joint development deal between the two companies on the CD. It's very important to remember this about two hundred pages down the road. He had the foresight to cement this partnership. But Ohga was not in charge when the downloading of songs became serious, and the new leadership did not view partnerships the same way.

Nobody I knew even considered the downloading of music when we set our CDs into a Sony Discman during the early eighties. We all knew about piracy. The sale of blank cassettes led to primitive cases of music theft—which some of us didn't even regard as theft at the time. The blank cassettes gave people the ability to record off the radio and rerecord cassettes. You know how we saw that at the time? We didn't care. At worst, it was insignificant. And at best, it was great marketing.

We were happy when somebody taped "She's Gone" off the radio and passed the cassette on to a friend. We thought it was wonderful because whoever heard it might go straight to the record store and buy *Abandoned Luncheonette*. And we knew

that if the person liked "She's Gone," he or she might buy tickets to Daryl and John's concerts and become a committed fan. We also knew that a committed fan was not going to settle for a bootleg, that he was going to go out and buy the quality recording.

There was very little time for a guy like me to sit around and wonder about the possibility of CD piracy in the early eighties. In fact, there was no time at all. I was in the middle of a revolution.

The revolution was every bit as influential as Elvis or the Beatles—but much trickier to identify because it wasn't attached to a singular musical act. It was a series of technological breakthroughs accompanied by the emergence of new platforms to showcase music: The Walkman in 1979. CNN in 1980. MTV in 1981. The CD in 1982.

When the Walkman arrived, cable TV was in its infancy. Only six years later, the release of "We Are the World" was beamed around the world by CNN's satellites twenty-four hours a day, and Live Aid concerts across the globe could be seen for sixteen straight hours on MTV.

What happened was so big that a guy like me could work ninety-six hours a week—or even try to squeeze in 120.

Just like when I was a kid running home from school to watch Dick Clark and *American Bandstand*, everyone ran home in 1981 to watch MTV. Only not for thirty minutes—but for seven hours straight. Or more. MTV became like wallpaper.

It was the first total music television channel, and the first time I saw its three-minute music videos was like another Elvis moment. You knew we were experiencing something that would create a powerful change. It was immediately clear that

a music video in heavy rotation hitting millions of people with pictures and sounds combined with the same song's heavy rotation on radio would strike every part of the consumer's senses and have an explosive effect. You knew that it had the possibility to create monster smash hits unlike ever before, and certainly it did, ultimately leading to millions of additional sales that were just not there until that time.

Hall & Oates were in just the right place at the right time to take advantage of the new network. They were on fire again after remaking "You've Lost That Lovin' Feelin'," originally a hit for the Righteous Brothers, for their *Voices* album, and they became one of MTV's most important early acts. So it was my job to get very friendly with the guys running the network: Bob Pittman, John Sykes, Les Garland, and John Lack. I brought Allen Grubman into MTV to discuss a deal for Hall & Oates. And, of course, Allen walked out representing MTV.

We were all finding our way with this new medium, especially Hall & Oates. To this day, when I happen to come across some of their early videos I find my hands covering my eyes. "Private Eyes," was basically two guys lip-synching in trench coats. These were low-budget productions, and Daryl and John were not particularly suited to the new medium. Now, you needed to not only be able to write the music, play it, and perform it onstage. You had to act it out for the camera—and not every musician is a great actor. A group from New Zealand that I managed at the time called Split Enz was much better at it. And as I began to manage John Mellencamp and Carly Simon, I observed that they had an affinity for it, too. Bands like Duran Duran seemed to be created just for the new network. It broke the lock of radio as a way of breaking an artist. Sometimes MTV took the lead over radio, and sometimes it could be groundbreaking even without Top 40 radio.

The new relationship between images and music created a whole new cultural experience that reverberated throughout the world. The fresh styles seen on MTV were embraced by the fashion industry. Marketers and every advertising agency on Madison Avenue followed these trends, which became a major influencer of consumer behavior and even flipped Hollywood upside down.

For the first time, corporate America really gravitated toward the music industry. I remember hearing a story about how Elvis Presley's manager, Colonel Parker, once offered to have Elvis advertise for free for a year for RCA. Of course, the record company, owned by GE, turned the offer down because execs were scared of a backlash from people who didn't like Elvis, some saying he was making "race" records. During the tumultuous sixties, the so-called "Generation Gap" pretty much ensured that there would be little synergy between corporate executives in suits and long-haired music stars in bell-bottoms. The magnetic attraction between corporation and artist really started in the seventies and exploded after MTV appeared. I was eager to forge these new alliances, and I actively pursued them for my artists, knowing full well what the benefits could be.

But at the time it wasn't always easy. When I'd brought a Beech-Nut Chewing Gum sponsorship to Hall & Oates, it should come as no surprise that the artist in Daryl saw this as a sellout. A lot of artists felt the same way at the time. It wasn't like it is now, when even Bono puts on sunglasses and is photographed in an open field with a Louis Vuitton bag. Back then, it wasn't cool for an artist to take money to associate with a product.

"This gum is in every candy store in America," I'd say. "Think of all the additional advertising and marketing you'll

receive in stores and with consumers who've never even heard of you before. Plus, the company is dumping hundreds of thousands of dollars into your lap."

The sponsor provided not only financial gain, but tens of thousands for tour support and additional funds that were coupled with the sales plans that the record company had drawn up. It also tied our products into our sponsor's distribution points, further providing a network of promotion for our music.

I do remember Daryl's and John's eyes lighting up when the next sponsor came to the table: Pontiac. Especially when I told them that in addition to the hundreds of thousands of dollars they would each receive, they'd get a brand-new car and so would each of their parents and other members of their families. It was like hitting the lottery. Pretty funny: We were all driving around in Pontiacs for three years. And GM and Pontiac got what they wanted. They were rubbing against the success of Daryl Hall and John Oates—the hottest-selling duo in the world at that time.

These new marketing advantages tremendously helped their *Voices* and *Private Eyes* albums go platinum, and then their *H2O* and *Big Bam Boom* albums go double platinum.

Following those massive successes, Hall & Oates were invited to sing on "We Are the World" along with Michael Jackson, Bob Dylan, Willie Nelson, Bruce Springsteen, Diana Ross, Ray Charles, Lionel Richie, and a choir of superstars that was the greatest assemblage of musical talent to ever stand in one room. I was one of the privileged few to be in the control room to watch it all, completely aware that I was witnessing the biggest musical event of all time. Eight thousand radio stations around the world played the single simultaneously, with proceeds going to help provide famine relief in Africa. Talk

about new platforms. Music and philanthropy were now married, and technology was the pastor.

A few months after "We Are the World" was released, Hall & Oates played at an all-day concert called Live Aid. The idea, generated by Bob Geldof, raised money to fight famine in Ethiopia by linking performances by some of the world's most popular artists at two venues—Wembley Stadium in London and JFK Stadium in Philadelphia. I met Geldof in the UK and we became good friends. The guys in my office were big fans of his band, the Irish phenomenon Boomtown Rats, so we offered to help in any way that we could. Bob did most of the booking and planning of the first Live Aid event out of Champion's Fifty-Seventh Street offices in New York.

Those who were watching that day walked away with many memories. Madonna, who would appear nude in *Playboy* the next month, came onstage in Philadelphia and joked that she wasn't "taking shit off" that day. Phil Collins performed at both venues, flying across the Atlantic in just under three and a half hours on the Concorde to make both shows. During a version of "It's Only Rock 'n Roll," Mick Jagger ripped off part of Tina Turner's dress, and she finished in leotards. The microphone was errantly turned off for the first two minutes of Paul McCartney's piano rendition of "Let It Be," and he later joked that he thought of changing the lyrics to "There will be some feedback, let it be..." It was Daryl and John who opened the prime-time portion of the show, televised by ABC before more than 100,000 people live in Philly, their hometown.

There was so much inside maneuvering to get Hall & Oates the prime position on ABC's portion of the show. Mountains had to be moved, as well, to position them on the cover of *People* magazine alongside Bob Dylan, Madonna, and Mick

Jagger. The issue came out shortly after the concert and gave them tremendous prestige.

The opportunities coming from all these new platforms—MTV, corporate sponsorships, philanthropy, new media—exponentially magnified the workload. If the phone rang twenty times a day in the seventies, it was ringing a hundred times a day in the early eighties. There were so many more possibilities to look into and follow up on. This period was a once-in-a-lifetime opportunity, and we took full advantage of every minute of it. It totally covered every inch of my day.

During this period in the early eighties, my son Michael and daughter Sarah were born. Being caught up in the musical vortex of the hurricane, working, working, working, it was impossible for me to notice how all-consuming it was. Only now do I fully realize—and fully regret—that the necessary time was not spent with my two oldest children at that point.

It was simply a period where you were either going to catapult into this new world or stay back and become a dinosaur. Everything I learned on the fly during this stage would set off the Latin Explosion more than a decade later. As you'll come to see, the corporate sponsorships that we lined up with Pepsi-Cola were so helpful at the World Cup in exposing and breaking open the careers of Ricky Martin and Shakira.

That's all down the road. But it started in the early eighties. By the time this revolution was complete five years later, the record business had become the music industry.

By the mideighties it was crystal clear that I wanted much more out of my life and career than to be just a manager.

In fact, there's one person I must credit for helping me see my way out of management and eventually up to the top at Sony:

John Mellencamp. Excuse me for being sarcastic when I say that. But the truth is the truth. There were many moments of working with John that made me want to run straight for the exit.

John was extremely difficult to get along with. What else can you say about someone whose own nickname for himself was Little Bastard? But maybe the way he treated the people working around him wasn't all his fault. At least I can see that there were reasons for it.

John came out of Seymour, Indiana. He was all heartland, a guy who grew up around fields, endless highways, telephone poles with long connecting wires, and a soda called Big Red, and he could express that life and all that came with it like no one else in the world. He was a poet and a minstrel of the Midwest. But he somehow got on the wrong track early in his career when he signed on with a British manager named Tony Defries. Defries had developed David Bowie's career, and he tried to turn Mellencamp into a pop rocker, an American David Bowie, even convincing John to throw away his last name. John's first album, *Chestnut Street Incident*, contained a series of musical covers like "Oh, Pretty Woman" and "Jailhouse Rock," but the album cover made him look like something he wasn't. It was released under the name Johnny Cougar. I'm not going to say that John was as heavily made up as Boy George in the cover photo, but he certainly didn't look like he was going out to work in a hay field. The album sold only twelve thousand copies, and for years John's career came to be a struggle to simply get his name back.

He changed managers, working in England with Billy Gaff, the guy who'd found Rod Stewart, and he'd had some success by the time we met. It was almost like you could see him trying to take back a little of his name one hit at a time. By his third album, he was no longer Johnny Cougar. He'd become *John*

Cougar. In 1982, after a breakthrough album called *American Fool* that sold five million copies with hit singles like "Hurts So Good" and "Jack & Diane," he had the leverage to resurrect his last name. He became John Cougar Mellencamp on *Uh-Huh*, which had a beautiful song that I'd use to define his work: "Pink Houses."

It was around this time that John was introduced to me through our mutual accountant, Sigmund Balaban. I'm not Freud, but it wasn't hard to observe at that first meeting that Mellencamp's past experiences had soured him toward managers. He thought that he didn't really need one. But Balaban insisted that I could take him to the next level.

"All right, Big Shot Charlie Potatoes," John said right off the bat. "I hear you're a tough guy. The guy who can make all this stuff happen. Well, what are you gonna do for me?" He was constantly challenging me. "Let's get one thing straight: we do it *my* way."

I certainly wasn't going to argue with him about his music. And when you hear a song like "Small Town," you know it's a classic that will be around for the ages. Not only does it have great lyrics, but the melody that went along with it is the sort that brings comfort to the masses of people who live that way. John also had the visuals down. He called up Jeb Brien, my right hand at Champion, and told him he'd seen the work of a photographer whom he wanted to shoot the cover photo for his next album. John was right. A beautiful photo of John leaning on a wood post and wire fence became the cover of *Scarecrow*. It went five times platinum. The only name across the top of his next album, *The Lonesome Jubilee*, was Mellencamp.

John had gotten his name back, and I was the guy who helped him do it, but he didn't quite see it that way. Even though we helped put him on top, the business side of the

relationship was a constant battle. He'd say things like, "Why the fuck should I pay you guys? I've got a Number One record. My daughter could book this fucking tour."

One time we got into an argument over an allotment of tour percentages, and he challenged me to an arm-wrestling match to settle it. "Okay," I said, "let's do it." We struggled to a draw and had to split the difference.

The best metaphor I can give you for our relationship was what was supposed to be a flag football game between his guys in Indiana and a bunch of my friends. Mellencamp had a team in what he called the MFL (the Mellencamp Football League), and he was always boasting about it. When I questioned just how good it was, he called me out. "What's the matter?" he said. "You New York pussies don't have the balls to come out to Indiana to play a little friendly football?"

So I rounded up the guys from my office, some of whom were jocks and sports fans, and some old high school football stars from New Rochelle, including Stormy (the Animal) Avallone, and flew the entire team out for the game.

After Mellencamp had called us "a bunch of pansy-ass poseurs from New York City," we'd bet a thousand dollars on the outcome. I quickly found out that he was more than a little concerned. We held a practice session the day before, and, sure enough, we caught Mellencamp on a hill above us spying on our plays with a pair of binoculars.

The game took place in a snowstorm. Mellencamp's beautiful wife at the time, Vicky, showed up to watch in a white jumpsuit and long white coat. It was supposed to be flag football, but it got physical quick. One of my guys broke a wrist, another came back to the huddle with a bloody nose, and a third with a chipped tooth.

"Okay, Animal," I said, "time to take the gloves off."

The Bronx descended on the Mellencamp Football League. Two of his guys went off with bloody noses. At one point, Mellencamp went up for a pass that was intercepted. John started punching the guy who'd made the interception, then stormed off the field. We won the game. Afterward, Mellencamp's wife walked over and unzipped the leg of her flashy white jumpsuit, took out the thousand bucks, and handed it to John. He threw it in the snow at my feet.

That moment sort of summed up our entire business relationship. Mellencamp is an amazing talent that I have great respect for on a musical level. And there was money in managing him for me and my company. But nobody likes to have to bend over to pick it up.

There had to be a better way.

VOICES

JANN WENNER

What was marketing in the old-time record business? It was: How do we get this on radio? Do we offer hookers, cocaine, or cash? That's what passed for marketing in the old-fashioned record business.

So that had to evolve. Because the other thing that was wedded to this Baby Boomer generation was the expansion of technology. That spread to music, and what happened was the music business went from a small American industry into a more mainstream art form with other platforms and larger revenues. The music was no longer confined to radio and payola.

MEL ILBERMAN
Music executive

It was during the early eighties when the music business made a major mistake—though it didn't show up until the late nineties. Piracy had always been a problem. There were plants manufacturing tapes in China. But when the CD arrived, it put out a much clearer sound that was just right for the pirating. In effect, the CD was the perfect instrument *for* the pirates. Music companies should have encoded those CDs with something to prevent copying back then. But the manufacturers were

looking for profit and somehow the record companies just missed it.

ALLEN GRUBMAN

Attorney

What really affected the record business in the early eighties was the CD. It sent sales through the roof, and that led to many changes in the industry that became apparent at the end of the decade. Initially, when CD sales went through the roof, artists who were recording were able to get much bigger record deals because sales were bigger and their catalogs had increased in value.

By the late eighties, the value of the independent record companies that had these artists and catalogs had soared. Independent labels owned by creative entrepreneurs started to be acquired by major record companies. Geffen Records was sold to MCA. Island Records was sold to PolyGram. Chrysalis Records was sold to EMI.

When my firm, in addition to representing superstars, started representing the sale of these independent companies, that materially affected our growth and made the firm much more successful and powerful. The record business turned into the music industry alongside this transition from independent to corporate.

DAN KLORES

Playwright/filmmaker

Being a talent manager is as good an experience as you can get in the entertainment industry. Because

when you're a manager, especially a young manager, you're making every mistake in the book, man. But you're learning, you're learning.

David Geffen was a talent man. Brad Grey was a talent man. Mottola was a talent manager. Irving Azoff was a talent manager. So why is that critically important? Because, afterward, when you walk over to the other side and become an executive, you know how to manage talent. You know what they want. You know how to cater to them, mold them, con them, make them feel as if they're great, know when to say no, how to say no.

You're never gonna know that if you come from the promotions or the A&R world. Never. Ever.

DAVE GLEW

Music executive

If you'd met Tommy in the early eighties during the MTV days, you would never have seen all the sides there are to him.

You'd have seen the manager, in which case you'd have bumped into the aggressive side, the generous side, the creative side. But there is so much more, and a lot of it didn't become apparent until after he became an executive—and these layers of personality were apparent only to people who spent a lot of time around him. He's very complicated.

He grew more and more famous with the marriages to Mariah and Thalia. But it's impossible to get an idea of who he is if you were relying on the newspapers or the trade publications. I don't think many people have an

inkling of who he really is. People know his name. The name is magic. We'd travel all over the world and people would know his name. It's a brand. Don't ask me why. It just is. What people don't understand is that brand has a lot of facets.

JEB BRIEN

Longtime colleague

Split Enz had an arrogant prick for a manager—a flamboyant fashion photographer named Nathan Brenner. One night Brenner got into a beef with Randy Hoffman. Not only did Randy work at Champion, but he was one of Tommy's most trusted and loyal friends. A beer bottle was smashed. But it was all show. Brenner had no balls.

A few days afterward, Tommy, Randy, and I were at a Grammy party in Los Angeles when Tommy spotted Brenner. Brenner was wearing a powder-blue satin brocade dinner jacket.

Tommy told Randy, "This is going to be your payback."

Tommy went to the bar and asked the bartender to make him a drink.

"Put it in one of those big highball glasses," he said. "Some tomato juice. A little milk. Some red wine. Bitters. Cranberry juice. Nuts. And throw in some ice cream."

The bartender was looking at Tommy like he's out of his mind. But he put everything in the glass, and then Tommy told him to shake it up real good.

Then Tommy took the glass and went over to the banquet tables, added a few more ingredients: blueberries, whipped cream, coffee, cheese dip. And he nonchalantly

strolled over to where Brenner was standing with this concoction in hand.

"Hey, Nathan," Tommy said, "how you doin'?"

Brenner gave him a what-the-fuck-do-you-want look.

Tommy said: "This is compliments of Randy Hoffman."

Then he tipped the glass over Brenner's head and emptied the entire contents all over him.

Brenner was freaked. He didn't know what to do.

"And another thing," Tommy told him. "You are hereby banned from entering the United States. You are never allowed to come back into this country unless I say you can."

"mmer of '69" • *Bryan Adams*

Boys of Summer" • *Don Henley*

ory Days" • *Bruce Springsteen*

Born in the U.S.A." • *Bruce Springsteen*

Want to Know What Love Is" • *Foreigner*

ery Time You Go Away" • *Paul Young [Hall & Oates song]*

"Heaven" • *Bryan Adams*

Small Town" • *John Cougar Mellencamp*

y You, Say Me" • *Lionel Richie*

u Give Good Love" • *Whitney Houston*

rivate Dancer" • *Tina Turner*

"Your Love Is King" • *Sade*

Are the World" • *USA for Africa*

"What You Need" • *INXS*

You (Forget about Me)" • *Simple Minds*

Broken Wings" • *Mr. Mister*

"Take on Me" • *A-ha*

"Shout" • *Tears for Fears*

Voices Carry" • *'Til Tuesday*

Promise • *Sade*

gs from the Big Chair • *Tears for Fears*

icted to Love" • *Robert Palmer*

Walk This Way" • *Run–D.M.C.*

ing in America" • *James Brown*

ake My Breath Away" • *Berlin*

Like an Egyptian" • *The Bangles*

The Sweetest Taboo" • *Sade*

igher Love" • *Steve Winwood*

reatest Love of All" • *Whitney Houston*

edgehammer" • *Peter Gabriel*

Manic Monday" • *The Bangles*

a Rock" • *Bob Seger & the Silver Bullet Band*

"Word Up" • *Cameo*

nga" • *Miami Sound Machine*

apa Don't Preach" • *Madonna*

C.K. in the U.S.A." • *John Cougar Mellencamp*

ords Get in the Way" • *Miami Sound Machine*

ing on the Ceiling" • *Lionel Richie*

Hometown" • *Bruce Springsteen*

t in the Dark" • Ozzy Osbourne

"You be Illin'" –Run-D.M.C.

"(You Gotta) Fight for Your Right (To Party!)" • *The Beastie Boys*

"In Your Eyes" • *Peter Gabriel*

Graceland • *Paul Simon*

"With or Without You" • *U2*

"Faith" • *George Michael*

"Bad" • *Michael Jackson*

"U Got the Look" • *Prince*

"I Still Haven't Found What I'm Looking For" • *U2*

"Didn't We Almost Have It All" • *Whitney Houston*

"I Wanna Dance with Somebody (Who Loves Me)" • *Whitney Houston*

"Brass Monkey" • *The Beastie Boys*

"La Isla Bonita" • *Madonna*

"Wanted Dead or Alive" • *Bon Jovi*

"Rhythm Is Gonna Get You" • *Gloria Estefan and Miami Sound Machine*

"Luka" • *Suzanne Vega*

"Dude (Looks Like a Lady)" • *Aerosmith*

"I Want Your Sex" • *George Michael*

"It's Tricky" • *Run–D.M.C.*

Bad • *Michael Jackson*

The Joshua Tree • *U2*

"Pour Some Sugar on Me" • *Def Leppard*

"What a Wonderful World" • *Louies Armstrong*

"Sweet Child o' Mine" • *Guns N' Roses*

"Paradise" • *Sade*

"Man in the Mirror" • *Michael Jackson*

"Red Red Wine" • *UB40*

"Welcome to the Jungle" • *Guns N' Roses*

"One Moment in Time" • *Whitney Houston*

"Angel" • *Aerosmith*

"1-2-3" • *Gloria Estefan and Miami Sound Machine*

"One More Try" • *George Michael*

"Can't Stay Away from You" • *Gloria Estefan and Miami Sound Machine*

"The Way You Make Me Feel" • *Michael Jackson*

"Monkey" • *George Michael*

"Hungry Eyes" • *Eric Carmen*

"Wishing Well" • *Terence Trent D'Arby*

"Father Figure" • *George Michael*

"Sign Your Name" • *Terence Trent D'Arby*

"Hey Mambo" • *Barry Manilow with Kid Creole and the Coconuts*

"Don't Believe the Hype" • *Public Enemy*

"Bring the Noise" • *Public Enemy*

Stronger Than Pride • *Sade*

Gipsy Kings • *Gipsy Kings*

"Smooth Operator" • *Sade*

"Summer of '69" • *Bryan Adams*

"The Boys of Summer" • *Don Henley*

"Glory Days" • *Bruce Springsteen*

"Born in the U.S.A." • *Bruce Springsteen*

"I Want to Know What Love Is" • *Foreigner*

"Every Time You Go Away" • *Paul Young [Hall & Oates song]*

"Heaven" • *Bryan Adams*

"Small Town" • *John Cougar Mellencamp*

"Say You, Say Me" • *Lionel Richie*

"You Give Good Love" • *Whitney Houston*

"Private Dancer" • *Tina Turner*

"Your Love Is King" • *Sade*

"We Are the World" • *USA for Africa*

"What You Need" • *INXS*

"Don't You (Forget about Me)" • *Simple Minds*

"Broken Wings" • *Mr. Mister*

"Take on Me" • *A-ha*

"Shout" • *Tears for Fears*

"Voices Carry" • *'Til Tuesday*

Promise • *Sade*

Songs from the Big Chair • *Tears for Fears*

"Addicted to Love" • *Robert Palmer*

"Walk This Way" • *Run–D.M.C.*

"Living in America" • *James Brown*

"Take My Breath Away" • *Berlin*

"Walk Like an Egyptian" • *The Bangles*

"The Sweetest Taboo" • *Sade*

"Higher Love" • *Steve Winwood*

"Greatest Love of All" • *Whitney Houston*

"Sledgehammer" • *Peter Gabriel*

"Manic Monday" • *The Bangles*

"Like a Rock" • *Bob Seger & the Silver Bullet Band*

6

Shock the Monkey

Which brings me to the brilliant, funny, articulate, twisted, blessed, cursed, powerful, instigating, addicted, charming, and vulgar man who never seemed to be more comfortable than when he was in the middle of a fight. That description, by the way, only mildly sums up Walter Yetnikoff. Walter was also the chairman of CBS Records Group at the time. Which means Walter was a king.

Unlike a manager, the kings running the big music companies didn't rely on a single artist to release a platinum record every year in order to prosper. They didn't have to deal with the situations I dealt with: like having Hall & Oates onstage in Australia while I was running around trying to track down a band member who hadn't shown up, and finally finding him doing heroin with some whores on a bus station bench. And then having to drag him onstage while the concert was in progress and listen to the asshole start playing Jimi Hendrix's version of "The Star-Spangled Banner." They didn't have

to pick up money thrown down in the snow by their artist's wife. The kings running the big music companies had contracts that paid them handsomely, that rewarded success with bonuses and offered security during the lean years. And that was where I ultimately wanted to be. That was it. My eye was on the prize.

There was one slight problem: the people who became kings didn't usually start out as musicians. They generally graduated with big credentials and diplomas from prominent universities, and many of them had law degrees. They worked their way up a corporate ladder or were plucked from the legal departments. But that actually made a guy like me very valuable to them. No, I was not another guy in an office. I had my ear to the street and I could find, develop, record, break, manage, and promote talent. Ultimately, that was the key to success at any record company.

It was very easy for me to strike up a friendship with Walter Yetnikoff. We hit it off right away. He had a law degree from Columbia, and his mind was the sharpest tool in the box. His timing was perfect. He moved into the top job at CBS after an accounting scandal pushed one legend, Clive Davis, out the door, and retirement eased out another, Goddard Lieberson. Walter took over in 1975 and got the most out of a roster of talented superstars, which would have been a staggering achievement for anyone at any time, but doing it while the record business was turning into the music industry made it monumental.

Walter's boardroom antics were notorious. He would show up for a very serious 9 a.m. suit-and-tie meeting wearing a schleppy suit and carrying a bagel and cream cheese after a night of revelry, shaking and crinkling the bag, and eating it with cream cheese coming out of all ends in front of the likes

of William S. Paley and Dr. Frank Stanton and other power-houses on the CBS board. He was a loose cannon. When Walter went to war, he went nuclear. And when his abuses overran him, he was totally insane.

While his timing was right, in many ways he was in the wrong place. The things he wished to accomplish were limited by the structure imposed by the starched executives above him and the power struggles between the fiefdoms below. I'd never had my vision narrowed by a corporate ladder, and I was able to give him ideas that would never have otherwise crossed his desk. Walter understood and appreciated what I did, and he began to think about what I could do for him. From the very outset, he looked for a way to bring me into the fold.

I can't recall exactly where we met—it must've been at some function back in the midseventies. When Walter saw what I had accomplished with Hall & Oates, the Savannah Band, and Odyssey, he was quick to offer me my own label. I accepted, and there was a celebratory party at the '21' Club packed with big shots from around the industry. But I hadn't counted on the ramifications. When the new head of RCA, Bob Summer, found out, he was furious. I'd signed a production deal with RCA not long before, and though there was nothing to legally prevent me from making the CBS deal, Summer felt betrayed. RCA had ponied up big-time for Hall & Oates, and basically funded my management company. Summer felt that RCA should be getting all of my talent and energy. He was prepared to pay more for it, but he didn't want me to leave. Remember, RCA was mocked at that time as the Recording Cemetery of America, and it was in dire need of fresh talent.

I didn't fully realize what a difficult spot I'd put myself in—along with Daryl and John—when I'd clinked glasses

with Walter and Grubman over dinner to toast the deal. My allegiance to CBS could've had a negative effect on the way RCA promoted Hall & Oates. And my first priority and my loyalty was to them. If I needed to go back and ask for more advances for Daryl and John, Summer might just say no. That was not a good position to be in.

Grubman and I went back to Walter, explained Summer's reaction, and asked him to let me out of the deal. Walter was a real mensch about it, a stand-up guy, and he let it slide. I could tell he wasn't happy, and he put some distance between us for a while. But I always wanted to make it up to him, and after a few months our relationship began to rekindle. By the mideighties, we'd become inseparable. I'd meet him at his office at the end of the workday three times a week and head off into the evening with him, which, for Walter, invariably led to all the excesses associated with rock 'n' roll.

Eventually, Walter's behavior led to his own downfall. I couldn't do anything about that. But one thing I was sure of: I did not want to go down with him. And he was definitely going to go down. We'll get into that later. But let me set the record straight here. Night after night during the mideighties I made sure he got home okay no matter what condition, and I mean no matter what condition he was in. And believe me, it was not pretty. He was my friend. In fact, our relationship gave me one of the few ways I could connect with my wife at the time because Lisa felt comfortable at weekend dinners with Walter and his wife.

Walter started watching what I was doing very closely in the mideighties. I worked with Diana Ross on an album called *Swept Away*, which went gold after her previous album didn't get off the ground. Diana had a difficult reputation. But from my point of view, the experience couldn't have gone smoother.

Then a great opportunity came to help Carly Simon make

a comeback, and we signed her to Champion Entertainment. Carly is an incredible, killer songwriter. How could anybody not love "Anticipation" or "You're So Vain"? But "Anticipation" came out in 1971 and "You're So Vain" was released in 1972. There were few hits on her five albums between 1979 and 1985, and when acts went cold like that there was a tremendous resistance at radio and retail when you tried to bring them back.

We had relentless sessions at Champion to figure out the right way to do it, but it all starts with the music. Carly came through with such a great song in "Coming around Again"; it then became the theme for the movie *Heartburn*, which starred Jack Nicholson and Meryl Streep. That was big, but we really wanted to push Carly over the top, and we came up with a way to do just that. We had recently produced two HBO specials for Hall & Oates. So we began to plan how we would set one up for Carly in the form of a homespun concert, although we knew she wouldn't respond well to the word *concert*. It was widely known in the industry that performing live was her greatest fear. But I was able to put it to her in a way that made her stop and consider.

"What if you could get a million dollars," I asked her, "and all you had to do was play in your backyard?"

"Really?" she said. "What do you mean?"

Of course, I explained, the million dollars wouldn't go straight to her. It also had to cover the execution of the concept. The idea was to have her sing in her backyard for an intimate audience of family and friends. The more we talked about it, the more she loved the idea and began to turn it into her own. It was her idea to shoot it in 35 millimeter, to have people come up to tell stories and read poetry. Something inside her bubbled to life.

151

Jeb Brien got the task of directing. We brought in an eighty-man production crew to build a set in the middle of a fishing village on Martha's Vineyard. That provided a great backdrop and we were surrounded by the panorama of Menemsha Harbor. About seventy-five of Carly's friends and family came to the event and watched it while sitting in beach chairs. It was more than a success. It was a blast for everyone, and it became the highest-rated concert special HBO had ever televised.

Walter never saw the sincerity in Carly's face when she thanked Jeb and me for helping to restore her career. But he got the big picture. Around the same time period that all this was brewing, he asked me to come in and produce the sound track for a movie project he was working on called *Ruthless People*. Walter was friends with the guys making the movie, and he got a producer credit. He also brought me in as music supervisor, and I immediately saw a way to take Daryl Hall down a new path. Daryl, as usual, was searching for new canvases, and working on another solo album with Dave Stewart of the Eurythmics. So one day when I was in the studio with them in London, I asked them to write the movie's theme song. We brought Mick Jagger in as part of the team. Daryl, Dave, and Mick wrote the song and sang it, and the directors loved it and everything else on the sound track. The movie, a comedy starring Danny DeVito and Bette Midler, was a blockbuster hit. Walter couldn't have come off looking or feeling better about it.

This made him feel even more that I could help him bigtime, and he knew he needed the help at the big monolith—CBS Records Group. He was the King, and his roster was stacked, but new acts weren't breaking through, and there was another king across the street at Warner Communica-

tions named Steve Ross whose group of experienced music impresarios—Ahmet Ertegun, Mo Ostin, and Joe Smith—were lighting up the charts with new talent and leaving CBS in the dust.

As everything converged, all of this was registering with Walter big-time. This made him feel that I could really help him to push the big monolith forward. Walter was looking for new blood, new ideas, and new energy. It was the perfect storm for both of us. We were just the right match...for a time.

I want you to fully understand what I mean when I say that Walter's mind was the sharpest tool in the box.

Here's a perfect example—a single situation. Walter was the chairman of CBS Records Group. But CBS Records Group represented only a part of the larger kingdom of CBS, Inc.

In 1986, the majority stake in the larger kingdom was purchased by Laurence Tisch. Tisch was a billionaire who started out by amassing a fortune in hotels and movie theaters and eventually became synonymous with the name Loews. He became the majority shareholder of CBS, Inc., with the blessing of William S. Paley, who over decades had turned a small radio outfit into the most respected radio and television networks in the world. Let me give you an idea of Paley's enormous clout: when John F. Kennedy was assassinated, the country turned to broadcaster Walter Cronkite and the CBS correspondents to find out what had happened. Which meant that at the bottom of it all, the nation turned with trust toward what William S. Paley had created.

When Tisch took over CBS, Inc., there was some deep cost cutting. This made it even harder for Walter to compete with the powerhouse across the street at Warner. Naturally, this

pissed Walter off, and Walter was not a guy to turn the other cheek. Walter's father had once whacked Walter's head against a wall when he was a kid, and the rest of Walter's life seemed to be a daily exercise in fighting back. Walter hated Tisch with a passion, and he became highly irreverent toward both Tisch and Paley.

Which might make you wonder, why didn't Tisch and Paley just give him the ax? Walter may have been the King to the thousands of people who worked at CBS Records Group and to everyone else in the music industry, but he was only a vice president at CBS, Inc. The bottom line was that Tisch and Paley were his bosses.

Walter just didn't give a shit. That was not only his personality. A lot of people in the music business at that time had that attitude. Music has always spoken to power. Music *was* the power. Walter wasn't a musician; he was an executive who worked in the Fifty-Second Street skyscraper that was famously known as Black Rock with all the other suits. But he felt attached to the artists. At the time, he was seen in the media walking side by side with the stars. This gave him enormous power, the power of association. If Tisch and Paley got rid of Walter, who knew what impact that might have had on the artists? Maybe the artists would want to leave, too. Music was a business that Tisch and Paley really didn't understand— and truthfully, they feared sex, drugs, and rock 'n' roll. They had an FCC license to worry about. On top of that, it didn't make sense for Tisch or Paley to upset the applecart, because Walter was selling a lot of apples. So instead of seeing Walter as the chairman of their record group, or as a vice president in their overall company, they, too, saw him as the King.

A lot of kings would have figured out a way to compromise and make nice with their bosses. Others might've said the hell

with this, left, and looked for a new kingdom. Walter's mind didn't work like that. Walter began to wonder: *How can I take this kingdom away from Tisch and Paley and keep it for myself?*

Walter noticed Tisch selling off pieces of CBS, Inc., that he didn't find a good fit for the company or that he could make a nice profit on. In the beginning of 1987 Walter began to formulate a plan. I felt like I was on the inside because he let me in on it as our late afternoons together extended into the evenings. Walter would look for a buyer for CBS Records Group and swing a deal. That way, he could have someone else pay to take Tisch and Paley off his back, and at the same time keep himself in charge. If you're wondering where somebody gets the chutzpah to do something like this, then you're just beginning to understand Walter. He knew that if he could put out the right hook and convince someone he trusted to put the right amount of money on it, then Tisch would bite.

Why? There were plenty of reasons. Tisch and Paley would be thrilled with the idea of getting a lot of cash for the company. They'd no longer have to have the good name of CBS smeared by any of the musicians on their roster who popped up in the news because of a drug bust or a rape charge. And there was the unspoken benefit: if Tisch took the deal, he could get rid of this huge pain in the ass called Walter Yetnikoff.

As Walter let me in on his plan, he began asking a lot of questions. *What do you think about this artist? How would you market this act? If you were in charge, how would you build a promotion department?* Walter didn't say anything directly, but I got the feeling that if he could pull off the deal, in some way he was going to bring me in to work with him. Maybe even install me just underneath him and let me run the company.

Walter's craziness was an advantage in situations like

these. He was also at his best when he had a singular objective that occupied all his time and thoughts. He went to Tisch with his idea, and Tisch gave him a number. If he was going to part with CBS Records Group, he was looking for $2 billion—an unheard-of figure at that time. Walter knew that if he got close, he could move Tisch toward the deal.

Disney passed. An attempt to bring in Mike Milken and the prepared-food magnate Nelson Peltz also failed. A couple of other suitors also couldn't reach the number. A lot of those people probably kicked themselves later on. They could've bought the company for $1.5 billion. Who knew that ten years later, we'd be able to drive the company to a valuation of $14 billion?

Walter kept at it. Eventually, he went to his old friend in Japan, Norio Ohga at Sony. Walter had a relationship with Ohga that dated back two decades because Sony was the licensee for CBS Records Group in Japan. Back in the day, it was easier to make a licensing deal in a foreign country than to create your own company with an expensive infrastructure.

Ohga, the baritone opera singer who was married to the famous concert pianist, and one of the driving forces behind the Walkman and the compact disc, was naturally intrigued by the deal. And he was in the perfect position to help pull it off. His ear for music had helped him rapidly ascend to the presidency of the Sony Corporation under founder Akio Morita. Walter could not have found a better partner.

For one, it would be easier for Walter to swing the sale to Sony because it was a huge company with a sterling name. He wouldn't be trying to sell it off to some corporate raider in a move that would attract bad press for Tisch and Paley. Walter knew he was working with the board at Black Rock. This *had* to be respectable. And two, Walter's bond with Ohga

would only strengthen his position of power after the deal was done.

When Walter told me, "I think I got a buyer. I think it's gonna be Sony," our talks went from being nebulous to being very clear. And I mean *very* clear. Once Walter had Sony in a position to do the deal, but before it was actually signed, he said: "I'd like you to come in and work with me."

I was excited, but some part of me must've conveyed hesitance about where I would fit in among the suits. I didn't wear suits after I left Chappell and became a manager. I wore jeans, like the musicians.

"Look, Tommy," he said, "I'm prepared to make you president of CBS Records."

For about half of my life it had been my dream to hear those words. But when I heard them, I was stunned. I was, and am, a realist. Bringing me in to run this monolith had to make anybody who didn't know me think Walter was completely off his rocker. Yes, I was seen as the manager behind the success of Hall & Oates and John Mellencamp. But I had no college degree, and absolutely no experience running a large multinational record company. How the hell was Walter going to sell me to Ohga as the new guy he wanted in charge? Oh, and one other thing: I'd also be the youngest president in the company's history.

Ohga didn't have any idea who I was. There had to be a big chance that he wasn't going to go for this.

Walter went to Japan to finalize the details of the deal in early '88. I was at home in Greenwich the moment the call came in. Walter had Ohga's complete trust. When Walter said that Ohga had agreed to let me run the company, I didn't know if I should jump up and down or start crying.

The deal made the front page of the *New York Times* and

the *Wall Street Journal.* I left Champion Entertainment and basically handed it to the guys who were in it with me.

A limo driver pulled up to my home to take me to Black Rock for my first day of work. I was dressed in a suit and carrying a briefcase.

Walter had given me the shot of a lifetime. He saw the potential inside me more than anybody else ever did. He believed in me, and he put me in the position to show what I could do to the entire world.

God bless Walter Yetnikoff.

It turned out that the house I'd driven by so many times when I was a teen and dreamed of owning one day, the one on the Westchester Country Club grounds in Rye, New York, had come up for sale at exactly the same time. So I put in a bid to buy it—and I got it.

Now, I had the job and the home that I'd always wanted to show Sam Clark. But there was no delight in seeing his reaction to my success. Sadly, Sam had passed away shortly before.

He'd been right about one thing. My relationship with his daughter was wrong. But at this point, there seemed to be nothing I could do about it. I had two beautiful kids whom I loved and couldn't even think of leaving, even though I was always working and saw them only on weekends. It was a terrible conflict. I wanted to be the father that my father was to me. But I just couldn't be. I was unhappy in my relationship with their mother, and I knew my kids could sense it.

Our marriage reached a point where one of our disagreements was so bad that I almost didn't show up at a surprise fortieth birthday party that Lisa had planned for me. It was on

a yacht. I can't even remember how I was tricked into getting there.

I couldn't orchestrate leaving my marriage the way Walter engineered his deal to break away from Tisch and Paley. My neighborhood and family had wired me to be married for seventy years, like my parents.

So I fixated on the new job. This huge career change would send my personal life spinning in a direction I could never have imagined.

There were people who thought Walter's antics and decisions had gone too far when he appointed me as head of CBS Records. "*Clive Davis* used to have that job. And Walter brings in *a manager?*"

But as I drove to Black Rock for my first day of work, I knew exactly what I was going to do. The company had become stagnant as far as breaking new artists, and had been surpassed by WEA—which was short for Warner, Elektra, and Atlantic music companies. All anyone had to do to understand the seriousness of the situation was pick up a copy of *Billboard*. The charts were a shocking report card for CBS. Many of the big names at CBS were sprinkled around the charts. But there were many more hits coming from Warner, and not only that, but a lot of the Warner albums were from new artists who'd never been heard from before.

Our chief competitor had a great overall strategy. It was clear to me that there was only one way to beat Warner Bros.: attack it at its own game. We needed to operate the way Steve Ross and his army did—only better.

Steve Ross was the greatest corporate architect of his time.

He was neither a music guy nor a movie guy. In fact, he had no background in the entertainment industry at all. But his philosophy created the largest media company in the world then. In order to understand that philosophy, you need to know a little about him.

Steve's father had lost everything in the Depression, and Steve got his start in his wife's family's funeral parlor business, which ultimately merged with the Kinney parking lot company. Steve grew those companies to the point where he could purchase the Warner–Seven Arts film studio, which he did in 1969 for $400 million, and he continued to expand. Two decades later, in 1989, he merged Warner with Time, Inc., to create a company with a valuation of more than $15 billion.

The secret of his success could very well have been developed early on. There is no place on earth where you are going to meet sadder people than in the funeral parlor business. Steve became an expert at making people feel good. By the time he took over the entertainment company, he was highly skilled at making sure all the talent around him was happy. I'm not talking only about the celebrated artists who were signed in all branches of the company. Steve treated *his executives* like talent, incentivizing and lavishly rewarding them for innovation and success. The executives at Warner flew on the same corporate jets that whisked movie stars and recording artists to the company getaway in Acapulco.

Steve had the best of the industry giants running the different music labels in his company. Mo Ostin was in charge of Warner Bros. Ahmet Ertegun was atop Atlantic. Great music men like Joe Smith and Bob Krasnow were leading Elektra. The head of each label ran his own company, was in charge of all of its services, and was completely responsible for the outcome of all the music that his company produced and

sold. Ross's music executives were not only getting the most out of talent like Led Zeppelin and the Eagles. They were hustling at the cutting edge, and they were driven by one thing: music.

This was a completely different outlook from the monolithic mind-set at CBS—the one that had been set up by William Paley and Goddard Lieberson, and eventually handed down to Walter Yetnikoff. CBS had generally been handpicking its chairmen from the business affairs and legal departments. So, we're talking apples and oranges from the start.

Underneath that chairman, there was an appointed president who basically ran CBS Records. But there was no Mo Ostin or Ahmet Ertegun in charge of the Columbia and Epic labels. These labels had many shared services and a corporate governance. Though this system spawned very talented executives like Clive Davis, its overall effects made the company stodgy and tired.

Cornerstone artists like Bruce Springsteen, Michael Jackson, and Bob Dylan, and the invention of the CD were really what kept cash registers ringing at CBS through the eighties. There was simply no burning desire in the management ranks to forge ahead. The pages of *Billboard* didn't lie. CBS didn't have a single hit artist in the burgeoning alternative music scene in Seattle as I headed into my first day of work.

The solution to this problem was very simple to me. The company needed to be turned upside down. It needed to be remodeled after Warner. We needed to set up Epic and Columbia as powerful labels and individual entities, bring in big-time execs, and incentivize success. This would be like shock therapy for a stiff and bureaucratic company that was often slowed down by executives concerned with maintaining the power of their fiefdoms.

Walter loved the idea to restructure and gave me the green light. So I pulled up to Black Rock on that first day extremely confident. There were a lot of people in the company who saw me as a manager who was out of his league, and predicted I'd be gone within six months. But the truth was that I'd never felt more secure in my entire life. I had a five-year contract. And it was a great contract, because Grubman helped me negotiate it.

There was no office ready for me on my first day at Black Rock. A crew would be hired to demolish the existing configuration down the hall from Walter's office—a big, beautiful corner spot—in order to build my new home. This sent a powerful message. I didn't move into a room that had been vacated by the last person in the job. I was going to tear down the old structure and create an entirely new one.

I brought in a company that the Kennedys might call— the design team of Parish-Hadley—and thought a great deal about every detail. I didn't want to mimic the office that Sam Clark had once worked in atop the ABC building. But I wanted people to feel the sense of sophistication and elegance that I'd felt when I first stepped into that office.

For years as a manager, I went to work in jeans. Now I was in a suit and tie. There would be no gold records in my new office. Those were outside in my music room, surrounding my piano. The ambience of that office was yet another way for me to shed the old skin and put on the new.

A lot of the old guard at CBS became shocked and outraged when word spread about the construction of that new office. But Walter got it. He was treating me the same way that Steve Ross had treated Mo, Ahmet, and Joe.

*   *   *

One of the first albums to be delivered to me had been recorded by Gloria Estefan. It was scheduled for release, but I immediately sensed that something was wrong.

It didn't feel like all the elements had really come together to create the image of a global superstar. As soon as I looked at the album cover, the videos, and the publicity shots, I could see Gloria's career veering down the wrong track.

The success of this album for the company, for me, and for Gloria was too important to just let it go. So I stopped the release cold. Inside the building it said that business as usual was no longer going to be the usual.

All of Gloria's previous albums had credited her band, the Miami Sound Machine, on the cover. This would be the first with only Gloria's name out front. That was why it was so crucial to get it right. The album had to be focused in a way that didn't compromise who she really was.

The essence of Gloria Estefan, if you asked anybody to define it, would be one single song: "Conga." It was a distinct blend of Afro-Cuban rhythm with great orchestrations, some pop, and a beat that could pull anyone onto the dance floor anywhere in the world. When you hear it today it's as current as the day it was recorded, and will be forever and ever. Gloria had it all: The Latin roots. The look. The rhythm of her music. I knew that if she was positioned correctly, she could become the next worldwide superstar.

My time with the Savannah Band, as hard and trying as that was, had given me the experience of working with a multicultural blend of people, Latin, R & B, pop, their musical rhythms, and their sense of style and imaging. That schooling broadened my knowledge and enabled me to apply some of that vision to Gloria and her Miami Sound Machine, and to take her pop Latin sound and help turn it into world music.

So one of the first things I did was reach out to meet Gloria and her husband and manager, Emilio, and tell them how I thought the album should be refocused. That meeting became my blueprint for what would become the entire Latin Explosion. It would also start a friendship that would change my life.

Gloria and Emilio were very humble. They had both emigrated from Cuba. Emilio almost died at sea when he returned to Cuba in a small boat to try to get his brother. Neither Gloria nor Emilio was upset that the album would have to be postponed and that I had suggested that we scrap all the images and the entire promotional campaign. They seemed overjoyed to have someone embrace who they truly were, who totally got them on every level, and who was willing put a huge amount of time, passion, energy, and money into their work. I was able to speak to them like a musician and see them through the eyes of a manager. Outside my office a sign read: "Thomas D. Mottola, President of CBS/Sony Records." But to Gloria and Emilio I was just Tommy and still am.

I immediately got on a plane and flew to Miami to immerse myself in Gloria and Emilio's world. Being in Miami felt as natural as it was on the night I saw Sinatra at the Boom Boom Room in the Fontainebleau as a boy, and the night I watched Wayne Cochran lift the roof beams off the Barn on the 79th Street Causeway. Gloria and Emilio made me feel like I was at home in their home.

I took so many trips to see them over the years that they now sort of blend together in my mind. But when I think back on those times I think of myself entering their kitchen in the morning wearing a pair of flip-flops and shorts, and having a half-dozen of Gloria's Dalmatians pin me up against the wall. The first time they charged me, the only clue I had that those

dogs weren't going to bite my balls off was Emilio saying in an accent that sounded like Ricky Ricardo, "Gloria loves those dogs...Gloria loves those dogs..." I also made the mistake of drinking the Cuban coffee they served me as if it were in an American cup—only to find out that it was really a version of Red Bull times ten. My heart started pounding so loudly the first time it happened I nearly asked Emilio to rush me to the hospital. But before long, I was sipping and enjoying. I loved the Cuban food. I loved their culture. It felt like the essence of what I grew up with on Arthur Avenue back in the Bronx. I loved seeing Gloria and Emilio as a couple. To be completely honest, I often stopped to observe the chemistry between them. Whatever that was, that was what I wanted in my own life, that was what I wanted in my own marriage. I loved every minute I spent with them.

There was some resistance in the company to the money I advocated spending on the marketing of that first album. I just steamrolled over everyone and grabbed some lapels in the international fiefdom to make sure that the entire company was completely behind Gloria everywhere in the world. Sometimes when you know you're right, you just have to voice your vision. It can't always be group consensus. Sometimes you have to follow a single vision no matter what the ramifications. And, of course, nobody had any complaints after *Cuts Both Ways* was released. It had a half-dozen hits. "Get on Your Feet" had that same magical feel as "Conga." If you want to see its enduring impact, all you have to do is go to YouTube and type in the words: "Steve Ballmer Going Crazy." That's right. *The* Steve Ballmer. The CEO of Microsoft opened a company speech a while back jumping up and down to that song. Talk about the beginning of the Latin Explosion.

"Here We Are" and "Don't Wanna Lose You" from the

same album made Gloria a Top 40 radio darling in the United States and all over the world. Not only did the album go multiplatinum at home, but she also had huge hits in Mexico and Brazil, the United Kingdom, and Australia. We sold millions.

We had opened the door and created the blueprint for the explosion to come down the road for Ricky Martin, Shakira, Marc Anthony, and Jennifer Lopez. In fact, it became the blueprint for every major artist we broke for the next fifteen years.

When I think back, the experience was more than opening the door. It was about taking the time to get it right. We'll never know what would've happened if that album had not been positioned properly. But we do know that a few bad choices at the start can cut short an artist's career or even destroy it.

The choices we made, and the choices Gloria and Emilio continued to make, were the reason she would go on to sing in front of Super Bowl crowds and why she is still selling out concerts more than twenty years later.

And, as you'll come to see, whatever I did to help Gloria and Emilio focus her career at that early stage was returned to me personally a million times over.

Unfortunately, you can't turn around a corporate culture with a single album.

I knew there needed to be huge changes. But I didn't really understand what I was up against until I began to get entrenched in the job. There were a lot of motivated employees, but there were also many who had been there for years, growing fat and happy, and simply collecting checks.

I'd sit in on a meeting to promote an album and would hear a lot of clichés but not a single compelling strategy. It

was all broad brushstrokes, without any of the nitty-gritty dirty work, as if everybody was riding on the artist's talent and the loyalty of the fan base. Yeah, it was great that we had that loyalty, but it was terrible to be on cruise control. Even worse, we weren't going out and signing the next big acts. The company had the greatest names in music, artists like Bob Dylan, Bruce Springsteen, Michael Jackson, Billy Joel, Barbra Streisand, Neil Diamond, Ozzy Osbourne, and Wynton Marsalis, to name just a few, but there were no artists in the budding alternative music scene. Those artists looked at CBS as a company resting on its laurels and living in the past.

Those artists had a point. We had a chief financial officer who kept bound ledgers as if he were working in the forties. It would be one thing if the guy had kept his nose in the books. But he went out of his way to block one of my first initiatives in the rebuilding of our music publishing company.

I'm sure this same guy was delighted two years earlier when CBS very foolishly sold its own publishing company, CBS Songs, to Stephen Swid and his partners. CBS got $125 million in return for its 250,000 titles, in what was then noted as the biggest deal of its kind. Let me tell you just how short-sighted that sale was: just three years later, not long after I took the job with CBS/Sony, that same catalog was sold to EMI for a reported $337 million. That's a 170 percent profit that Swid and his buddies made on those CBS titles in just three years. And that's not all. Worse, CBS/Sony was slowed by a non-compete agreement that prohibited it from getting into the publishing industry for a certain number of years afterward. Here's the ultimate irony: What started as CBS Songs grew into the world's largest music publishing catalog called EMI Music. Sony recently paid EMI $2.2 *billion* to get its catalog back.

My time at Chappell had taught me the importance of a strong publishing catalog. The art of songwriting is the basis of the whole industry, and copyrights were then—and most certainly are now—the most valuable assets in the business. A small Nashville company, Tree Music, had many country gems, and it was available for $33 million—an ideal first step for us. Yet the financial officer kept asking Walter to knock the idea down. I got Walter to overrule his objections, and Tree became part of a publishing company known as Sony/ATV, but who had time for foolish obstructions? If this guy were still around years later, I'm sure he would've also objected to our acquisition of the Beatles' catalog in a deal that was split with Michael Jackson. The CFO just didn't get it, and I couldn't even bear to be in the same room with him. "Tommy," he once told me, "you don't understand. CBS is like a giant ocean liner. You're trying to turn it around too fast."

"Not only am I going to turn it around fast," I snapped at him, "I'm going to turn it into a speedy PT battleship."

This CFO had to go. We needed to break apart the fiefdoms that constipated the company. We needed to get as many people as we could on board the PT boat and leave those behind to sink with the *Titanic*.

As you can imagine, this made many of the people running the old fiefdoms very nervous. When I was appointed to the job, many people in the company thought that I'd last only six months. When that didn't happen, several of the old executives started to put imaginary bull's-eyes on my back. But none of these executives knew about the immediate connection I'd established with Norio Ohga.

Ohga not only supported his executives' visions in a way that reminded me of Steve Ross. But remember: he himself had started out as an opera singer. Music was his life. Even

though he was running the biggest electronics giant of the era, he was, in his soul, an artist, and that was where we connected.

"We need to develop new talent," I told him during a private lunch with Walter. "Aggressively."

I explained that in order to do this we'd have to revamp the entire corporate structure. I was asking for tens of millions of dollars to do so, and I was asking at a time when the music company was operating at a loss. Not many people in their right mind would ever ask a new boss for this kind of funding at such a difficult time. But after thinking for a moment, Ohga said, "Do whatever you have to do. Just bring us the hits and develop the new stars of the future."

Walter watched the relationship between Ohga and me unfold like a proud father cutting loose a son he believed in. And when Sony decided it needed to make another move in the entertainment business, he immediately enlisted my help.

Sony had developed a videocassette magnetic tape called Betamax in the seventies that could film home movies and also be used to play Hollywood classics at home on Sony equipment. It was a great product, superior in a lot of ways to a competitor with a different design—VHS. There was one problem. The consumer wanted only one format. Even though Betamax was in many ways a cut above VHS, it lost out, because it didn't have its own content that would force the public to accept Sony hardware.

Sony's founder, Akio Morita, didn't want what happened with Betamax to happen to any of the company's future hardware formats. From his earliest days at the company, Morita understood the importance of both creating new technology and maximizing the value of his brand. When he first brought the transistor radio to America in 1955, people warned him

that it would never sell in the U.S. under the name of an unknown Japanese company. One American company told Morita it would place an order for 100,000 transistor radios on the condition that these radios be sold under the American company's name. Morita said no. His vision was to create cutting-edge technology with the name Sony on it. He wanted people all over the world to know that name, trust that name, and seek out products with that name. Protecting the company's technology and refusing to compromise the brand were the essence of Morita's philosophy.

The simplest way to protect future hardware, then, was to develop and control the software—the content. If Sony was putting out its own hit movies and music simultaneously on products that could be served up at home and only on Sony equipment, it could manipulate the market to accept and purchase its hardware.

What happened to the Betamax may seem like a topic that's sitting in the dustbin of history. But it's important to note here. Because the philosophy behind Sony's reaction to the fall of the Betamax would inevitably hinder the company ten years later when Napster arrived and Sony needed to be open to sharing technology. Sony wanted to control it all.

Bottom line for the moment: Sony was now in the market for a movie studio. Ohga reached out to Walter to locate the right one, and Walter called me in to help. I suggested what I thought was the most logical thing to do: bring in the most powerful guy in Hollywood. The same guy who had once asked me to back away from the book that led to the making of the movie *Goodfellas*. That was Mike Ovitz.

Ovitz flew into New York to meet with Walter and me, and he suggested that we try to buy Columbia Pictures because it was available and had a great catalog. The three of us began

to meet and talk regularly to figure out how we could secure the movie studio.

So a typical day in my first nine months at CBS/Sony looked something like this:

Implement ideas on changing the culture of the music company.

Run the Columbia label until I placed the right person in the job.

Organize Gloria's new album campaign and get it launched.

Check sales and promotion on Michael Jackson's *Bad* album and tour.

Follow up on Michael Bolton's *Soul Provider*.

Figure out a launching pad for New Kids on the Block.

Introduce Harry Connick Jr. to the world.

And devise a strategy for Sony Corp to buy Columbia Pictures.

It was like living in the middle of a 24/7 hurricane, going to meeting after meeting after phone call after phone call, then hitting the recording studios all night after work. Every lunch was a working lunch, every dinner a working dinner. There just wasn't enough time in the day to do everything that needed to be done, so the work bled over to the weekends, and even then there wasn't enough time.

I knew that we needed the help of people who were as obsessed and committed as I was to pull all this off. We needed gladiators to compete with all the other companies in the industry to push this company where it should be. Fortunately, there were three things going for me from the start.

First, I knew what I didn't know. That meant I knew that I had to bring in people who could guide me in the areas where I was inexperienced.

Second, my time as a manager had given me the opportunity to work with almost every record company in the business. So I knew exactly where these people were.

And third, the executives that I needed just happened to be only a few blocks away from my office.

Walter didn't really believe I could get the people I wanted for my executive team.

When I showed him the first name on my list, he looked at me as if I were trying to hire Yoda away from *Star Wars*.

You think you can get Mel Ilberman?

Hey, no harm in asking. I certainly knew Mel well enough to ask. I'd had years of experiences working with Mel. The first being almost a ten-year period at RCA between the midseventies and early eighties when I was managing Hall & Oates, the Savannah Band, and Odyssey. Mel was a tough businessman who would always say no—especially to most managers. But he took a liking to me, and after he'd say no, he'd pull me aside and give me fatherly advice. *Look, kid, here's how you do it.*

My second experience with Mel was after he left RCA and moved to PolyGram Records when I was managing John Mellancamp. Even though Mel was an executive at the record company and I was the artist's manager, we sometimes felt like we were on the same team—especially in the case of Mellencamp, who was difficult for both of us to work with. Mellencamp brought us close in a way that no one else could have.

The bottom line on Mel was that I trusted him with my life and, at almost sixty, he knew how to run every single division

inside a record company. Business affairs. Creative services. Promotion. Marketing. Accounting. Finance. Sales. Distribution. International. A&R. I had worked with all these divisions on my own as a manager. But Mel actually operated them from the inside, and he had great insight into how to manage large groups of people.

Walter thought I had no shot at bringing Mel on board—particularly because he knew that Mel was under contract to PolyGram and was working for a guy who'd once worked for him, and with whom he had a falling out, Dick Asher. But I'd been in constant touch with Mel—and I knew something that Walter didn't. The timing was perfect. Mel had grown disenchanted working with Asher. So I called Mel, and we met at a little coffee shop on Seventh Avenue very close to the PolyGram offices.

I laid out to Mel everything that I wanted to do. He listened carefully and grasped the situation immediately. He thought it would be a great last stop for him. He'd get a powerful position and, at the same time, be able to mentor and guide me at the top. That made me feel incredible—it told me he truly believed in me.

Mel's contract was almost up, and he was going to have to ask Asher to let him go. But he seemed confident he could get a release. "Let's shake hands," he said. "I want to do this." And Mel pulled it off.

Walter was shocked to find out that Mel was coming aboard. Walter and Norio Ohga really respected Ilberman, and you can imagine how it made them view me when Mel agreed to come work at my side.

I then focused on a direct raid on Warner. If I was going to elevate Epic and Columbia from imprints to powerful labels, I

was going to need execs to compete with the heads of Warner, Elektra, and Atlantic. That was why I wanted Dave Glew. Dave was executive vice president and general manager of Atlantic Records. He was the very backbone of the company, and he had tremendous experience in sales, marketing, and distribution. Just what I needed. I thought I had a shot because I knew that Dave would never have a chance at the presidency in his current company.

At first, Dave said no. But I set up a secret dinner between him, Walter, and me specifically on a Friday night. Very shortly after all the small talk ended, I cut to the chase, looked him in the eye, and said: "I know you said no. How would you like to be the president of Epic Records?"

He was stunned.

I wasn't finished. "What would you need from us to take that job?" I asked him.

Now, his mouth was open.

It was perfect timing because Dave was between contracts. His new contract with Atlantic was sitting on Sheldon Vogel's desk unsigned. Dave went home that night and talked it over with his wife, Ann. He took out the infamous yellow legal pad that hardly ever left his side and wrote down everything he desired. I'm sure he thought I would say no to many of his requests. When he finished running down everything on his list, I said: "Are you done?"

"Yes."

"Okay, you've got it."

But I told him if he wanted this job, he'd have to sign the contract over the weekend. I knew that once Ahmet Ertegun, Doug Morris, and the corporate brass at Warner got wind of what was going on, they would never let Dave go...and I was right.

On Monday morning, Dave went to work, and he told Ahmet.

"You can't leave," Ahmet said, "you're under contract."

"No," Dave said, "I'm not."

It didn't take long before telephones were ringing around the Warner Communications building like alarm sirens. The war was on. The next thing Dave knew, he was being summoned to the office of Steve Ross. Ross tried to up the ante, matching the deal I gave him, and then throwing in something like fifty thousand shares of WCI stock, which at that time had great value because of Atari.

When Dave told Steve that he'd already signed a contract with CBS/Sony and that he'd be leaving, he was immediately ushered out of the building by security guards.

That was music to Walter's ears. Perfect—a war with Steve Ross. Walter never met a Goliath he didn't love to hurl stones at.

Next I needed to fill the top job at Columbia Records. I wanted to bring in Don Ienner. Don was Clive Davis's head of promotion at Arista Records. They were a perfect combination. Clive made Whitney Houston's records. Don got them on the radio. Those were the two critical components for success in the music business at that time. End of story.

I'd had a chance to work closely with Ienner when I helped move Hall & Oates from RCA to Arista in the late eighties. Ienner had a chip on his shoulder. He was a bully, loud and brash. He was sort of like the hotheaded Sonny in *The Godfather,* and after his first few years at Columbia a lot of his staff was wishing that he was on his way to the tollbooth. He was definitely a bull in a china shop, and I knew every aspect of all these traits. But that was precisely the kind of energy that I needed to move that division of the company forward at that time.

Don had a contract with Arista. But he had a verbal agreement and a handshake with Clive Davis that if he really wanted to leave and he had a much better opportunity, he could do so.

The opportunity to become the president of Columbia Records was certainly a much better opportunity. Even though Clive kicked and screamed, he had to let Donny go. He'd given his word. Now, my two main labels—Epic and Columbia—had excellent leadership.

I was happy to have my core team in place. I didn't realize that there was a crucial player missing until I met her a few months later. Sometimes you don't see things until they're right in front of your nose.

VOICES

DOUG MORRIS
Music executive

It struck me as odd, initially, when Tommy got that job. Tommy was a very good manager, a very clever guy who got his records played and his groups on MTV. He knew how to move and work the system.

What no one knew was that he had the kind of taste to really be a top executive. He's not a financial guy. But who cares? You can get twenty accountants to do that. The guy who can pick the artist and pick the song is the rainmaker. And no one knew he could do that. You couldn't know until he got the chance. He got the chance—and he was great.

BILLY JOEL

I had no concerns about Tommy when he took over. He's got the street smarts. There's that line from the song: "Tommy Mottola lives on the road." He spent a lot of time working firsthand with bands on the road. So he knew all the idiosyncrasies of what goes on with the band and the musicians and the songwriters. He lived it.

So I thought it was a good blend, a good balance. Walter was a corporate animal, an attorney, and he dealt with the higher-ups, the guys in the golf pants, as we used to say.

The great thing about dealing with Tommy is he's very direct. He'll say: "We don't think there are as many singles as there were on your other albums." He's straight ahead about it, and I don't have a problem with that. He encouraged me to do my part, and I knew he would follow through on his end.

A lot of the time, what he did was a complete mystery to me. I didn't know a lot of aspects to that end of the business. I knew things in general, but he was the guy who could get things done. And the more direct you were with Tommy, the more effective he seemed to be. So I came to have every confidence in him.

MEL ILBERMAN

There were many aspects in the operation of a record company at which Tommy had no experience. The financial statements, he had no clue. He also did not have the experience of managing within a large company where so many interrelated factors are involved. What he did, very wisely, was bring in the help he needed—a guy like Dave Glew. Tommy picked good people. And that's the most important trait to bring to a role like that.

Another thing. In a normal company, there are very few bosses who would accept hearing *You're wrong.* I had no problem telling him that, or telling him to stop if I thought he was going in the wrong direction. Tommy might argue for a minute or two. He might get pissed off for a minute or two. But he always listened. And he would never be upset afterward. Not many bosses could accept that positively.

JIMMY IOVINE

Music executive

I had met Tommy early on when he was an aggressive young publisher and manager. When he got the job at Sony, my ex-wife said something very funny.

She said: "Oh, this is interesting. Party's at Tommy's house."

And I said: "You know what, you're probably right." And he proceeded to throw an incredible party. I mean, he did a great job over there. Hustled, and got the right people working for him.

We were competitors—Doug Morris and me were in competition with Tommy and those guys over there. We had our ups and downs—like the Lakers and the Celtics. It was always cool.

The greatest gift Tommy had—the greatest gift any of these guys that have lasted for a long time or really made a mark have—is you can hear songs and you know talent. It's that simple. Then you have to learn how to get it out and market it. But first you gotta start with a good product. Without a great song, you ain't going anywhere. You just can't get off first base. I mean, who wants to hear Elvis Presley sing a bad song? Nobody wants to hear bad songs. That's why the Beatles were the Beatles. It's all in the song.

And then you marry this right song with the right artist, or they write it themselves, and that's when the magic happens. Then you help that magic grow, which is the part that no one understands, because it just happens to be inside someone. It's instinct. Tommy has those instincts.

7

The Wind

In October 1988, I threw a party for a friend of mine who had once gotten the feeling that I'd wanted to hurl him out the window.

Jerry Greenberg had gotten chewed out by all of his bosses at Atlantic for releasing Hall & Oates. But he was a brilliant exec who went on to become Atlantic's youngest president after Ahmet Ertegun rose to CEO. There were no hard feelings between Jerry and me. Business is business, and it didn't stop us from becoming close over the years. Jerry had left Atlantic to go out on his own, but his new company hadn't worked out. Didn't matter to me. He was still a great record man. He was living in Los Angeles, and I was sure he would be a great presence for us on the West Coast.

We gave him his own label, an imprint. It was a joint venture, but it used the services of Epic to promote, market, and sell. That was a great fit also because Jerry had worked at Atlantic for at least a decade with Dave Glew. It may sound like

a minor decision based on everything else that was going on. But it's impossible for me to calculate the impact of the decision to bring Jerry in, and the single night that occurred in October of '88 that came along with it.

The party on that particular night celebrated the launch of Jerry's new label and the signing of an English pop band called Eighth Wonder featuring Patsy Kensit, who went on to become an actress and star in *Lethal Weapon 2*. When I walked in, it looked like so many other typical music business parties. But when I walked out, I held something in my hand that would change my life.

An old friend of mine, a singer named Brenda K. Starr, was at that party, and she walked over to me and handed me a demo tape.

"What is it?" I asked her.

"Just listen to it," she said. Then she nodded to a honey-blonde-haired girl across the room. I found myself staring into brown eyes that were staring back at me in a way that demanded attention.

"That's my friend," she said. "Her name is Mariah."

Mariah had been one of Brenda's backup singers. There was a really brief hello. But it was a common hello. There are a lot of parties, a lot of hellos, a lot of beautiful young singers, and a lot of demos.

After I left the party and reached my car, something inside me wondered if she could really sing. So I slipped the tape into the player. At first I thought there was some mistake. The music had R & B and gospel qualities that made it seem like Brenda had given me the wrong tape. That couldn't be the blonde chick that I met, I thought. I waited for the next song. It blew me away. It was amazing music, an amazing voice, but my overriding feeling was confusion because I thought there

had to be some mistake. The third song played, then the fourth. By that time my confusion was gone. It didn't matter whose voice I was hearing. An unbelievable energy was running through me, screaming, *Turn the car around! That may be the best voice you've heard in your entire life!*

It took me about three days to track Mariah down and arrange a meeting in my office. She showed up with an older woman wearing dark glasses who didn't say a word. Her mother. Mariah was eighteen years old.

"Is that you on the tape?" I asked her.

"Yeah," she said.

"I love it," I said. "I'd like to sign you to our company."

She was sleeping on a mattress on the floor of a girl-friend's apartment and had been working as a waitress and a coat-check girl. Needless to say, she was thrilled. Developing Mariah was going to be a long process, and I believed it best to connect her to people—like Grubman and the management team at Champion—who would understand how to nurture her.

There was one hitch. Mariah told me that she'd signed a production agreement that linked her music and earnings to the keyboard player on the demo tape—Ben Margulies.

"Can I meet him?" I said.

"Sure," she said.

"When?"

"Just come down to the Woodshop."

That very night I went down to the little studio where she and Ben worked. It was called the Woodshop, and it really was a woodshop, filled with machines for cutting and turning wood to make furniture. There was sawdust all over the floor,

and the smell of glue and fresh-cut wood filled the air. In the back of this shop was a small space where Mariah and Ben worked with a couple of keyboards.

Mariah stood in front of me, singing a cappella, and then Ben joined in on the keyboards. When a voice comes at you like that from only a couple of feet away it completely occupies your space, your ears, your eyes, and your universe. It was like hearing that demo tape times ten. I was overwhelmed by the breadth and power in her vocals. She had a seven-octave range that peaked with a high-pitched whistle that almost knocked me to the floor.

It reminded me of the emotions that ran through me the first time I heard Daryl Hall and John Oates play and sing acoustically in a room back at Chappell Music. Only this was magnified. It was raw, but that was the beauty of it. Her voice was the Hope Diamond.

I went back to the office the next day and told my business affairs department, "I don't care if you lock her lawyer in your conference room, do not let him out until you have a deal."

Once it was signed, Mariah got an advance to move out of her girlfriend's apartment, get her own place, and start work on her first album. There was no timetable. My goal was for it to be right. Didn't matter if it took a year, a year and a half, or two years, because we were creating the world's next superstar. If the first album wasn't right, her entire career could fall apart before it even started. But if we got all the music right on that first album and positioned it correctly, then everything I envisioned could actually happen. It was that simple.

The only complication was how the arrangements would work with Ben Margulies. He had written more than a few good songs with Mariah. But I was certain that he didn't have the chops to produce them. I knew I would eventually have

to extricate Mariah from that agreement, and the first step toward doing that was to let Ben try to make the first album even though there was no possibility that he could pull it off. I started to think about a backup plan immediately, knowing it would take a few months for the situation to come to a head.

As all this was transpiring we were finalizing the details to bring Ienner to Columbia from Arista Records. Don and I were sitting in a car and I slipped Mariah's demo into the cassette player. When Don heard Mariah's voice he went crazy.

"In addition to giving you all the things you asked for," I told him, "in addition to giving you a deal that is totally unheard of, this is going to be the first project you're going to work on. Together we'll make Mariah bigger than Whitney."

It was a defining moment. Don had promoted Whitney, and he knew exactly how talented Mariah was just by hearing that voice on the demo.

I kept going by the Woodshop to check in on Mariah's progress. We had a great chemistry when we talked about the music, and when it came to work she was as obsessed and fanatical as I was. Mariah had been flirtatious from the moment I set eyes on her at the launch party. I did everything in my power to resist. But a few months later there was a moment when it all began to change.

I had just come back from a business trip to Miami. I'd spent four or five days working with Gloria and Emilio and, in my spare time, had been able to enjoy some sunshine. I was wearing a jacket and tie and had a great Miami tan when I went to the Woodshop to see how Mariah and Ben were doing. Mariah looked at me, and said: *"You look great!"* The tone of her voice went beyond my clothes and the tan, and everything went into slow motion. I looked into her eyes and she stared back at me, and then we quickly turned back to work.

Those three words—"*You look great!*"—were intoxicating to me. Those three words—and the way she said them—opened the door to a forty-year-old's crisis and I stepped right on through. There was no time to think about it. Everything else in my life was moving at a thousand miles an hour. This was no exception.

After a while, I went to see my therapist about it. I told her how Mariah and I had met, how she looked at me, how she made me feel. "I think," I told her, "I'm falling in love with this girl."

Often, therapists listen to you and then frame what you're telling them so that you can see the full picture and reach your own conclusions. But this therapist was a wise old broad who pulled no punches.

"Tom," she said, "stop right there. Forget it! It's not going to work!"

She tried to make me see that I'd been blinded, and she listed the reasons why it couldn't possibly work. But I didn't want to see that Mariah was roughly the same age as I was when I first walked into Sam Clark's home with a 45 in my hand. I didn't want to see that Mariah was from a broken family and had grown up without her father around, and for the most part had gotten by on her own.

What didn't work, the way I saw it, was the marriage that I was in. And what did work was the strong bond based in music that I'd seen between Gloria and Emilio Estefan. I'd seen that bond work for Sharon and Ozzy Osbourne. And later, I would come to see how it worked for Celine Dion and René Angélil. René is twenty-six years older than Celine. He launched her and manages her career. Age doesn't matter when it works. When it works, it works.

"*Absolutely* forget it!" My therapist put the hammer down again. "This will never work!"

The therapist kept trying to make me see Mariah as someone who'd been through a difficult childhood. All I could see was what Mariah was about to become.

"You don't understand," I told the therapist. "Mariah is going to be the biggest star in the world. She's going to be as big as Michael Jackson."

The therapist took a deep breath and stared at me as if I were totally delusional.

"Great," she said. "Then just develop her as a recording artist. This is a girl who's had a lot of family issues. Remember, the apple doesn't fall far from the tree. Tom, don't do it."

I didn't like hearing the word *don't* come out of her mouth. The sound of that word did everything she didn't intend it to do. It was as if she'd thrown kerosene on a fire. Smashing through the word *no* was a big reason for my success. Hey, I had no MBA and I was now the head of CBS Records. Who would've said yes to *that* twenty years earlier? Just as I had willed everything to work in my career, I believed I could also will Mariah and me to work out.

"Tom," the therapist said, "you're in denial."

She must have realized she really needed to put the hammer down because she went so far as to get me to see that I was trying to fix myself by trying to fix Mariah.

This time she'd really rung my bell. I went back to see Mariah that night, and at one point told her that I didn't know if it was good for her, good for me, or good for both of us to continue our intimacy. Mariah looked at me, confused, but really didn't say much. I left early.

That feeling lasted about two days before my emotions and obsessions and my denial overwhelmed me again. I thought: *Life is short. Fuck it. This is what I feel. This is what I'm going to do.*

There really was no time to reflect on it. Everything in my

life was moving in fast-forward. That was perfect for me in a business sense, because it fed my machinery beautifully. It's just the way my brain works. I was trying to turn around the company in one minute. Trying to help Sony buy a movie studio the next. Turning Gloria Estefan into a global superstar the minute after that. Then spending all night at the Woodshop.

I went off with Mariah without thinking about the possible consequences and repercussions, or the effect that both might have on my children.

How the hell this happened to the razor-sharp Bronx street kid who would've grabbed a buddy in the same situation by the lapels and then slapped him silly—I'll never know.

Everything around me was in such sharp focus that it was impossible for me to comprehend that I was making this mistake. Not long after I met Mariah, I saw a unique talent in another woman. This woman did not seek me out with a demo tape. She did not seek me out at all. In fact, at the time she didn't want to work with us. But as soon as I met her, I knew that I wanted her alongside me riding shotgun.

This is what happened. As part of an overall strategy to be competitive developing new bands, Columbia was trying to make inroads into the rock and alternative scenes in Los Angeles and Seattle by signing a band called Alice in Chains. But we just couldn't get a deal done.

When I asked why, I kept hearing the same name.

"Well, Michele Anthony..."

"Michele Anthony says..."

"Michele Anthony..."

It got to the point where I wanted to scream: "Who is this Michele Anthony and what is her problem?" The only

two things I knew about her were that: (1) Michele Anthony was the daughter of Dee Anthony; and (2) coming up in the business the way I did at the time of the British Invasion, Dee Anthony was like a god to me. That is, if a god measured about five feet five and weighed three hundred pounds.

Dee was a charismatic street guy from the Bronx who managed Tony Bennett in the early years and later went on to work with some of the great British bands and talent like Jethro Tull, Traffic, and Peter Frampton. He had a larger-than-life persona, so I was naturally curious about his daughter and why she kept refusing to let us sign Alice in Chains. I went to Los Angeles to meet her.

What was supposed to be a casual meeting over drinks turned into a four-hour dinner. Michele and I had an immediate connection. Musically. Historically. Emotionally. Business-wise. Not to mention the whole Italian-Jewish thing—her mom was Jewish and her dad was Catholic. It was like meeting somebody in your family whom you somehow never got to know when you were growing up. I instantly trusted her as if I'd known her all my life—and still do to this day, twenty-five years later.

We talked about everything. Michele had been raised around the musicians that her father managed because they often stayed in her home. As a kid, she'd tagged along with Dee when he'd go to meetings with Ahmet Ertegun and Chris Blackwell and Jerry Moss. She'd gone on tour with Dee as a teenager, and at three in the morning he'd stuff the night's take into her handbag before they left the Fillmore, figuring that nobody would suspect the cash would be in the hands of a fourteen-year-old girl. Michele saw the music industry through the eyes of a manager—just like me—only she wasn't a manager. She'd gone into law, and she was working for a high-powered firm in Los Angeles, alongside lawyers like Lee Phillips and Peter Paterno,

while simultaneously doubling as a mother hen for bands at the center of the alternative rock scene in L.A. and Seattle.

The combination of her experiences, her point of view, her skill set, and her connections in the alternative music world was as unique as Mariah's voice. I didn't want to let her leave the table until she agreed to join my team.

"Okay, listen," I finally said. "I want to make you an offer."

"What are you talking about?" she asked.

"I want you to work for the company."

"Are you kidding me? All the people who work at CBS are living in the past. I know you're trying to change the culture. But I wouldn't work in that company for anything in the world!"

She went on a riff about how awful the company was to work with when it came to new young bands and how nobody in L.A. or Seattle would do business with it. "There is no A&R in your company," she went on. "And your business affairs department is draconian." I tried to hold back a smile. But I couldn't help myself. She was dead-on. Every one of her criticisms of the company was exactly what I was trying to change.

My mind went into overdrive. "Not only do I want you to work for the company," I told her, "I want you to come in and ride shotgun."

"What does that mean?" she asked.

"I want you to be the corporate vice president underneath me and Mel Ilberman overseeing the activities of all the labels. I want you to change business affairs. I want you to bring in A&R people."

"Are you kidding me?"

"No, I'm not."

It didn't faze her at all. She still said no. "I don't want to leave my artists," she said. "I'm committed to them."

"What do you think, we're selling shoes here? If you think

you're doing good for your artists now, wait until you see what you can do for them from *inside* the company."

Then she told me she didn't want to get involved in record company politics. "At least with my practice," she said, "if I don't get along with an artist, we part ways. In a corporation, I'm stuck."

"There are no politics in the company," I told her. "No politics." Well, there was Walter. But he was beyond politics. *Of course* there was politics. But the fiefdoms that created political tension at CBS were exactly what I wanted to tear down.

I was not going to stop at anything to bring Michele aboard. I knew in my gut that quadrupling whatever she was making at that law firm would be the best investment the company could ever possibly make. But she was perfectly happy where she was and completely attached to her artists. So I had to reach her another way. "Why don't you come in and get to know everybody before you make a decision?"

The dinner ended, but the conversation didn't. It went on for weeks. I called her every day. I was relentless. Finally, Michele agreed to come to our New York offices. Mel and I talked for a couple of weeks prior to her arrival, and we had the meeting well scripted. Just before she walked into my office, she went to see Mel.

"I'm not going to take the job," Michele told him. "I'm just not arrogant enough to think I know how to run a company this size. There are areas of this operation that I just don't know."

Mel said: "Here's what we're going to do. You're going to come into this company and do exactly what you're great at doing. And then I'm going to teach you anything and everything that you don't know."

Remember, Mel was like Yoda. He saw a curiosity in her

eyes, an understanding that she could go to a whole new set of places and take her artists with her.

"Not only that," Mel said, "but after I train you, you can have my job."

"I don't want your job!" Michele said.

But Mel had made his point. In an instant, the corporate horror and vicious politics that Michele feared had been wiped aside. What Michele saw was Mel's pure generosity and an education that she could never get anywhere else.

Before she left the building, she took the job. She was only thirty-four years old. It was an out-of-the-box hire, and the management community in the music world was stunned. But I knew our company had just gained instant credibility and integrity in an area of music that it didn't even have a foot in. Michele gave us access to artists and producers who were just not engaging with the company. Alice in Chains signed with CBS/Sony. Then Michele brought in rock A&R specialist Michael Goldstone. Then came Pearl Jam. Then Rage Against the Machine. One after the next.

But this was more than a huge change for the company in a single branch of music. It was like I'd been given another arm. Mel was my right hand. Michele became my left.

Now, my team was in place. We were about to really sail. That was just when Walter Yetnikoff started rocking the boat. Even though I was steering, it began to feel like Captain Ahab was walking the deck.

Walter no longer had to answer to Larry Tisch or William Paley. He'd gotten a $20 million signing bonus and a new contract from Sony, and Tokyo was far, far away. He began to act as if he had absolute power.

One night, Walter and I were eating dinner at Café Central when Bruce Springsteen came in. Bruce was with his wife-to-be, Patti Scialfa, along with Sting and his soon-to-be wife, Trudie Styler. They sat at a table in the middle of the restaurant.

Bruce was trying to avoid Walter. But it was a social setting, and I was sure that at some point Bruce was going to get up and come over to say hello. He didn't. Instead, Walter got up, walked over to Bruce's table, and hit Bruce in the back of the head. It wasn't a vicious smack. It was the kind of smack that said: *What, you don't come over to say hello to me?*

Ohhhhhh, shit, I thought. I was ready to crawl under the table. First off, you don't hit a man in the back of the head with his fiancée sitting right next to him. That's crazy to begin with. But to do that to somebody who'd never caused you problems? Who'd brought you success after success over the years? And who'd long been one of your cornerstone artists?

Sure, the artists realize the guy in charge is writing the checks, and there must be respect that comes along with that. But like in any business dealing, it's the good spirit coming from both sides that makes the relationship work. And here was Walter slapping the Boss in front of an entire restaurant!

From across the room I carefully watched Bruce's face turn red. At first, he was obviously stunned. But he didn't react even though he was smoldering inside. Bruce knew better than to get into a fight with Walter. I didn't know what was going to happen, but my guess was it wasn't going to be good. So I started walking toward the table to try to defuse the situation. Before I got there, Bruce looked Walter straight in the eye and said, "Don't you ever do anything like that again. I'm not that little kid anymore that you used to push around. Do you understand?"

Now Walter was stunned. In his mind, *he* was the Boss, not Bruce, and he couldn't fathom Bruce's reaction. It was a defining moment and a permanent breakdown in their relationship. I'd been around Walter so long that I'd gotten used to this sort of behavior. But that slap was an unmistakable omen. I had the feeling that Walter Yetnikoff might soon go overboard. And I began to wonder if he was going to take me down with him.

I was in an incredibly difficult situation. It was impossible for me to distance myself from Walter. Not only had he given me my big break, but we were on the verge of pulling off a deal even more audacious than the one that maneuvered the sale of CBS Records to Sony. Walter and I were orchestrating Sony's deal to buy a movie studio, and if it worked out, it was going to be monumental for him, and anything that was monumental for Walter would be great for me, as well.

The movie studio deal immediately lifted my profile in Tokyo. They were impressed that I quickly had identified the right candidate and brought Mike Ovitz into the discussions. Soon, the three of us began to formulate a plan. Once all the pieces were identified, it seemed easy and beautiful to put them all together. Mike, Walter, and I would be able to synergize on a full-blown entertainment company.

There was a lot riding on this deal. If we were successful, Walter would be closer to the executive hierarchy in Tokyo— and so would I.

It was stunning to think how far things had come in so short a time. Not long before, I was picking up John Mellencamp's cash in the Indiana snow and trying to convince Carly Simon to sing onstage. Now, as this deal took shape, I was sitting with Walter and Sony's founder, Akio Morita, at Chasen's restaurant, the Hollywood hangout famous for sending its

chili to the set of *Cleopatra* in Rome at the request of Elizabeth Taylor.

Everything was all set. Sony had brought in the same rep it had used to help negotiate the deal to take over CBS Music, Mickey Schulhof, to work toward a deal for the movie studio. Ovitz was about to come in with an offer to run the studio. And then came the unexpected.

Ovitz sat down with the Japanese and asked for an enormous figure simply to pull off his end of the deal. When the Japanese heard Ovitz's number, a call must've gone out for oxygen. The meeting sharply concluded and the Japanese stopped the negotiations. Nobody was counting on Ovitz asking for that much money or the Japanese refusing to negotiate. It was the worst thing that could've happened. The Japanese were insulted, and Ovitz was out.

As soon as Walter heard what happened, he called me and I went down to his office. He was freaked. It was as if all the blood had drained out of his body. We were both freaked. Of course, it wasn't *our* fault. Ovitz had essentially negotiated himself out of what would have been the biggest deal of his life. Walter was beside himself. I wouldn't say that it sent him over the edge. But it added to his anxiety and frustrations, and from that point on his abuses accelerated.

"We've got to come up with another plan!" he said. "We can't lose this deal!"

Walter reached out to Jon Peters, the ex-boyfriend of Barbra Streisand, who had produced hits such as *Flashdance*, *Batman*, and *Rain Man* with his partner, Peter Guber. They were hot at the time, and they seemed like the perfect solution. Guber was especially charming, the ultimate salesman, and not likely to alienate the Japanese.

Guber went to Japan, got along great with the execs at

Sony, and moved a deal forward quickly. During this time, Mickey Schulhof inserted himself into the mix between Sony Tokyo and Sony Entertainment. He was a good friend of Norio Ohga's—they were both aviation fanatics and pilots who sometimes got behind the cockpit of company planes—and he had Ohga's full confidence. It looked like Walter had averted disaster by making that call to Jon Peters, but there was still a huge problem that needed to be solved. Guber and Peters were contractually obligated to Warner Films. Extracting the two from that contract meant a war with Steve Ross. This would normally have been right up Walter's alley—except this time Steve Ross had all the ammunition.

Warner sued Sony for $1 billion for the loss of Guber and Peters. Steve Ross started squeezing Walter in the settlement negotiations, and Walter was not the kind of guy who liked to be squeezed. He liked to do the squeezing himself. But this time he was in a vulnerable place, and he was pushed aside in the negotiations. In order to free Guber and Peters, Sony had to surrender half of the Columbia Record Club, trade plum real estate with Warner for property of lesser value, and give Warner cable television rights to the Columbia Pictures library. Anyone who picked up *Variety* read that it had cost Sony nearly a billion dollars simply to free Guber and Peters. The entire purchase of Columbia Pictures was seen in the industry as a notoriously bad deal for Sony, and it was during this period that Walter started spinning out of control. We're talking bizarre behavior. He was seen walking around the office with a riding crop and yelling, and people around the office came in to work wondering if a secretary was going to get smacked in the ass.

Walter's dream deal ultimately closed in the autumn of 1989. Sony purchased Columbia Pictures for $3.4 billion and received two film studios, a television unit, and the Loews the-

ater chain. Peters and Guber were given one of the most lavish contracts ever extended to run a studio. And the settlement with Warner was sealed. You'll excuse me for not dwelling on any celebratory moments. For one, Walter was not around to celebrate. His behavior had escalated to the point where it was necessary for him to check in at Hazelden Treatment Center in Minnesota for rehab.

And second, the purchase would become known as one of Hollywood's great failures after the studio burned through money like a blowtorch. Five years later Sony had to write off losses of nearly four billion dollars. And that would have an impact on a lot of people down the road.

I stayed focused, and all the obstacles and turbulence around me would vanish when a great song or album came along. One particular moment around this time still stands out. I remember meeting Billy Joel at the Hit Factory recording studio to hear the tracks for his new album—*Storm Front.*

Most of the artists liked to be in the room when my team was hearing their work. Some would not. Some would prefer that we listen, digest, and get back with our reactions. But I remember Billy watching our expressions as one song started playing. I wish there had been a video camera on my face at that moment, because I'd like to see what I looked like when I first heard those lyrics.

My God, I thought, *you've gotta be kidding me.*

Billy was rapping and singing newspaper headlines as only he could do. It was somewhere between Walter Cronkite and LL Cool J. The song was like a history lesson, a rap record, rock 'n' roll, and pop music all blended into one stunning anthem that was set to an incredible, high-voltage music track.

"We Didn't Start the Fire" was absolutely riveting. I made him play it in the studio at least six more times to fully digest it. I think we grew more stunned with each playing. The more I asked him to play it, the happier Billy got. Moments like those were the high points for me. Getting to fully engage with Billy on that day, to appreciate the full vision of his work and to see how proud he was to present it to us.

When my team walked out of the Hit Factory we were overwhelmed and elated. One of our artists had just created one of his best pieces of work ever—and we were on the brink of breaking something special to the public.

Billy was an established icon putting out his twelfth album, but he had just taken his art to a new place. That was our starting point. We clearly knew who his audience was. But it was now our job to reenergize his core audience and broaden it without compromising it. As soon as that song was released it shot to the top of *Billboard*'s Top 100. Eighth graders were looking up references to the lyrics and writing history papers about:

Little Rock, Pasternak, Mickey Mantle, Kerouac
Sputnik, Chou En-Lai, "Bridge on the River Kwai"

In the midst of all this excitement and enthusiasm over *Storm Front*, we couldn't lose focus on a much broader responsibility. There were close to four hundred other artists signed to the label worldwide, and so many of them deserved the same attention. Might be classical, country, or R & B. Each artist was different, and each one needed to be handled, marketed, and sold differently.

The point is this: All the details surrounding the launch of *Storm Front* were different from the strategies used to release Gloria's next album. In that case, we were carefully consider-

ing the Latin market. And we certainly wouldn't be applying the strategies for Gloria when we released a New Kids on the Block album.

New Kids were stalled when I arrived and it took a mall tour to break them wide open. That tour went right to the New Kids' audience. All their fans congregated in malls and we teamed them up with a pop phenomenon at that time named Tiffany, who had a big hit. At first, only a hundred kids showed up. Eventually it turned into a thousand and then it steamrolled into thousands more. All of a sudden radio stations started getting phone calls to play "Hangin' Tough," and the kids were leaving these concerts and walking straight to the record store to buy the album.

After a few months, "Hangin' Tough" shot to the top of the charts. New Kids ended up selling more than 80 million CDs and won two American Music Awards; they had a forty-four-city tour sponsored by Coke, a cable television pay-per-view special that broke all records at the time, and an animated Saturday morning cartoon show. In a few years they were atop the *Forbes* list of highest-paid entertainers, over Michael Jackson and Madonna.

The strategies that got this band started and that process will probably never be talked about again, and the people who pulled it off will never be remembered. That's a shame because there was a real talent and skill to this process. Especially when you compare it to blowing up a singer overnight on a one-hour singing contest on television. Sadly, the next year, you can't even remember that artist's name.

After more than a few months of work on Mariah's album, it was clear that she was going to need a new producer.

Ben had written many of the songs with Mariah, and in the beginning he was a good collaborator. But the public would never be able to recognize just how good those songs were because he didn't have the skills as a producer or as an arranger. He just wasn't capable of taking the songs past what I'd first heard on the demo tape. On top of that, the album needed more variety in the songwriting department.

I turned to my backup plan. We made a win-win agreement with Ben that gave him a handsome check and Mariah the freedom to record with any producer she pleased. Ben was named a cowriter on many of the songs that were released on that first album and received royalties. What's fair is fair. Ben had believed in her, and worked with her, and he was rewarded. By the time Mariah's second album came out, he'd received payments of millions of dollars.

Once Mariah was free, I called Narada Michael Walden, one of the greatest pop producers and drummers ever, to come in to produce. When you hear Whitney Houston's "How Will I Know" and "I Want to Dance with Somebody," you're also listening to the work of Narada Michael Walden. He'd been awarded a Grammy for writing Aretha Franklin's "Freeway of Love" in 1985 and another in 1987 as producer of the year. Narada was at the top of his game. There was only one problem, at first. When I asked him to work with Mariah, he resisted. He thought Mariah was really talented, but he didn't want to take on an unknown artist. It's not often that the head of a large music company directly calls a producer, though, and I told him what a priority it was for us, how it was going to be something special, and how much we as a company really believed in her. To be perfectly honest, I really twisted his arm. Later on, he would thank me profusely for that twist.

We already had "Vision of Love," which is a unique kind

of ballad. In fact, it was one of the most unique songs I'd ever heard. It allowed Mariah to show all her vocal abilities, and gave the audience an idea of her full range. We knew it would be our first single.

But we wanted something more. We didn't want to put out an up-tempo tune as the second single. We wanted another hit, of course, but we also wanted to make a statement. We wanted people to know that Mariah would be one of the best singers of all time. We wanted the second single to be another ballad. That was highly unusual, and highly risky. Nobody would ever release two ballads in a row. It could represent death. But I loved the unconventional approach. Once the world had an idea how good Mariah really was, then we could come out with an up-tempo hit.

Mariah was not comfortable with the switch to Narada Michael Walden. When I look back now, I can see that her whole issue of feeling controlled started right here. Because of the split between her parents, she'd spent a lot of time alone and was used to doing everything her own way. When she worked with Ben she pretty much did whatever she wanted.

I was trying to give her the freedom to go after her dreams. But that freedom came with responsibility—something she was absolutely not used to. She was, after all, nineteen years old. Now she had a very, very successful producer telling her how *he* wanted her to sing. Narada was the type of producer who'd ask Whitney Houston to insert a little laugh in "How Will I Know"—and he made that little laugh memorable. His suggestions worked for Mariah, too, and although Mariah was not happy complying with many of his requests, the album started to take shape. I asked her to *please* put up with the process because, the fact was, Narada was doing a great job.

The entire game plan was coming together. A unique

promotional tour was being set up to introduce Mariah to radio and retail outlets. The concept was to give the people working in radio and retail a similar experience to what I felt when I first heard her in the Woodshop. We'd take her from city to city and have Mariah sing for them in carefully chosen intimate settings with only a piano player and three backup gospel singers. Our international team was prepped and on board. Our strategy was set, but just as everything was beginning to come together on Mariah's debut album, I got a phone call. Life, of course, always takes its own direction and one never knows what will happen from one minute to the next. As the line goes: Man plans. God laughs.

I had asked Gloria and Emilio to take an extended tour to help promote the *Cuts Both Ways* album, and they'd gone along with the idea. They were heading for an appearance in Syracuse in March 1990 when a call came into my office. There had been a terrible accident. Gloria, Emilio, and their son, Nayib, who was nine years old at the time, were badly injured on the road in their tour bus.

I kept trying and trying and trying to reach Emilio, but couldn't. It was all confusion in the first few hours. The news started coming in, and it was devastating. Their tour bus had stopped in traffic on a snowy interstate in Pennsylvania behind a jackknifed truck, and a tractor-trailer just plowed into them. There was an explosion. It must've been the equivalent of getting hit by a tank.

Gloria was thrown from the couch where she'd been sleeping and hurled across the bus. Her back was broken. The bus door ended up inches from a steep embankment, and paramedics had to lift Gloria out through the smashed front

windshield. We got word that she might end up being a paraplegic.

Nayib had a broken collarbone. Emilio had minor head injuries and a cracked rib, and was badly shaken up. Finally, I got through to Emilio's brother, who was running their business at the time. Then Emilio. He was obviously medicated, and he sounded like he was in shock.

"The doctors said Gloria has to have this surgery tomorrow," he told me. "They say that there's a good chance that she won't be able to walk right again."

As soon as he said those words, I begged him to hold off. "Please give me some time to research everything. Give me an hour. Let me see if there are better alternatives and get you options to consider."

Emilio said he'd wait, and I got on the phone with all the doctors I knew until I had drilled down deep enough to find the man recognized as one of the best spine surgeons in New York at that time: Dr. Michael Neuwirth.

I called Emilio back. "Look," I told him, "you're in a community hospital that doesn't ordinarily deal with this type of surgery. There's an orthopedic institute at NYU that specializes in this type of surgery and that has one of the best surgeons in the world. This is the place to do the surgery."

Emilio didn't say yes at first. I'm sure he went back to Gloria, who was medicated and probably still in shock. But after calling back again and again and again, I convinced them to get on a medevac helicopter that we had standing by and fly to New York the following day. They landed at a heliport on the East River.

I met the ambulance at the hospital and saw Gloria strapped down to a gurney, her head in a protective cage. To go from "Get on Your Feet" to that gurney...I don't want to linger on that image any longer than I have to.

We went inside and waited for Dr. Neuwirth to make a diagnosis and tell us what could be done. He came back and told us that Gloria was fortunate the break had come near the waist. But the nerves controlling movement in her lower body had been pinched, bent, and nearly severed when the impact fractured and dislocated the two vertebrae. The surgery would be delicate, but if it were successful, she might be able to walk again and possibly have full movement again. There was no guarantee of a complete recovery. One never knew what the outcome might be. But it certainly was better than thinking she'd be crippled for life.

Waiting through the surgery on the following day was agonizing. I never knew four hours could last that long. Dr. Neuwirth came out and told us he was very confident that it had been a success. That was a huge relief. But then the blood rushed out of us when we heard how he'd inserted two eight-inch surgical steel rods inside her to align her vertebrae and fuse them. I'll never forget going into the recovery room and seeing Gloria lying there, helpless, through the tears in my eyes.

What can you do? You look for the little things to bring a smile. Emilio was able to go out, and I took him to one of my favorite Italian restaurants at the time—Sal Anthony's on Irving Place. He loved the food. He loved it so much that every night I would take bags of food from Sal Anthony's over to the hospital for Gloria and Emilio.

After a couple of weeks in the hospital, Gloria was stable enough to get into a wheelchair and into a private plane that flew her home to Miami. The rehab was going to be brutal. She would have to retrain nearly all the muscles in her body— and she did. It took her more than one year. When she next returned to New York she was able to walk into Sal Anthony's. For years and years afterward, until it closed, whenever she and Emilio were in town they would always go to that restaurant.

VOICES

EMILIO ESTEFAN

I've been lucky to have a lot of friends—some for more than forty years. Tommy is special.

Tommy was the right person when the accident happened. He's the kind of guy who knows what he wants, and he got the doctor, the hospital, the helicopter—and he got them right away, all within one hour. You're never going to go halfway with Tommy. You call Mottola, he's going to be in charge. And he always comes through. I love him like a brother.

8

Nothing I Could Do

Looking back, I cannot remember a dull moment. Just when things seemed to be calming down and getting back on track, another storm would blow in. During this period, two new hurricanes were brewing: Hurricane George and Hurricane Terence. That is, George Michael and Terence Trent D'Arby.

I loved George Michael's music. I thought his *Faith* album was one of the most outstanding pop albums of all time. He wrote and sang the songs, played various instruments, and produced nearly every track. The sparseness and sonics with which he recorded it was brilliant. It was so spectacular and complete that it served as a reference model for me on how to make great pop music albums. No words could express how excited I was to have a new George Michael album on the way.

George was like a modern-day British version of Elvis and had been ever since he was twenty years old, when he hit it big in a duo called Wham! He had hits like "Wake Me Up before You Go-Go," along with a fantastic stage presence and looks

to kill. Then he went out on his own and put out *Faith*. The sky was the limit for George Michael.

We were leaving him alone as he prepared his new album, so we had no idea about the concept, what the music was going to sound like, or what the visuals were going to be. Then we started to get tiny hints from our people in the UK, who pampered him, that something was not right, and that we needed to prepare ourselves for a new direction.

My antennae went up. When an artist becomes so big so quickly and then wants to make abrupt changes, there's a good chance he's going to take a wicked left turn. I'd seen it happen at the beginning of my career, having watched dozens of other artists do the same thing.

George Michael's career had taken off like a NASA missile launch, and he had been denied the benefits that an artist like Bruce Springsteen got while developing over a long period of time. In the first five years of playing live and making music from his heart and soul, Bruce had a chance to evolve into a clear vision of himself. That clarity allowed him to change direction over time and develop into another clear vision. As Bruce kept growing, he took more turns, and even more diversity entered his music and performances. He allowed his audience to grow along with him. But there was always enough of what his audience got in the beginning that allowed them to go along with any new steps that he would make.

George Michael did not have that luxury. All he had was a rapid trajectory of success, and I believe it overwhelmed him. Living in London is like living in a little village filled with tabloids, and the fame that was cast upon him took over his life. Everything he did was written about on a five-times-a-day basis. Cameras followed him wherever he went, and it became unbearable for him. It overwhelmed him, to the point where he decided

he was going to flip everything that had made him successful upside down. The only way for him to go forward, in his mind, was to put out his next album with no imagery. None. No visuals at all. Now, imagine Elvis Presley deciding to put out an album or filming a movie without putting his face on it. That's where George Michael was headed. Worse yet, it was very clear with the elements he was choosing that he was abandoning his prior audience. It's every artist's choice to reinvent themselves—Madonna does it at every turn—but you don't disrespect your prior fans.

When we got wind of this, a few of us immediately went to London to hang out with him, understand what was going on in his mind, talk it through, and listen to the music. I took some walks with him in the streets and tried to explain to him what he'd created and what the expectations were going to be from his audience. I was very direct. "What you want to do is going to be problematic," I told him. "We are extremely nervous that your audience will not respond in a positive way. We think it could backfire."

He didn't care. He wanted change. Period. He didn't use those words, but it was definitely not up for discussion.

Hall & Oates had made me a certified veteran of abrupt change, but this was severe. At the end of the day, though, I was back in the same place. Even if we didn't think it would further the artist's career, we stood together and supported George Michael's vision. So my team and I went back to New York to deliver the news to the troops. "There is no way George is going to change his mind. We will figure out everything we can do to get behind him and make the album successful."

The album art arrived in New York and we all stared at it in amazement. The cover was a cropped photo from a famous picture taken in 1940 called "Crowd at Coney Island." The entire photo is jam-packed with people. It was as if George Michael

had taken the lens off himself and turned it on the masses that had been looking at him. Then the video for the first single came in. The only appearance of George Michael was the back of a black leather jacket. No face, no head, no body. This guy was a sex symbol, and all there was of him was the back of his jacket! Maybe he didn't even realize what he was doing. But it was clear to us. George was turning his back on his audience—figuratively and literally. That video was like watching a Kafka dream and a Fellini movie all in one. This isn't really the video, right? There's another cut of this somewhere and he's in it, right? There was another essential element: the music. The music on this album was very good. But it certainly did not have the distinctive clarity and the undeniably clear pop hits that *Faith* did.

Then the album was released. It was called *Listen without Prejudice, Vol. 1*. To say it was not received well would be an understatement. It came out and hit a brick wall. There was backlash everywhere—from his fans to MTV—and the album predictably sold only a third of what *Faith* had sold.

There was only one way for George Michael to point a finger, and it was at Sony. So what did he do? He tried to get out of his recording contract by suing the company as if we were responsible for the terrible sales of this album. If you can imagine how personally disappointing the experience was for me, it would only get worse for both of us. I will get into all of this a little later.

My team went through a similar disappointment with Terence Trent D'Arby, but for different reasons. All of us had such great expectations for him, and I was in love with his music. In my eyes, Terence was positioned and destined to become one of the biggest stars in the world. He had potential to be up there in the Michael Jackson and Prince category. As a writer, singer, and performer, this guy was one of the most outstanding talents of all time.

He had been born in Manhattan and grown up in Florida, with a dad who was a Pentecostal minister and a mom who was a gospel singer, then gone off to Europe to serve in the Armed Forces, and then moved to London. He completely absorbed England and acquired a British accent. When I met him I would never have known he was from New York. But there was an incredible homogenization of styles and blends of music that filled his head and dreams, and ultimately created some awesome music and classic songs.

He put out his first album, *Introducing the Hardline According to Terence Trent D'Arby*, in the middle of '87. It sold a million albums within the first three days of its release, but I could sense it was still at the beginning of its trajectory when I arrived at CBS/Sony a few months later. I took the time to meet and connect with him. The more I saw, the more impressed I was. His star quality stood out the moment he appeared in the studio, a young handsome man, perfectly groomed, with a meticulous appearance. When you watched him live onstage, with his R & B band and horn section, it was like watching a cross between a male Tina Turner and Michael Jackson—but with maybe even more range. There was a freshness to him that made me feel as good as I did when I was fourteen in the Canada Lounge in Mamaroneck watching the Orchids. You'd listen to a classic ballad like "Sign Your Name" and then an up-tempo song like "Wishing Well" and realize it had come from his debut album, and you couldn't even begin to contemplate what this guy could be capable of over the course of a long career.

I couldn't wait to hear his second album. I called him up and asked him to bring it to New York. Stunning all of us, he showed up looking like Lou Reed after a "Walk on the Wild Side," with his hair dyed into a yellow shade of blond. Looking at him gave me creepy flashbacks of a night at the

Capitol Theatre in Passaic, New Jersey, years earlier when Hall & Oates had opened for Lou Reed. The stage manager and road manager were frantically running around searching for Lou as Lou's band started to play onstage. Nobody could find Lou. Finally his managers opened a dark dressing room door and saw him standing in a shower facing a wall.

We all tried not to let Terence's physical appearance sway our take on his music. But as his next album began to play, everybody in the room thought: *This same guy who made that first album can't be the guy who actually made this one.* The music was all over the place. Unfortunately, so was his personal life at that time. I could tell there were influences moving his mind and his creative process. Some of the songs felt like pure noise. By the time the album was finished, I knew it in my bones: *Okay, we've got trouble. Big, big trouble.*

At the end of the session we all sat with our mouths open. My team and I put it straight to Terence: "Man, you have all these great things in you, every ingredient to go all the way. And we're not talking about our vision of you. This is not us trying to make you into something or take you somewhere you don't want to go. We're just asking you to look at what you created before and look at where you are with this album. The vision of your first album was pure and clear, and this is all blurry. What happened?"

He looked at us vacantly and said: "Man, this is what I'm feeling now. This is what I'm hearing."

He looked and sounded like a different human being. What could I do, except think: *Oh, boy, here we go again.* Only this was more than a left turn. It felt like this could end up being the left turn of no return.

Neither Fish nor Flesh was released in October 1989, and it just didn't have it. Here we were, blessed with these great artists, and feeling like we were going to get a chance to help

take them to even greater heights. But in the cases of George Michael and Terence Trent D'Arby, despite our all-out efforts to globally promote their albums, we ended up watching them fall, and there was absolutely nothing we could do about it.

The closer Mariah's album moved toward completion, the more I started drilling deep down into it. Narada had produced the first single ("Vision of Love") and we had the third single ("Someday") that I thought we needed. But we still didn't have the single that I really wanted to pull off our strategy—that second big ballad.

The more I listened to the songs that Narada produced, the more I intuited that something else was going on in the music. There seemed to be an ingredient that was adding to the overall composition but that was not easy to identify. It was more than simply Narada at work. I didn't know what it was, but I could sense it.

I kept listening and listening and asking questions, and eventually realized that this ingredient was a keyboard player who was in on all the arrangements and sounds. His name was Walter A.

That wasn't his full name. That's just what everyone called him. His full name was Walter Afanasieff. But no one had time for that mouthful. So I called him and asked him to come to New York to meet with me. I knew little more at first than the fact that he was a talented keyboard player who was helping Narada with some of the arrangements. The more I asked around, though, the more I heard great things about him from artists like Michael Bolton and people in the Whitney Houston camp. He was a quiet guy, and when we met he didn't volunteer much about his past. He showed no trace of an accent. I could've been talking to a guy born in San Francisco. Only later would I

learn that he had Russian parents, that he'd been born in Brazil and was classically trained. There were Russian and Brazilian sounds and rhythms in his DNA that came out of him in ways that nobody would expect. I had no idea that we'd develop him into one of the most talented and original producers I'd ever work with. But from the start it was like recognizing in him many of the talents that David Foster had when he, too, was just a recording session piano player and I'd brought him in to do his first production on a Hall & Oates album. All I can tell you is that from the moment I sat down with Walter A., I had a good feeling. We offered him an exclusive production deal and he accepted. He was being mentored by Narada, but now he would have the financial freedom to further develop on his own.

The first job I had for him was to get together with Mariah and come up with our second single—the monster ballad. He was thrilled, and so was Mariah. She felt a good chemistry with him at the start.

"I need you to write the ballad and record it in a week," I told them. "And you need to hit it out of the park."

To say we were up against the clock would be a joke. The clock had struck twelve. We'd already showcased Mariah before retailers in nine different cities with the famous R & B piano player Richard Tee, and she'd just killed it. There were no fancy gimmicks, no backdrops, no costumes. Just her, the piano player, and three background gospel singers. Our distribution division had primed retailers to clear merchandising space. The entire company was under mandate to make Mariah's debut album's release in June 1990 our top priority. Everything was set, except for one thing. That second ballad. The CD was already at the presses in order to be manufactured and released in time for Grammy nominations. We were risking that schedule by calling in Walter A. for that second ballad.

A few days later I went into the Hit Factory studios, where the two were writing. Walter A. put his hands on the keyboard and Mariah began to sing "Love Takes Time." I can't describe the feeling, but when you know a hit, you know a hit. Now, they had two days to record it. I went back and asked Mariah for one final vocal change in the bridge, and she was happy she made it, because it really lifted the song. It was off to the pressing plant. Now, we had our one-two-three punch.

We wanted that first punch to land right between the eyes of Arsenio Hall. *The Arsenio Hall Show* was one of the most popular talk shows at that time—and certainly the coolest and the hippest of the late-night shows. Ordinarily, there'd be no way to get Mariah on a show like that before she'd already had a hit album. Mariah was a complete unknown who'd never sung before a large audience in her life. She was shy, and there was a deer-in-the-headlights quality to her. But after watching her move the retailers and radio people, I was willing to take the risk. So I called up Arsenio, asked him to put her on, and sent him the album. We got the green light.

The curtain came up on a darkened stage. Mariah sang "Vision of Love" and ripped the crowd apart. The response started a groundswell that rose to a crescendo a few days later when she sang "America the Beautiful" at the NBA Finals. The game was between the Detroit Pistons and the Portland Trailblazers at the Palace outside of Detroit. For a couple of minutes she took over not only the arena but also the coast-to-coast telecast. When her voice reached that high-pitched whistle toward the end of the song, the cameras focused on basketball players looking at each other in disbelief, and when she finished, the announcer simply said: "The Palace now has a queen."

We were on exactly the path I had hoped. It was everything I had planned for, and it almost seemed like it was too

good to be true. The response was like hitting a gusher. The album sold millions, and I felt like I was walking on air. And if *I* felt like I was walking on air, I knew I could never imagine what was going on in Mariah's head.

Having been a manager and having seen how easy it is for everything to turn cold, I tried to keep her balanced as best as I could. *"Keep your feet on the ground,"* I kept telling her. "This is gonna be a long journey, and if we are not careful, it can stop very quickly. We've got to stay focused. *Just keep your feet on the ground."*

I also knew exactly where that ground should be: the recording studio. When the first round of publicity ended, there was going to be a lot of work to be done. We had a plan to avoid the sophomore jinx by hitting the public so fast that it wouldn't even know it'd been hit.

It was a good thing we were able to get Mariah launched at that point, because the company would soon be at a standstill. Somehow things got worse when Walter Yetnikoff returned from Hazelden. The treatment center had removed the alcohol and drugs from Walter's life—but not the underlying problems that Walter had been using them to anesthetize.

Now that he was sober, he was paranoid and enraged—mostly enraged. For the company, that wasn't the worst of it. The immediate problem was that Walter had final authorization on all the deals we were making, and he stopped signing contracts to push new and developing projects through. The company was becoming totally paralyzed. The office had an uneasy quiet and stillness like just before a tornado approaches, and you never knew if it was darkness on the edge of town or coming straight for you. It might depend on what side of the bed Walter woke up on. But you knew it was coming. Eventually the blur of insanity

was going to blow through and hit someone or all of us. All Walter wanted to do was go on three-hour rants, get into fights, and knock down whatever bridges he had remaining.

He was taking on Steve Ross, who had replaced Larry Tisch as his favorite punching bag. He was lashing out at Michael Jackson and feuding with Bruce Springsteen's manager, Jon Landau. He even took on a guy that nobody in the industry would mess with—David Geffen.

"Hire a private detective and get some dirt on Geffen," he'd tell me. I would just listen and, of course, I didn't do it. Then he'd call and tell me to investigate Michael Jackson. Of course, I didn't do that, either. Then he'd call me ten times the following day to see if I had the detectives and the dirt.

He berated Grubman every time they met. Allen had to put up with it because he represented so many CBS artists and there was a lot at stake financially. But it got to the point where I couldn't watch Walter abuse him. Then Walter ordered the business affairs department to stop talking to Grubman. Then he barred Grubman from coming into the building. Then he ordered that I not speak to Grubman or have anything to do with him. Grubman represented so many of our company's superstars. How could I not talk to him? It was just crazy, and it went way beyond that. Walter put me in the worst possible position. The man who gave me my big break was telling me not to speak with my dear friend. Walter was tearing at my loyalty.

It got to the point where there were piles of deal memos and contracts sitting on Walter's desk for a month waiting to be signed. Here we were desperately trying to build the music company of the future to compete and sign new artists, and everybody in the company who was busting his ass was having his hard work boomerang back in his face. When Walter wouldn't sign the contracts, it looked like we were insulting

the managers and lawyers of the new artists. People would ask me over and over: "What's going on? Why is it taking so long?" It got to the point that I didn't know what to tell them. Walter was my boss. All I could say was: "The contracts are on Walter's desk." All the lawyers in our business affairs department were pulling their hair out. Everyone inside the company became aware of the situation, and it wasn't long before word reached the entire industry from coast to coast, and then traveled more than six thousand miles across the ocean to Japan.

I tried to get Walter to look at himself in the mirror. I would urge him and beg him, at times, to try to confront the situation for his own sake, also pointing out that the company was 100 percent paralyzed.

"Leave me alone," he would snap.

This had never happened between us before. Walter had driven a wedge between himself and everybody around him, and now he was driving a wedge between himself and his last supporter—me. His office became a bunker. He closed the doors and wouldn't let anybody in—including me, and I was used to going into his office ten times a day.

This was headed only one way. I could see that he was going over the edge, and I certainly didn't want to be attached to him when he went off that cliff.

There was just no reaching Walter. Mickey Schulhof, Sony's rep in the United States, tried to set up meetings with him to understand what was going on. Walter would berate him and call him Mickaleh Pickaleh. Walter had a special name for everyone in Yiddish. Sometimes being around him was like listening to Jackie Mason on crack. But it wasn't funny when he told Mickaleh Pickaleh to leave him the fuck alone. You can imagine how well that sat with Mickey. Not only was Walter in denial, he just didn't care about anything.

Stories started getting back to management in Japan through Schulhof. Mickey was more than Sony's rep. He was a confidant to Norio Ohga. About a month or so after Mariah's album came out, Ohga came to New York to talk to Walter about his behavior. Now he had a formal warning, but we all knew it wasn't going to do any good.

By that point, I tried to stay away from Walter as much as possible. I could only get in trouble if I didn't. Walter had pissed off so many of the wrong people, and a groundswell was building to take him down. When you're making Michael Jackson's camp angry and disgusting Bruce Springsteen's manager and humiliating Allen Grubman and sniping at Steve Ross—and conspiring to take down David Geffen—you're basically shaking your fist at a tidal wave.

Schulhof told me that Ohga would be coming to New York for meetings at the beginning of September, and it was not difficult to guess what was going to happen. As the day approached, the entire office seemed to go silent. It was as if the whole company had shut down.

Mickey had already told Ohga that a change needed to be made. But when I was called in to meet with Ohga and Schulhof, Ohga was very thorough. He asked me about all the allegations to see if they were true, and if the company was now at a standstill. Then Ohga and Mickey brought my entire team in and asked variations on the same question: "Are you able to do business? Can you tell me what's happening?" They all told him that the company had basically been stopped cold.

Within an hour of these meetings, Walter was summoned to meet with Ohga. Norio walked out of that meeting very solemn, like he was leaving the funeral of his best friend. The next day, he and Schulhof called me and my whole team in for a meeting.

There were about six of us in that room. "It is with great

sadness that I tell you this," Ohga said. "A very terrible thing has happened. I have had to tell my good friend of more than twenty years that he will no longer be employed by this company." He took a deep breath and continued, "I am very fond of Walter and always have been. But this is not my own private company. I have an obligation to our shareholders."

It took no more than sixty seconds for Ohga to say those words. He stopped and remained speechless. It was all very awkward. He did not get up and leave. Nor did he ask us to leave. He just sat there in silence. Finally, all of us just looked at one another, stood up, and walked out the door.

There was a big play in the media about Walter's firing. They called it a palace coup. It came to be known as the Labor Day Massacre, because it happened just after everybody came back to work following the September holiday.

The media turned it all on me. These are things I've learned to accept. You know how it goes. When someone gets whacked, it's always easy to point the finger at the guy who's closest. Especially when his last name ends in a vowel. It made for much more sensational headlines.

Sony Tokyo was stunned by the press's reaction, confused and not sure what to do. So Ohga immediately moved Mickey Schulhof into Walter's corporate position. This insanity had really spooked the executives in Tokyo, and it was now time for things to settle down.

I certainly felt terrible about what had happened to Walter. But there was nothing, nothing, nothing, *nothing* I could do about it. In the end it came down to him or all of us. I just wanted the company to function again.

People in the industry who remember the headlines have no idea what really went down. The clearest way to describe what happened is also the saddest: Walter Yetnikoff cut his own throat.

VOICES

MEL ILBERMAN

Let me tell you something. Walter Yetnikoff was a
brilliant guy. Not too many people would have had the
genius or the balls that Walter Yetnikoff had to bring
Tommy in. If Walter had not been working for a Japanese
company, it probably would not have been allowed. You're
not going to be able to give that job to someone who
has no experience of working in the structure of a large
company. But Walter intuited what Tommy could do.
Walter was a wonderful guy. He just had his issues. Those
issues put him through a rough time and they caused him
a lot of problems.

JON LANDAU

I had a very complex relationship with Walter Yetnikoff
over the fourteen years we worked together. Twelve of
those years were very, very good. The last two were a
deterioration that nobody wants to revisit.

SHARON OSBOURNE

Walter Yetnikoff was completely ignorant about music.
He was nothing more than a star-fucker. He treated artists
like they were objects, not human beings. On top of that,
he was the poster boy for misogyny.

Yetnikoff took more drugs than any artist I ever worked with. He made Ozzy look like an absolute beginner. Tommy never got caught up in all that drug nonsense; he was much too smart. When Tommy took over at Sony, he was the only executive in the industry who really cared about music and the artists. The first thing he did was to move a piano into his office. These other executives had calculators, but Tommy had a piano.

RANDY JACKSON

Music entrepreneur/*American Idol* judge

I often refer to Tommy when I give this example because he was so smart.

I met Tommy when we were still mad young. I was working with Narada Michael Walden—this legendary producer—and Tommy came to San Francisco with this great new artist—Mariah Carey. We started working on Mariah's first album.

In these producer teams there are always guys behind the scenes that are doing most of the work as the producer grows. When you start out as a producer, you're doing all the work by yourself. You've got one or two projects, whatever.

But you start to grow and then you've got ten projects and you can't do it all. So you need to bring in a B team and a C team.

The smart people go into the studios and look around. Okay. I know who the producer is. But who's the one really making this happen?

Tommy was astute enough to see that Walter A. and I were doing a lot of the work. He saw something in us that he could definitely use to help nurture Mariah's career. Walter became a staff producer at Sony. I became the musical director for Mariah's show, and later, an A&R guy, a senior VP at Columbia Records.

It all kind of snowballed from there. Tommy believed in us and in our talent, and he believed that we knew something that could enrich Mariah. So my hat off and my props to him for believing.

P. DIDDY (AKA SEAN COMBS)

When I went to meet Tommy for the first time, I felt like I was meeting the Godfather. One of the things that Tommy and I have in common is our backgrounds. Coming from an inner-city New York background, him coming from an Italian neighborhood, me from a black neighborhood, we're all trying to make it out. We're all trying to make a better way.

One of the things people may not really realize about Tommy Mottola is how hands-on he is. There are a lot of executives that stay up in the ivory tower. They don't go to the studio. They don't get their hands dirty. They don't talk to the producer who doesn't have a hit yet. But Tommy was always accessible. He was around, always listening to the music, and he was smart enough to ask questions. He understood the importance of melody, the structure of a hit record.

I think one of his greatest attributes was working with the music in the studio, really cultivating the music, really

pushing artists for greatness, and really assisting artists. Sometimes you could tell somebody you want more, and you leave 'em there with the problem. Tommy was able to say that he wanted more, then he would come up with the solution for how to get more.

CORY ROONEY
Music executive

Tommy really knew his instruments. It was amazing to me sometimes. He would say, "You know what this needs? This needs a cello right here. You need this kind of string line." He'd pick up the phone: "Get somebody to bring this." And I'm thinking, *This is crazy.* But by the time it shows up and it starts to take form, I'm thinking, *He really knows what he's doing.* Sometimes he would sit at the board and actually mix the records himself. Sometimes he would sit in the studio with us and write melodies and lyrics. He couldn't take credit for it because he was the chairman of the company, but he would actually sit and write lyrics with us.

HARVEY WEINSTEIN

Tommy is a talent magnet. He's a throwback to the icons in the entertainment industry. In my business, he'd be like an Irving Thalberg or a David O. Selznick, a guy who could make a movie.

He's an artist. He can go in and tell a producer what's wrong with the song. He's not one of those guys who just says, "Hey, man, thanks a lot for the record, and we'll market it to the best of our ability." No, he can go

head-to-head with somebody and say, "This is what it's all about."

In our world, those are the guys who created this business. Those who inherit it are something else, but the guys who created our industry are guys like Tommy Mottola.

Boyz II Men

use You Loved Me" • Celine Dion

ys Be My Baby" • Mariah Carey

"Tha Crossroads" • Bone Thugs-n-Harmony

Not Gon' Cry" • Mary J. Blige

"Fantasy" • Mariah Carey

Gangsta's Paradise" • Coolio

"Lady" • D'Angelo

"Wonderwall" • Oasis

"Ironic" • Alanis Morissette

enever, Wherever, Whatever" • Maxwell

irtual Insanity" • Jamiroquai

Shadowboxer" • Fiona Apple

"Macarena" • Los del Rio

Give Me One Reason" • Tracy Chapman

o Will Save Your Soul" • Jewel

ssing" • Everything But the Girl

ange the World" • Eric Clapton

"No Diggity" • Blackstreet

Fastlove" • George Michael

"Just a Girl" • No Doubt

sh" • The Dave Mathews Band

"Doin It" • LL Cool J

uled the World (Imagine That)" • Nas

The Score • Fugees

It Was Written • Nas

Break My Heart" • Toni Braxton

e in the Wind 1997" • Elton John

"Foolish Games" • Jewel

e Missing You" • Puff Daddy and Faith Evans

t Nobody Hold Me Down" • Puff Daddy

Believe I Can Fly" • R. Kelly

ow Do I Live" • LeAnn Rimes

o Money Mo Problems" • The Notorious B.I.G.

Want You" • Savage Garden

very Time I Close My Eyes" • Babyface

All by Myself" • Celine Dion

All Coming Back to Me Now" • Celine Dion

et Garden" • Bruce Springsteen

Karma Police" • Radiohead

"Angels" • Robbie Williams

"Building a Mystery" • Sarah McLachlan

"Fly Like an Eagle" • Seal

Buena Vista Social Club • Buena Vista Social Club

"You're Still the One" • Shania Twain

"Truly Madly Deeply" • Savage Garden

"All My Life" • K-Ci and JoJo

"No No No" • Destiny's Child

"My Heart Will Go On" • Celine Dion

"Gettin' Jiggy Wit It" • Will Smith

"My All" • Mariah Carey

"Been around the World" • Puff Daddy

"I Don't Want to Miss a Thing" • Aerosmith

"This Kiss" • Faith Hill

"Ray of Light" • Madonna

"Uninvited" • Alanis Morissette

"Brick" • Ben Folds Five

"Car Wheels on a Gravel Road" • Lucinda Williams

"Deeper Underground" • Jamiroquai

"Doo Wop (That Thing)" • Lauryn Hill

"Can't Take My Eyes Off of You" • Lauryn Hill

"Gone Till November" • Wyclef Jean

"The Boy Is Mine" • Brandy and Monica

"Adia" • Sarah McLachlan

"My Way" • Usher

"What You Want" • Mase

"Feel So Good" • Mase

"Spice Up Your Life" • Spice Girls

"A Rose Is Still a Rose" • Aretha Franklin

Vol. 2...Hard Knock Life • Jay-Z

Surfacing • Sarah McLachlan

"One Sweet Day" • Mariah Carey and Boyz II Men

"Because You Loved Me" • Celine Dion

"Always Be My Baby" • Mariah Carey

"Tha Crossroads" • Bone Thugs-n-Harmony

"Not Gon' Cry" • Mary J. Blige

"Fantasy" • Mariah Carey

"Gangsta's Paradise" • Coolio

"Lady" • D'Angelo

"Wonderwall" • Oasis

"Ironic" • Alanis Morissette

Shadowboxer • Fiona Apple

"Macarena" • Los del Rio

"Give Me One Reason" • Tracy Chapman

"Who Will Save Your Soul" • Jewel

"Missing" • Everything But the Girl

"Change the World" • Eric Clapton

"No Diggity" • Blackstreet

"Fastlove" • George Michael

"Just a Girl" • No Doubt

"Crush" • The Dave Mathews Band

"Doin It" • LL Cool J

"If I Ruled the World (Imagine That)" • Nas

The Score • Fugees

It Was Written • Nas

"Un-Break My Heart" • Toni Braxton

"Candle in the Wind 1997" • Elton John

"Foolish Games" • Jewel

"I'll Be Missing You" • Puff Daddy and Faith Evans

"Can't Nobody Hold Me Down" • Puff Daddy

"I Believe I Can Fly" • R. Kelly

"How Do I Live" • LeAnn Rimes

"Mo Money Mo Problems" • The Notorious B.I.G.

"I Want You" • Savage Garden

"Every Time I Close My Eyes" • Babyface

"All by Myself" • Celine Dion

"It's All Coming Back to Me Now" • Celine Dion

"Secret Garden" • Bruce Springsteen

"Karma Police" • Radiohead

"Angels" • Robbie Williams

"Guantanamera" • Wyclef Jean

"Criminal" • Fiona Apple

"Building a Mystery" • Sarah McLachlan

"Fly Like an Eagle" • Seal

Buena Vista Social Club • Buena Vista Social Club

"You're Still the One" • Shania Twain

"Truly Madly Deeply" • Savage Garden

"All My Life" • K-Ci & JoJo

"No No No" • Destiny's Child

"My Heart Will Go On" • Celine Dion

"Gettin' Jiggy Wit It" • Will Smith

9

No Ordinary Love

Two days later I was sitting in Mickey Schulhof's new office reviewing all the deal memos and contracts. Within twenty-four hours we got every one of them signed and our company began firing on all twelve cylinders.

My working arrangement with Mickey was easy and great. He kept it simple. He was not a music guy. So he let me do what I knew how to do. His timing couldn't have been better. Imagine stepping into that job just as Gloria Estefan, Mariah Carey, and Celine Dion were starting to bloom.

After everything that had just gone down with Walter, it felt great for everyone to be back to normal. In January 1991, I was sitting in the front row at the American Music Awards. It was a huge night. Gloria Estefan was returning to the stage for the first time since her accident. Just before she appeared, a video had shown the television audience and the crowd at Shrine Auditorium in Los Angeles footage of the crashed tour bus and of the gurney rolling Gloria toward the ambulance.

When it ended a hot single blue spotlight cut through the darkness and focused directly on Gloria center stage. The entire crowd erupted to its feet. As the ovation grew louder and longer, I looked at Emilio sitting next to me, then at ten-year-old Nayib next to him, then at Gloria, and uncontrollable tears came running down my face. One of the most emotional moments in my life came when Gloria began to sing "Coming Out of the Dark."

Less than a month later, I was accompanying Mariah to the Grammys. She'd been nominated for five awards. Out of respect for my children, I purposely was not seen much in public with Mariah as my divorce with their mother unfolded. But unfortunately the marriage ended up where it began. It started on the wedding pages of the *New York Times* and ended up in all the newspapers. Once it was official, I felt freer to be out with Mariah, and the Grammys was our big first step.

Twice Mariah's name was called. The first award was for the category that we had really hoped she'd win: Best New Artist. The second time was for the Best Female Pop Vocal with "Vision of Love." Winning a Grammy on your first album is surreal—like a fairy tale. And as Mariah stepped away from the podium we had already ensured that the fairy tale would continue. There would be no sophomore jinx. Plans were in place to avoid it before there was even a chance that it could hit.

The first four singles we released from Mariah's debut album each shot to Number One. And now we were preparing to release the first single from her next album, *Emotions*, so quickly that people were bound to think it was still from the first album. When they finally realized that it wasn't, we'd have already whet their appetite to immediately buy her second album. Bam. Bam. Bam. Bam. Bam. Exactly what I'd seen

Elvis do when I was eight years old. To this day, Mariah is the only artist to ever have her first five singles go to Number One on the Billboard Hot 100, and no other solo act—including Elvis—has more Number One singles than Mariah.

I can only now wonder about the expression on my therapist's face when she tuned in to the Grammy Awards and saw Mariah thank God for that first Grammy, and then Tommy Mottola for believing in her. Although my therapist was certainly right that I was in denial, she could no longer call me delusional—at least in terms of Mariah's success. My gut sure had been right about her talent, even though my emotions and the whirlwind got the best of me and made me drop my guard.

I'd also found reassurance in the bond I saw between Gloria and Emilio, and the commonality that they shared through music. Celine Dion and René Angélil shared a similar connection, and even though they were not publicly linked when I met them, it was easy to see the chemistry.

I met Celine and René in 1989 as she was making the leap from singing in French to her first album in English—*Unison*. Celine didn't really speak much English at the time—just a few words here and there—but she had the voice of an angel, and much more. Her ears are so sharply tuned, and she is such an incredible vocalist, that she could study the phrasing and words phonetically and then sing songs clearly in English even when she didn't have a full grasp of the language. I remember being in the studio and listening to her sing for the first time "Where Does My Heart Beat Now." It was stunning. There was no question that Celine was going to be huge.

She created her own lane and musical style. It was different from those of Whitney and Mariah—more down the middle, more pure. She had an uncannily perfect pitch. In that respect,

she might be the best singer I've ever heard. There is something in her voice that will always stand up to time, and when I hear Tony Bennett sing today in his late eighties, I sense that Celine's voice will have the same magic at that point in her life.

The question was: how do we introduce this special voice to the world? We needed a master plan to launch her. A few months later, a brilliant opportunity came along. Disney had come to us with a big animated film, *Beauty and the Beast*. We could pick anybody on the label to do the title track. So, of course, I chose Celine, and brought in Walter A. to produce. The song, written by Alan Menken, called for a duet, so we paired Celine with a great singer named Peabo Bryson. There couldn't have been a better mass-marketing opportunity. Disney was putting tens of millions in advertising and marketing behind the film, and it ended up nominated for an Academy Award in the Best Picture category.

I remember going to the screening, hearing the title track, and thinking: *That's it.* A few weeks later, the song became a hit around the world. It was a beautiful time and the future couldn't have looked more promising. While all this was going on, we were preparing the release of the great Michael Jackson's first album in four years.

We had so much respect, and cared for Michael Jackson so much, that we bent over backward in 1991 when we at Sony renewed his contract. I can't say it was *the* largest recording contract ever offered up to that time as it was reported to be— but it was certainly one of the largest.

Here's what you need to know about it because it sets up everything to come. Even though Michael was happy with the final negotiation, he wouldn't sign the document unless the

accompanying press release announced it as a billion-dollar deal. By no means were we paying Michael a billion dollars. But if that was the press release that Michael wanted, we figured out a way to do it for him. Yes, if his albums sold along the lines of *Thriller* and *Bad*, a case could be made that the sales of those albums would total a billion dollars. So we were able to spin it in the press in a way that pleased Michael. But if I recall correctly, the actual advance was somewhere around $35 million. Which I guess made it another normal day in the life of Michael Jackson, because he lived in a world of fantasy, where all dreams come true.

I remember going to meet with Michael at the presidential suite at the Four Seasons. When I walked into his four-thousand-square-foot penthouse, I couldn't believe what I saw. The suite was filled with life-size, fully clothed mannequins. Twenty-four of them, all in different outfits. It was eerie. Like walking into a wax museum. It spooked me out. I asked Michael what the deal was with the mannequins, and he said, "Oh, I just like them. They're my friends." He brought them with him everywhere he went. When I made the mistake of complimenting him on his friends, the next day he sent me two of my own, fully clothed and decked out in their regalia. They went straight into the storage locker.

Anybody who punctured the balloons that Michael blew up around him was not around Michael Jackson very long. In other words, if you said *no* to Michael one time because it was the right thing to do, you'd be gone. During the fifteen years of overseeing Michael's career at Sony, I think he went through at least five managers and different lawyers, not to mention temporary mentoring from Prince Al-Waleed bin Talal of Saudi Arabia. I would have to have numerous meetings with Al-Waleed about Michael's career, as crazy as that sounds, going past two floors

of security people at the Plaza Hotel to get to the prince's suite. There were also meetings with Mohamed Al-Fayed, who owned Harrods and who truly cared for Michael and took care of him many times when he was in need.

But there was virtually nobody around Michael who could speak truth to him because he was Michael Jackson, King of Pop, and he was writing the checks. He surrounded himself with people who said *yes* simply to be around him or because they were cashing his checks. *Michael, what would you like? Michael, how would you like that? Michael, we can do this. Michael, of course we can do that. Yes, Michael. Yes, Michael. Yes, Michael, yes.* That put me in somewhat of a unique position. I was in charge of Sony Music—and Sony was writing *his* checks. I didn't confront him very often. But I might have been the only person in the world who was able to say "I don't think that's right" to Michael Jackson. From the beginning, part of him resented that, but mostly he respected that.

In November 1991, Michael released *Dangerous*. There were two huge singles on it—"Black or White" and "Remember the Time"—and it would be hard for anybody to call that album less than a colossal success. *Dangerous* ultimately sold 32 million units. But everyone who heard the record at Sony knew that it was not going to have the same impact as *Thriller* or *Bad*. When it came to sales numbers, something was always off balance with Michael—and it's easy to see why. All you have to do is look at his trajectory from his days with the Jackson 5 through the moonwalk to "We Are the World." The world had never seen a performer quite like him ever before. But it was *Thriller* that really separated him from even himself. Not only did the album win a record-breaking eight Grammys, it also became the largest-selling album of all time. The accompanying videos and the theatrics of the world tour were

astonishing. I knew *Thriller* was going to be huge the instant I heard it, but nobody had any idea that it would go on to sell 100 million. Nobody! Anybody who tells you that he or anyone else predicted that is full of crap!

As we watched the meteoric rise of this album from the sidelines, we saw how stunned executives were about the reaction and the incredible sales that snowballed day after day. I arrived at CBS/Sony shortly after his next album came out. *Bad* sold 45 million units. *Forty-five million* is an insane number. And yet, it was a frightening figure to Michael. "You've got to turn this around," he'd tell me, "so it can sell more than *Thriller*." It was an unrealistic situation to be in. But there was nothing about Michael Jackson or his universe that was realistic, and he put his expectations on the back of the company.

When *Dangerous* came out four years after *Bad*, there was nothing I could do other than to tell Michael that I had sent out a promotional army to make way for his album, and that he had to look at the numbers realistically. There was not another album out there selling 32 million units. Not even close! So you can see how differently our views were of the same numbers from the start.

Anybody would have signed Michael Jackson for an enormous amount of money. He was arguably the biggest star in the world in any category of entertainment, and he was making the company money hand over fist. So you just had to deal with unrealistic requests when one of his managers would come in and ask for millions more for short films—MJ never called them "videos"—and more displays in music stores and more ads on television. More, more, more, more, more...

I just had to deal with it when Michael would wake me at three in the morning and ask me to commit to selling more than a hundred million. I'm not talking about one 3 a.m.

phone call. I'm talking about dozens. And that doesn't count the 3 a.m. phone calls that Dave Glew was getting from him. But it was okay. I understood the fear and insecurity, having lived with the emotions of so many artists right from the start.

You just dealt with it, even when reports surfaced of him trying to buy the Elephant Man's bones and living with his pet monkey, Bubbles, not to mention the rumors of sleepovers with young boys. You just dealt with it. You managed it. You managed it the best you could day in and day out. It was clear that the rumors and his strange behavior were hurting his popularity. The calls would come in from Toyko. "Are these things true? Is everything all right?" All I could say was, "As far as the music goes, everything is okay. We're managing it."

But Michael was very right about one thing. As high as those numbers were, and as profitable as they were for the company, they *were* shrinking.

Mariah was now perfectly positioned. She was a blend of soulful essence and pop hits, which was exactly the appeal that Berry Gordy used when he had black artists sing great pop songs to put Motown on the map.

Everything in her short career had unfolded as if it had been perfectly choreographed. The debut on *Arsenio*. The marketing that helped push sales of her first album past 30 million units. The two Grammys. The release of the single "Emotions" months before it came out on her second album—which built a groundswell of anticipation and allowed her to avoid the sophomore jinx.

We wanted her to stay in the studio just a little longer after the *Emotions* album was released to write some more hits since she was on such a roll. It was not just a matter of selling CDs.

I'm a creator and a builder, and I've seen these situations come and go so many times. When an artist comes along and is so prolific, it's always critical to take advantage of that creative energy and document as much of it as possible. On top of that, we wanted to continue to finish the rock-solid foundation of her career that had been meticulously blueprinted. If we got it right, that foundation would always support her no matter what musical styles or changes she would undertake or directions she would want to go in.

I explained that this foundation would give her a rare opportunity. "Look, if you keep putting out all this diverse music and have hits," I told her, "you'll have the opportunity to become iconic like Barbra Streisand." I explained that if Barbra wanted to do a Broadway album or an album produced by the Bee Gees, she had the latitude to do so at any point in her career. "If you can get to that point," I told Mariah, "everything you do will be a new plateau." On top of that, she would have the benefit of a more diverse audience: kids, black and white, moms and adults. Quite simply, the career we were trying to build would allow her to have it all.

But Mariah felt that the workload wasn't giving her the time to go out and celebrate her success. Looking back on it, this was totally understandable. She was twenty years old and never really had a childhood to begin with, not to mention money or success. She was a perfectionist in the studio, dissecting and correcting every note if she had to, and she'd redo any line or word if it was not to her liking. When she threw herself into her music there was no holding back or anything left afterward. It was grueling, and I understood where she was coming from. I loved and respected her, and I supported all of her dreams and desires. But I had also seen dozens and dozens of times how instant success had unraveled

the lives and careers of so many other artists. All the classic stories you've heard about and all the ones that you haven't. The process is so demanding, so delusional, so surreal, and you live in such a bubble, that unless you walk a fine line and have people around you to help keep you grounded, there's no possible way to make it through. I don't care who you are. That overwhelming force will get you. You can't argue with history—and history repeats itself over and over.

Having seen it all, my feeling was that there'd be plenty of time for Mariah to celebrate just a little ways down the road. I'm not talking ten years, just a few. I encouraged her to stay focused on the big picture. Those suggestions began to form very tiny cracks between us. In the beginning they were unnoticeable, though, because for us in so many other ways this was the best of times.

We were living together now, and for the first time in her life Mariah had a sense of stability at home, a sense of grounding, a sense of family, a sense of financial security, a sense of real love and true caring. I'm not talking out of school and I'm not breaking any news here. She's told her story in the press and on TV time after time, as if the interview process were a form of therapy. The story of her upbringing has been well expressed in the media in precisely her own words. She'd grown up amid the difficulty of having interracial parents at a time and in a place that was not very accepting. She's told the story of being asked as a kid in elementary school in Long Island to draw her parents, and when she drew her father as a black man and her mother as a white woman the teacher said something like: "No! No! No! Why did you do that?" as if her picture were wrong. Her father was ostracized, people in their Long Island neighborhood set her family's car on fire, and

these tensions ultimately led to her parents' separation. This left Mariah scarred and often fending for herself.

There have been so many stories in the press about Mariah and me, with me being described as a Svengali, restrictive, controlling, and on and on. Lots of crap. But I had to continue to take the hits because I was the chairman of Sony Music, and so I remained above the fray and never responded. When squeezed, my only statement would be: *I continue to be her biggest fan. She is one of the most talented people to come along in entertainment. I will always support her in all of her endeavors.*

The irony here is that in the end I was the one who was restrained. But I'm free to speak my mind here. If you've read George du Maurier's novel *Trilby*, you know that Svengali is a fictional character who hypnotized people and controlled them with evil intent. So that characterization is simply bullshit. No, I did not hypnotize Mariah. No, I did not hypnotize her into selling 200 million albums. No, I did not chain her to the recording studio in the mansion we built after we were married. I was running through cement walls for her, trying to give her all I had learned from the day I set eyes on Elvis Presley at eight years old. But, hey, we all know that everyone has their own way of seeing things. And that includes me.

Our relationship at the start provided all the good things that came along with a loving family. The gifts I had gotten from my parents growing up were extended to Mariah— including the home-cooked meals that I had learned at my grandmother's knee and prepared for her. Even though my parents didn't quite know how to assess my new situation, they welcomed Mariah with open arms. That made her feel good and she gave that warmth back to them. Nobody, including

Mariah, will tell you that back then she didn't soak it all in, love it, and appreciate it.

Look, I'm not trying to shrug any responsibility here. It was absolutely wrong and inappropriate for me to become involved with Mariah. And I'm not saying this because there was a generation gap. Thalia and I are a generation apart. And that angel that dropped from the sky and I are still together and enjoying fourteen (and counting) of the best years of our lives. Celine Dion and her husband, René, are also a generation apart, and they have been together for more than twenty years. When the arms you're in are the right arms, age doesn't matter.

I should have listened to the piercing voice of my shrink and maintained my distance. Even today, more than twenty years later, when I see Mariah go over the same ground in interviews, I want to say that I am truly sorry for any discomfort or pain that all of my good intentions inevitably caused her, and most of all for the scars it left on my two oldest children. But it was confusing for me, because I went in with a good heart and, by the way, it was Mariah who asked *me* to marry *her*.

We had a *musical* connection. She had the talent— tremendous writing and vocal abilities—and I knew how to help her get the most out of it, and I also was fortunate enough to have the power and the means to execute everything that I knew. Early on, our dreams and our daily conversations were completely aligned. It's very possible that she could've achieved the same success if we'd never gotten any closer than Mariah Carey the singer and Tommy Mottola the chairman of Sony Music. Looking back, that would have been the ideal collaboration for both of us. I wish somebody as strong as I was would have locked me in a room and smacked me around until I finally understood that before I dove in blindly and got

involved. Many people did warn me. But with all the elements surrounding me in my personal and professional life, I drank my own Kool-Aid—the very thing that I scream at everyone else not to do. All I could see was a fairy-tale collaboration and success.

As we headed into 1992, Mariah and I were in total agreement when it came to what needed to be done next. Her vocals on the song "Emotion" were so unique—and there were places where Mariah sang through a succession of high notes like a bird—that critics began to wonder if her voice was being manufactured in the studio.

One of the reasons these rumors picked up steam was that Mariah had never gone out on tour. The critics and the masses had not seen her live, so there was no way for anyone to dispute these claims. Of course, I knew how amazing Mariah's voice was. So did everybody else at Sony. But that didn't matter. Public opinion can make or break you. I was always acutely hypersensitive to any issue—good, bad, or indifferent—that dealt with consumer thinking and behavior. And I've always liked to attack things that are a cause for concern. So we didn't waste any time.

We simply had to show the world that Mariah's voice was one of the greatest ever—and we figured out the perfect way to do that. *MTV Unplugged.*

MTV was the biggest promotional force in the industry by this time, and its *Unplugged* series had become one of the hottest shows of its time. Its purpose was to show stars outside the studio and give the audience a realistic performance in a natural state with only pure and raw talent coming through. It got off the ground in '89 and was given a big boost when Paul McCartney performed on it in '91. So we made a deal for Mariah to showcase her voice in front of a small crowd on MTV.

There was some risk involved. Mariah had come out of nowhere and gone straight to the moon. She didn't have the opportunity to grow and develop in small clubs and venues. All the years it took artists like Bruce Springsteen, Billy Joel, and Bob Dylan to piece themselves together at these tiny, noisy, smoke-filled locations were the invaluable experiences that made them the pillars of music today. Mariah had to develop her own style in concert, and that was going to take time. But the entire company stood behind her and we rolled the dice.

She stepped on the *MTV Unplugged* stage in a black leather jacket and jeans, and right off the bat she shattered any rumors of her "studio" voice with a rendition of "Emotions" that sent high notes through the roof and into the clouds. She went through her hits with only a microphone in front of her and a piano, violinists, guitarists, drums, and a choir behind her. For a closing number she delivered a rendition of the Jackson 5's "I'll Be There" that is the second-best rendition of that song in history—and from my point of view will always hold that position.

Fans deluged MTV with requests to replay the concert, and the network aired it three times as often as the usual *Unplugged*. Because of this live appearance, there was never any question about Mariah's voice again.

There were times I got to pause and reflect for a moment, and only a moment, because there was never any more time than that with a thousand moving parts flying around and a hundred holes in the dyke that needed to be filled.

But there was this one particular day I remember heading to the studio to see Bruce Springsteen. As I walked over, my mind drifted back to a night many years before when I

saw Bruce setting a crowd of only a hundred people on fire at Max's Kansas City with an early rendition of "Rosalita." Then it flipped ahead to the first time I'd heard "Born to Run," and the power in the imagery of the line "strap your hands across my engines." When I heard that line I had to stop and pinch myself. And now we were headed to the studio to hear Bruce Springsteen play his new work, and I was going not as a guest, nor as Hall & Oates' manager opening the show at Max's Kansas City, nor as an observer, but as the head of the company and a conduit to help his music reach a larger audience.

Bruce and Jon Landau decided to release two albums simultaneously in early 1992: *Lucky Town* and *Human Touch*. I had no idea what I was going to hear, but I was filled with anticipation and excitement. This was the first work from Bruce that we'd received since I had started at Sony.

We heard so many great songs in that session. But one song still stands out for me: "If I Should Fall Behind." The lyrics captured the way I feel about people who are near and dear so powerfully that I almost began to cry, and I had to get up and take a break. I just loved it, loved it, and will love it forever. If you asked me what it was that allowed me to get up in the morning and move my body and brain at a thousand miles an hour and try to turn Sony into the biggest music company in the world, it was a song like this.

One of our many strategies was to always look outside the box and try to use our own sense of creativity to connect all the dots. One of the best connections we were able to make for Bruce Springsteen came along in the same period. TriStar Pictures was working on a film starring Tom Hanks and Denzel Washington called *Philadelphia*, and the director, Jonathan Demme, needed the title track. So we brought the idea up to Bruce's manager, Jon Landau.

It's important to pause here to talk about Jon, because you can't really talk about Springsteen without talking about Landau. And you certainly can't talk *to* Bruce unless you talk *to* Landau. Bruce was fortunate to have a guy who was so obsessively committed yet so in tandem with his thinking, his artistic vision, and his music, as his manager and filter. Nobody got to present an idea to Bruce unless Jon Landau heard about it first and fully believed it would be in Bruce's best interest, and then, maybe...maybe...*just maybe* Jon would mention it to Bruce.

At first Landau laughed at us.

"Look," I said, "this movie is powerful. It's about a man dying of AIDS. Can we at least get Bruce to a screening?"

Bruce did attend that screening and was deeply moved. Then Bruce and Jon met Jonathan Demme and Tom Hanks. It was a marriage made in heaven. Springsteen's title track lifted the movie to higher ground and made "Streets of Philadelphia" resonate even more deeply. When you think of that film you think of the song, and when you hear the song you think of the movie. It may seem seamless when you sit in a theater. But the feeling I got watching the two come together was almost addictive. I couldn't wait to do it again.

Timing is everything, and as luck would have it, in that same period we were able to do the same thing for Sade when the opportunity came along to create a theme song for the movie *Indecent Proposal*.

Sade's sexy and smooth sounds were a paradox from a business perspective. Her songs rarely hit Number One, but at the same time they always seemed to be playing—and not just on the radio. When "Smooth Operator" was released you almost couldn't escape it. You couldn't walk into a little boutique, an upscale restaurant, or a spa without hearing it. To this day, I

reach for Sade's greatest hits to put on in my home whether it's downtime, dinnertime, or anytime. I must've played "No Ordinary Love" three thousand times over the years. That's no exaggeration.

I remember the look on Sade's face the night I told her that over a quiet dinner. We were discussing the launch of her upcoming album and she was filled with joy, but almost a little embarrassed when I said it. She didn't like any overt attention, and certainly not the glitz and glare of the bright lights. She was a much more introspective soul. She'd record her albums and then disappear for years. That was Sade. But upon the release of this new album, *Love Deluxe*, we were looking for a major launching and marketing tool. When a film opportunity came along we jumped on it, and Sade didn't have to do anything. The song was already recorded and a perfect fit. All we had to do was connect the dots.

Cut to Robert Redford, Woody Harrelson, and Demi Moore in *Indecent Proposal*. The plot had the ideal setup. Harrelson and Moore are married and gamble away everything they own at a casino in Vegas. Redford comes along and offers Harrelson a million dollars to sleep with his wife for a night. Harrelson takes the deal. It's almost impossible to describe the emotion that "No Ordinary Love" injects when the cameras hone in on Redford and Demi on Redford's yacht. The music just electrifies the scene, ignites the senses a hundred times more than pure dialogue ever could. Every time you hear the song you think of Demi Moore rubbing the money all over her body.

As soon as we all attended the screening, we knew that it was going to be the ultimate fuel for Sade's album—and it was. The album was in stores months before the movie came out. Once *Indecent Proposal* was released, radio jumped on the album big-time and the phone lines lit *up*. That single movie

scene alone incrementally sold millions of additional CDs around the world for Sade.

We were having such phenomenal success plugging our music into movies—and most of it was happening outside of Sony's own Columbia Pictures. The synergy Walter, Ohga, Morita, and I had hoped for when we first tried to set up the purchase of the studio worked on *Philadelphia*, but didn't materialize much outside of that. The successes we were having, though, from *Dances with Wolves* for Kevin Costner, to launching Celine on *Beauty and the Beast*, to *Indecent Proposal* and *Philadelphia*, led us to the idea of starting our own separate sound-track division that was unique in the industry. With Glen Brunman as president, Sony Soundtrax was born and became one of our most profitable divisions. How's this? The song that Celine Dion sang years later for *Titanic* would bring in more than a *billion* dollars in sales.

Sometimes connecting the dots led me to places I could never have imagined. For instance, like the song "Hero"...

One night, when Mariah and Walter A. were in a writing session for Mariah's next album, I stopped by the studio to see them just before heading off to dinner.

I'd gotten a call that day from Columbia Pictures. They were working on a film starring Dustin Hoffman and Geena Davis called *Hero*, and Epic was handling the music. We were thinking of asking Gloria to sing the title track.

I told Mariah and Walter A. what the story line of the movie was, then I asked them if they could come up with the theme song. Walter A. started playing some notes and a possible intro for the song. He and Mariah seemed headed in a good direction, so I went off to dinner.

Mariah and I in the good days... *Credit: Sony Music*

Early 90's after party for the Grammy Awards in Los Angeles at Jimmy's Restaurant—such great memories. Bottom row (left to right): Walter Afanasieff, Celine Dion, Mickey Schulhof, Mariah Carey, me, Michael Jackson, Brooke Shields, Dave Glew, Tracey Edmonds, Babyface. Crouching down in front of Brooke Shields is Daryl Simmons, and next to him is LA Reid. Back row (left to right): Richard Griffiths, Michele Anthony, Tony Bennett, Peabo Bryson, Mary Chapin Carpenter, Regina Belle. At far right is Shelly Lazar, aka MFTQ (motherfucking ticket queen). *Credit: Sony Music*

Madonna and me at my pre-Oscar party at Asia de Cuba, Los Angeles, March 1998.

With founder, chairman, and CEO of Sony, Akio Morita, and violinist Midori.
Credit: Sony Music

Left to right: Sony Corp Chairman and CEO Norio Ohga, my mentor and Japanese godfather, me, and Nobuyuki Idei in Tokyo, February 1996.
Credit: Sony Music

NYC Grammy after party: Robert De Niro, Billy Joel, and me. *Credit: Sony Music*

George Michael and me at his Madison Square Garden show for the *Faith* album. *Credit: Sony Music*

At the *Vanity Fair* party for the Tribeca Film Festival, April 2011, with Michael Douglas and Robert De Niro. *Credit: Dick Corkery*

With Billy Joel and
Michael Jackson
at one of our after
parties. *Credit: Sony
Music*

Michael Jackson and
me—over 100 million
albums sold! *Credit:
Sony Music*

Michael looking great
that year at our Grammy
party. *Credit: Sony Music*

GOOD FELLAS: Nick Pileggi, Chazz Palminteri, Police Comissioner Ray Kelly, Harvey Keitel, Robert De Niro, me, Jerry Inzerillo, and Quincy Jones at the Tribeca Film Festival *Vanity Fair* Party, April 2011. *Credit: Dick Corkery*

2000 *Vanity Fair* Music Issue with then-Chairman of Universal Doug Morris and Allen Grubman. Shot at Sony Music Studios on West 54th St, NYC. *Credit: Jonas Karlsson*

My surprise fiftieth birthday party in Miami, thrown by Gloria and Emilio Estefan at the Cardozo Hotel.

With Jennifer Lopez at her album-release launch for *On the 6. Credit: Sony Music*

Shakira and I at the after party for the first-ever Latin Grammy Awards.

Julio Iglesias starts the Latin explosion.

Ricky Martin, me, and Marc Anthony after MTV's Video Music Awards, 1999. *Credit: Sony Music*

Lauryn Hill and me in 1999, the year she won five Grammys. *Credit: Sony Music*

Joe Pesci and me. "Omerta." *Credit: Sony Music*

With the incomparable
Barbra Streisand.
Credit: Sony Music

With Joe Perry, Tony
Bennett, and Steven
Tyler at a Sony Music
Grammy Party. *Credit:
Sony Music*

Me, Jada Pinkett Smith,
and Will Smith at the
movie premiere of *Men
in Black*, outside Planet
Hollywood on West Fifty-
Seventh Street in New
York City.

At the after party for the first-ever Latin Grammy Awards, September 2000. Left to right: Michele Anthony, Justin Timberlake, Jennifer Lopez, me, Gloria Estefan, Melanie Griffith, and Antonio Banderas. *Credit: Sony Music*

My birthday dinner at Da Silvano Restaurant, with Will Smith on the left and Thalia on the right.

Left to right: Me, Diddy, Patti Scialfa, and Bruce Springsteen at Spy Bar in Soho, NYC. *Credit: Sony Music*

Thalia and I in Los Angeles at the Sony Grammy party with Destiny's Child. Left to right: Michelle Williams, Kelly Rowland, Beyoncé. *Credit: Sony Music*

Like a rolling stone... *Credit: Sony Music*

Thalia, the love of my life, and I, just married, leaving the altar at Saint Patrick's Cathedral, New York City, December 2, 2000. *Credit: Jimmy Ienner Jr.*

Thalia and I at the ranch in Aspen for an *Architectural Digest* spread... "The Bronx Cowboy." *Credit: David Marlowe*

Celine Dion listening session for a recording with the Bee Gees at the Hit Factory, New York City. Left to right: Robin Gibb, Barry Gibb, Maurice Gibb, Celine, me, Billy Joel, Joe Pesci. *Credit: Sony Music*

One of our great Halloween parties: the Donald, me, and Steve Stoute as Don King. *Credit: Jimmy Ienner Jr.*

Left to right: Andy Garcia, me, and Elton John with my good buddies Danny DeVito (front) and Joe Pesci (far right) at a Grammy after party. *Credit: Sony Music*

A little advice, from the "Other Boss," George Steinbrenner (seated), and PR guru Howard Rubenstein. *Credit: Kevin Mazur*

At dinner with friend John O'Neill, a former FBI special agent and counterterroism expert (The Man Who Knew).

President Bill Clinton, Tony Bennett, and me at the annual Peace Memorial event in Washington, D.C. *Credit: National FOP*

With Gloria and Emilio Estefan. President Clinton has an incredible sense of humor and a way of making everyone feel at ease. *Credit: National FOP*

Once again at the annual Peace Memorial event in Washington, D.C., with (left to right) New York City police commissioner Ray Kelly, me shaking President George W. Bush's hand, and Marc Anthony. *Credit: National FOP*

Top of Aspen Mountain, "Mi Adorada Familia," with Sabrina and Thalia, who is holding Matthew.

With our baby girl, Sabrina, at her first horse show in Greenwich, where she won a blue ribbon.

Africa, a dream come true.

When I returned at about eleven that evening the two were still working. They'd come up with an almost completed song that they wanted me to hear. As soon as Mariah began singing I started to get chills. Halfway through the song, I couldn't take it anymore.

"Stop! Stop! Please stop."

They looked at me like I was losing my mind.

"What's wrong?"

Wrong? Nothing was wrong. It was almost too much to take.

Confused, they continued to stare at me. For me, it was like being in the room the first time Frank Sinatra started to sing the outline to "My Way," or Barbra Streisand on her first run-through on "People," or Elton John finding the right melody to the lyrics of "Candle in the Wind." It immediately gave me a sense that fifty years from that moment people would still be listening to Mariah sing that song.

"This could be one of the best songs I've ever heard," I told them. That made them happy. But I wasn't through. "This song is so good that it is not going to be in the movie. This song is not going to be recorded by anyone else. Mariah, this is your song. You have to sing this. This will be part of your legacy. This song has to be on your next album. This is going to be one of the biggest songs in your career, and maybe the biggest. It will become a standard—a classic."

The smile drained away from Mariah's face. "I'm writing this song for somebody else. I can't sing a song like this. It's too white-bread—it's just not me."

Mariah always struggled with her desire to take her direction much more into hip-hop. And it's understandable. She had grown up with gospel and R & B, and hip-hop had become the music of her time and generation. It was part of

the fabric of who she was. I got that. Though she had agreed to write "Hero," she didn't necessarily want the association of singing it.

"Please, listen to me," I said. "Make it your own. Sing it with your style, with your passion and your soul. Make it your own."

She and Walter A. went back to work and she did just that, and then she recorded it. We brought in the best mixer at that time, Mick Guzauski, who worked for us on so many hits. I remember sitting next to him at the recording console for the entire mix.

It was hard to imagine that Mariah really didn't have strong feelings for the song by the way she sang it. Her entire being was infused into it. Great lyrics. Great melody. Great singer. Great production. It not only had everything, it had everything for everybody, and the message was so strong and universal.

The song could be about a young girl whose father was a hero to her. It could be about a teenager being tested. It could be about anyone who stepped up when the moment called for it. It could resonate with *anybody*. A six-year-old girl could be uplifted by it just as easily as a seventy-year-old man. Mariah and Walter had created a work of art that contained all the ingredients that—once we turned on the Sony machine— could be taken over the top and turned into a standard.

It was so apparent to everybody except Mariah. When she listened to the recording she became apprehensive. Down deep inside I believe she really loved it, but she might've been embarrassed by it in front of the hip-hop community. My sense was that it was much more about that than her feeling for the song or the record. The bottom line is that nobody was putting words in her mouth. The song came from her own soul. It just wasn't the direction she wanted to be going in. Her

next album, *Music Box*, was a great mix of styles. But for her, "Hero" was not even a small piece of that pie.

I saw "Hero" as Mariah's missing piece. This was the magical piece that was going to open up every demographic to her. Now, everyone all over the world was going to be hooked into her music.

Generally, it's almost impossible for any artist to have it all. They're always categorized as either pop, or pop and adult contemporary, or R & B, or hip-hop. Nobody, but nobody, had the ability to span all radio formats and demographics. This song gave Mariah what you could only dream and wish for if you were building a career. Everyone at Sony fell in love with that song. So it was not just me being obsessive and delusional about how fantastic it was and how great an inclusion this would be on her next album. The way I saw it, keeping "Hero" off *Music Box* would have been like nobody ever hearing Tony Bennett sing "I Left My Heart in San Francisco." Mariah wasn't happy about it. But "Hero" was on her next album. This had to be another example for her of seeing me as being controlling.

I really don't think she got it until "Hero" became a hit in every country of the world, and teenagers were writing her letters saying that they were considering suicide before hearing that song and recognizing there was something greater in themselves to strive for. Or until she was asked to sing "Hero" in a duet with Luciano Pavarotti at a fund-raiser for Kosovo. Or until she was asked to perform it to help heal hearts after the devastating attack on the World Trade Center. Or until she was asked to sing it at Barack Obama's inauguration. Or maybe until I saw a television special during which she played it for her twins while they were still in her womb.

She was just a kid when she wrote that song, but she probably didn't get it until she turned into an adult.

*　　*　　*

It's important that you see the flip side. There were so many times when my instincts got completely overruled by an artist. Let me give you a great example. At about the same time, I went to Miami and had a meeting with Gloria Estefan that was unlike any that we'd ever had before.

For months, Emilio and I had been discussing where Gloria would go with her next album. It was a crucial time. We had built all of this momentum. With every album she put out she drew more passionate responses, broader demographics, and greater sales. As the saying goes, the pump was primed. Gloria could now release a pop album, attach it to a world tour, and easily double the sales of her last album. But Emilio had come to me with a different approach: an album totally in Spanish that was a tribute to their Cuban roots.

I had heard Gloria sing a song called "Mi Tierra" and thought it was fantastic. But releasing an all-Spanish album next was a risky move. It could narrow her audience just at the time we were set to radically expand it. It made much more sense to launch an album like that on the heels of the next pop success. Whenever I mentioned the Spanish album—whether it be in our New York offices or to execs operating in our territories around the world—I got serious pushback.

I knew we'd have to figure it all out the next time I visited Gloria and Emilio in Miami, and so did Emilio. When he approached me he was a little nervous. "Gloria wants to talk to you alone," he said.

We were like family, but Emilio handled the production and business side for her, and Gloria never had cause to talk over a topic like this with me—much less ask for a private meeting. It was odd and quiet when we sat down in the backyard of her

home on Star Island. We were beneath palm trees and looking out over water, but there was a very slight chill in the tropical atmosphere around us, and as soon as we started talking a quality came out in her that is hard to describe. But I'll do my best. It was a steely conviction, something that was probably always inside her but had surfaced after the accident. The mental strain and the power that came through the experience, along with the physical strength she'd derived from the grueling workouts, had given her another dimension. She got right to it. She said that she wanted to do her next album completely in Spanish.

"Look, Gloria," I said. "It's a great idea. I love the idea. The music is incredible. But let's just get one more pop album out while we still have momentum, and we'll release the Spanish album right afterward. The pop album will put wind into the sails of the Spanish album."

"I want to come out with the Spanish album *right now*," she said.

The way she said it was not aggressive, but it made me feel like I was a stack of weights that she was determined to lift.

I didn't want her to see me as a stack of weights. I wanted her to understand all the potential risks an artist takes when changing direction. I needed to put on my softest pair of velvet gloves.

"Gloria," I said, "sometimes the artist's work and the public's appetite are not aligned. You can take the consumer to new places, but it works best and more smoothly if the new sounds are rooted in something familiar. That familiarity is what makes people feel comfortable when they reach for your album. Once you're off that track, there's always a risk you can alienate your audience."

We talked about the nuances of this for about half an hour. When I was finished, she said: "I understand, Tommy.

I thank you, and I love you for thinking it through so thoroughly. But this album means *everything* to me. And it's what's inside me *right now*."

I sensed in that moment that the album she wanted to do was the culmination of everything that had happened to her. Not only the accident. But everything from the time she had immigrated to the United States as a little girl from Cuba. She wasn't running away from a certain style of hits because she was bored and needed to experiment. She was running to a fire that was burning inside her.

It was not a left turn to her. It was a right turn. And I got it.

"Okay," I said. The company had never thrown itself behind a foreign-language album as if it were a pop album. I knew the velvet gloves were going to have to come off the moment I left Gloria because there were going to be a lot of walls to smash through to help make this album successful.

We stood and embraced. "I believe in you," I told her. "And I believe in this music. We'll do it. Nothing will stop us. Let's go."

Mi Tierra was not only a beautiful work of art that was honored with a Grammy. It not only became the biggest-selling album ever in Spain. The single reached the Top 40 as far off as Australia. *Mi Tierra* became the biggest-selling Spanish album ever produced at that time, selling millions of copies. We'll never know what would've happened if she'd released it after a huge pop success. Doesn't matter. I'm happy to tell you that Gloria was right.

VOICES

GLORIA ESTEFAN

I was so emotional, so nervous when I came out on that stage. Tommy was sitting front row center. He was the first person I saw. He was crying like a baby, and I forgot all about how nervous I was.

CELINE DION

Tommy knew about the business—but he was very sensitive. I've seen him cry more than a few times. That's important to me because I have based a lot of my life, and a big part of my career, upon emotions.

I don't want to work with people who are not sensitive and emotional. It's nice when you work with somebody who's got so much power—but who is also sensitive. I don't know if there's an expression like this in English. But in French we say: *Une main fer dans un gant velour.* It means "An iron hand in a velvet glove." That's Tommy. He understood very quickly when we first met that I was shy, nervous, and kind of intimidated. He talked business with René, but with me he tried his best to make me feel as comfortable as possible.

JON LANDAU

You know, it can be a difficult spot when the artist and the manager are playing new music for the record company.

I've had executives look up at me after hearing an album and say, "Huh? What was that?" They just couldn't relate to it, and when that's the case it's hard to conceal.

Tommy was a very intelligent listener. Occasionally, he would react with visible emotion, and he could express what he was feeling very well.

What made it different in the case of Tommy is that Tommy used to be a manager. So he understood where I was coming from. Let's say that Tommy and I were negotiating on a particular point with the artist way, way in the background.

One of the things that I could say to Tommy is, "Let's just think about this from Bruce's point of view." If there was a point that looked unfavorable to our side, I was the one who would have to take that back to Bruce.

And Tommy understood that very well. Because he knew how that felt as a manager. That was helpful. It's not like he'd say, "Okay, I'm going to give you a billion dollars because I see it your way." But it enabled us to have a very freewheeling discussion.

GLORIA ESTEFAN

Tommy and I had our first and only fight over *Mi Tierra*. But in the end, he understood how important it was to both Emilio and I to pay homage to Cuba, and he got behind it in a big way.

There is no middle ground with Tommy. He sees something he likes, and he knows what light to shine on it. He puts all of his guys behind whatever he does. He believed in us and he took the risk. Another thing about that album—he did great things with that cover.

When Tommy says yes, he will do everything he can to make an artist a success.

CORY ROONEY

One of the things I learned from the experience of "Hero" is how you can overshoot something. At one point, Mariah purposely tried to sabotage the song by making it really soulful and gospel. And Tommy said, "Okay. Cool. Now sing it the right way."

You know, if you just kind of clean it up and keep it right down the middle, you can broaden the whole song, and everything that truly needs to come out of the song will then come out. Just listening to the A and B performance of "Hero" and seeing the outcome, it made me realize, this guy knows what he's talking about. And it's not that he didn't respect gospel music. Listening to gospel music is one of the things Tommy loves to do most. It's just that he knew the difference in how a person should sing that song for it to appeal to the masses.

DAVE MARSH

To succeed in the record business, you have to understand the subtleties of race relations in America. For instance, Tommy knew how to position Mariah on the edge of three racial groups: black, white, and Latin. That was Tommy's skill. He did a hell of a job with Mariah, and it wasn't easy. Lots of people have good voices. Few of them succeed. Fewer still have the kind of success that Mariah had.

DAVE GLEW

There's an important piece of this puzzle that is often overlooked. One of the shortcomings of the Warner, Elektra, Atlantic system—and I saw it because I was there for almost twenty years—was that they had two companies. They had a U.S. company with all these powerful executives, and then there was an international company.

When I was at Atlantic, we in New York had very little control over our marketing and our release schedules in Germany, France, and the rest of the world. Because of this, we could not break bands on a global basis. If we released, say, a Phil Collins record in the U.S., sometimes that record would be released a little later internationally. So we couldn't make that record a global priority.

I kept saying, "Tommy, look, if we can take a Mariah Carey, a Gloria Estefan, a Celine Dion, and you can push a button, and release each record at the same time in every country in the world—the impact on our bottom line is going to be enormous. Enormous!"

We couldn't do that at first because when Tommy came in he didn't have control of international. But once Tommy got control of international, he could market and muscle our records globally, and he took over the world. If you sold 300,000 Mariah Carey CDs in Korea and 2,000,000 in Japan, the numbers really started to add up. The cost of making that record, in most cases, was already paid for by the U.S. company. The videos were used all over. So the long profit was huge.

People will never realize what Tommy did for Mariah—I don't even know if Mariah realizes it herself.

But look at it this way. I'm at Epic thinking about releasing a Michael Jackson CD. I would move that Michael Jackson release date a week to give Mariah and Columbia a window so that Epic and Columbia were not competing against each other around the world. Because remember, if you came out with a Michael Jackson CD and a Mariah Carey CD at the same point, they would be fighting for radio time.

Tommy could juggle releases, make sure each artist always had these windows of opportunity around the world, and then he'd put the company's entire muscle behind each release. His global vision is what made Sony Music so powerful in the nineties.

10

Fairy Tales Don't
Come True

When I look back on all the music that we released in 1993, and consider everything else that unfolded during those 365 days, I can only scratch my head and wonder how there was ever enough time to pack everything in. This single year of my life could write a book of its own.

This was the year when Mariah released "Hero" on *Music Box*—which ended up selling more than 30 million and became one of the biggest-selling albums of all time.

It was the year that Celine broke through all over the world with *The Colour of My Love*—which included three Number One singles.

It was the year that Gloria came out with *Mi Tierra*.

And the year that Barbra Streisand's *Back to Broadway* hit Number One on *Billboard*'s Top 200 album chart.

Those four releases would have defined a great three-year period for almost any music company in the world.

But now add the crowning achievement of Billy Joel's career—*River of Dreams.*

And Pearl Jam, which now showcased our new strength in the alternative/rock music genre, when *Vs.* not only topped *Billboard*'s Top 200 album chart, but at the time broke Sound-Scan's record for selling more than any other artist in one week.

Plus Michael Bolton adding to his succession of hits with *The One Thing.*

And Harry Connick Jr. closing out the year with the best-selling holiday album in America—*When My Heart Finds Christmas.*

Everything that had been set in motion from the day we began to make our plans in 1988 began to galvanize in full view of the public and the brass in Tokyo during this one year. Not only were we on top of the charts, our numbers were off the charts. Profits rose by 40 percent in 1993, and Sony management in Japan responded by promoting me from chairman of Sony Music North America to chairman of Sony Music Entertainment Worldwide. The international fiefdoms were now under one umbrella. We could now mandate and seamlessly focus an army of fourteen thousand people around the world to help break and establish more artists and have even bigger hits.

Nineteen ninety-three also was the year I was married to Mariah. And the year I had to go to England to testify in a suit filed against Sony Music by George Michael. And also the year that Michael Jackson was first hit with charges of child molestation.

But I'd like to linger a little on another defining moment in 1993 that told the world we were just beginning our ascent.

It was the year that we launched Sony Music studios, the most creative recording facility in the world.

The Sony studio made sense in every way—creatively and financially. It would allow lots of dollars that were being spent in outside studios to now be spent internally with us. Once word of the Sony studio spread, it became *the* destination for artists in every crack and crevice around the world.

I remember the day I laid the plans out to Norio Ohga. I told him there was this jewel of property on West Fifty-Fourth Street and Tenth Avenue directly down the street from the renowned studio called the Hit Factory. It was the old Twentieth Century Fox Film studio, with an indoor pool that was used in the Esther Williams movies back in the forties. The facility that we had envisioned would be dramatically different. Our facility would provide rooms for preproduction, in addition to cutting-edge recording studios and mixing facilities. It would also contain one of the best soundstages, with ceilings high enough to rig up concert lighting so artists would be able to rehearse their live stage shows before setting off on tour. Artists would also be able to shoot their videos at the studio, then take them upstairs to one of the best video-editing services anywhere. The concept was for artists to complete the entire creative process all under one roof. Almost before I could finish my pitch, Ohga responded: "I love it! This will uniquely separate us from everybody else. This is what our philosophy should always be. What will it cost?"

I took a deep breath, looked him straight in the eye, and told him: "Between forty and fifty million."

Then it was Ohga's turn to take a deep breath, but he didn't blink. He looked me straight in the eye and gave me the nod. Once again, Ohga got it.

Shortly after the ribbon cutting, a who's who of recording artists came through the doors. The studio also became a creative hangout where A-list actors would drop by to hang out with some of the musicians. This went way beyond celebrity. They would also end up doing looping sessions there because they liked it so much. People from MTV and all the best video directors and musicians were constantly bumping into each other day after day, night after night, starting friendships and sparking ideas. Many hits came out of casual conversations in those hallways.

It became my destination every day before and after dinner. So many of those artists were recording for other record companies, and every now and then they'd invite me into their recording sessions. I was hearing their music weeks before the execs running the artist's label.

If their contracts were expiring, or if they were disenchanted in any way with their record labels, our studio certainly made them think that we were a better team and a better home for them because of the way that we took special care of our artists.

Sometimes I'd even have a little fun with the executives of other labels who were friends of mine while we were in phone conversations. I'd drop a line on them, like: "Hey, congratulations, you've got a really big hit on the way."

"What are you talking about?" they'd ask.

"I just heard it last night," I'd say.

When I think back on the wedding to Mariah, all that's left in my mind is a stop-action still frame—the kind of publicity shot that might be in the newspaper the next day or that I see still floating around the Internet.

My mind just doesn't remember the wedding like it was a flowing movie. In fact, I can't remember anyone dancing. I know that I did my best to create a fairy tale. But for all the meticulous planning, I can't even remember the name of the band or any—and I mean *any*—of the songs that were played at the reception. So in reality it was just a fairy tale.

I can tell you that it was at Saint Thomas Episcopal Church on Fifth Avenue. I remember there were a lot of flower girls, and Mariah had my friend Vera Wang design her wedding gown. It seemed like the entire music industry turned out. The reception following the ceremony took place at the Metropolitan Club overlooking Central Park—sort of cold, stiff, and proper. But when I press myself to think back on it, the images that come to mind now are what I didn't see at the time, but that came out later. One of those images was of my daughter Sarah crying during the ceremony and my son Michael hugging her and trying to comfort her. Sarah was twelve. Michael was thirteen. They felt terribly out of place and uncomfortable, and they knew in their bones what I simply couldn't feel.

So many people understood beforehand that it just wasn't right and tried to tell me time after time as best as they could. I remember talking with Mickey Schulhof in his office just a week before the wedding and him saying to me, "Let me just shoot straight with you. She's an artist on the label and you're twenty years older than her. If it lasts five years, nobody's gonna criticize you. But if it ends within twelve months..."

It's true, I wanted to get married, but it certainly wasn't like I was forcing this on anyone. There was nothing in Mariah's past that leaned toward marriage at all whatsoever. In fact, the idea of marriage was the furthest thing away from her universe, and to her *marriage* was probably one of the most frightening words in existence. Any inference to it in conversation

early on really didn't go anywhere. So I just sat back, left it alone, and stayed away from the topic. I can only now wonder if marriage was a way for her to close some of the cracks she noticed coming between us, because I was completely taken by surprise when she sprang the idea on me. At about midnight while we were renting a house in Florida, she just turned to me with a smile and said: "Hey, why don't we get married?"

Me being me, I would've gotten an engagement ring to pop the question. But it didn't happen that way. I was both empty-handed and stunned.

Even though marriage meant only anxiety and anguish for her in her upbringing, I think when she thought this through she figured it would make me happy. The two of us had an intimate and genuine care for each other. And it could've been her way of giving back after I had given so much to get her to where she was.

There was no reason to be concerned with pushback from inside the company. Sales were going through the roof, and Mariah was not only on top of the world but she was one of the biggest-selling artists in Japan. The idea of getting married soon morphed into creating a fairy tale. There was detail after detail after detail being handled by a small army.

The stitching of a special compartment in one of Mariah's shoes to fit a sixpence for good luck came from that old British custom: "Something old, something new, something borrowed, something blue, and a sixpence in her shoe." So much for that good luck!

The fifty flower girls were all Mariah's fans. Mariah took part in designing the wedding cake.

All I can tell you about these forgotten details that I'm trying to dredge up and pull to the surface is that I was just trying my best to make Mariah happy. And when the wedding

ended, it felt like we were both happy. The only thing left to complete the fairy tale was to build her a castle.

So that's what I tried to do next—completely blind to the fact that fairy tales don't come true.

My honeymoon had barely ended when two very unpleasant situations arose. The first came when charges that Michael Jackson had molested a thirteen-year-old boy filled the airwaves. A few months later I had to go to England to testify in a trial against an artist whose music I loved dearly—George Michael.

There are few charges more serious than molestation, and in the case of Michael Jackson there was little we at Sony could do but step back and wonder how it would play out. It was our job to handle the public relations as it pertained to his music and recording career, but we couldn't do anything in these legal matters other than support him in any way he asked. Looking back now, it's obvious that Michael's career had already peaked by this time, though he refused to acknowledge it. Living in a delusional bubble permitted him to think these allegations and the press reports were not going to affect the way people thought about him. The reality is his career was certainly never the same from the moment that charge hit the airwaves.

Earlier in 1993, we had tried to reignite passion for his *Dangerous* album with a halftime performance at the Super Bowl. He appeared to pop out the top of the scoreboard seconds before being shot up through a stage at midfield amid fireworks. A couple of weeks later he sat down for an interview with Oprah Winfrey that was seen by 90 million people. But the topics everyone was talking about the next day had little to do with music, but as his celebrity would have it, about the

Elephant Man's bones and all of the physical abuse Michael endured as a young boy from his dad. *Dangerous* did get a boost from these appearances and the surrounding publicity, but certainly not the kind of sales we saw when our new management team had taken over in 1988 and had given his previous album, *Bad*, a second wind.

We didn't know the exact impact the charges would have on his career and would only get a reading of the scope when his next album came out. While we knew that his loyal fans would stand by him, there was no doubt all the publicity surrounding the facts, rumors, and innuendo behind the cash settlement between Michael's insurance carrier and the boy's family was going to turn a lot of people away.

While all this was playing out, I had to go to London in the fall of '93 to testify in a trial against George Michael. We would never go to court against recording artists unless there was absolutely no other alternative, and in this case there was no alternative. We worked for months trying to settle the dispute with George even when we knew we were in the right. But George just took things too far and sued us, and I believe deep down inside it was really bad advice from his manager and his attorneys, who were arrogant and pompous in thinking that they would get a release from us at Sony and attract a huge payday from another record company. I knew that simply was just not going to happen.

George somehow managed to describe the situation surrounding the marketing of *Listen without Prejudice, Vol. 1* as "professional slavery." His suit claimed that he was a victim under British and European laws of restraint of trade because he had no say in the way Sony had promoted his last album and might promote future albums.

The way we saw it at Sony was this: George brought us an album that was transitional—take that any way you like—and

different from *Faith*. Which is fine; after all, he's the artist and it is his music. But if the hits aren't there, that isn't our fault. The way we saw it, George was the whole package. That package included the great music on *Faith* and the incredibly youthful handsome guy in a leather jacket and jeans that put him over the top—just as it had for Elvis back in the day. George simply had an emotional rebellion to his success and he lashed out at anything he had done in the past. It was like watching somebody who subconsciously wanted to hurt himself. After all was said and done, the new album sold only a third as many CDs as *Faith* did and, of course, the artist is never to blame. In his mind, and in the minds of the inept management surrounding him, only Sony was to blame. Good luck, buddy.

It was unfortunate because, as I said from the start, George was an artist that I, and everyone else at Sony, had put up on a pedestal. I loved and respected this guy's music and was so eager to help him get to new platforms and greater heights.

But you can't make the public love a product, and you can't make the consumer go to the store and buy it. Nobody was better than our team at Sony when it came to marketing and promoting and presenting an artist's new album. We were world renowned for our great distribution, so this album was everywhere that people could see it. We got it played around the world, positioned perfectly in record stores, featured on television shows, and written about in newspapers. But ultimately, something has to catch the attention of the public to make it *compelling* so enough people will buy it. You just can't get around this simple truth: ultimately, the consumer genuinely has to want to buy it.

Music isn't like a sweater that you might need on a chilly autumn day. It isn't something you can pick up, feel, examine, and try on. You can't cook it like a steak and put it in your

mouth. Music is something that's in the air. It has to appeal to all the senses. We had to have a sense of how this ethereal product would sell, and then we needed to prepare the most meticulous and detailed way to sell it.

We organized dozens of listening sessions in every corner of the world where up to a hundred people sat in a room to listen to the music that was about to be released. Through all of this we stood by and supported our artists—especially George Michael. Even though so many of our promotional tools had been taken away by George, we didn't back up for one second. There were millions of dollars on the line, so we motivated and inspired our army of troops to promote George's new release.

Even though we were handling the most talented artists in the world—often with kid gloves—and giving them the respect and the time and the support that they were entitled to, at the end of the day we were still a business. A *big* business. A business with $7 billion in sales every year, and it was my job to not only nurture all those artists but to report to a board of directors. That board cared about one thing: numbers. If my numbers weren't in line or ahead of projections, then the score on my report card wouldn't look good. So I was faced with a minute-to-minute, night-and-day juggling act of those two dynamics. On one hand, I was dealing with pressures that said: *Make the numbers.* On the other I realized that I was selling a product that had somebody's soul in it.

At the time, Sony had close to four hundred artists who, by the way, were all in need of its promotional dollars. We were just like any other business. And just like any other business, when we saw that one of our releases or new products wasn't going anywhere, we would have to make cold, hard decisions about how we would be spending our marketing and promo-

tional budget on other releases that could be surging toward the top. That was how our business worked—and if it didn't work like that, there would be no business at all.

Yet when I went over to England for the trial my mind was filled with doubt. Even though the evidence is clear in a lot of murder cases, sometimes the murderer gets off. What was that line? *If it doesn't fit, you must acquit.* We also didn't know how cultural differences could affect the case, because George Michael walked on water in the UK. Or how the evidence would play out in a court system that made me feel like I was watching a movie on HBO about medieval times. How the hell could anyone guess what might happen when you've got to look up at a judge with a long white wig on his head and call him "my lord." Can you imagine a kid from the Bronx in this movie? All I could do was testify, tell the truth, and state our case.

Months later, I was back in my office in New York, when my assistants were ringing my intercom incessantly and there were loud knocks on my door. It was my general counsel. I was in the middle of an important discussion, but I had an idea what he had come to talk about. The decision from the courts in the UK had come down, and it was overwhelmingly in our favor. The people who'd misguided George had really screwed up badly. Not only had he lost the case, but under the judge's ruling he was now on the hook for all the court costs, and the charges for our UK lawyers were in excess of $15 million.

Sure, I was glad we won. But there was nothing in this situation that I was truly happy about. I knew George wasn't happy, and at the end of the day all I wanted to do was make the best of the situation. There was a silent period for a few months. Then his attorneys approached us and asked if they could buy George out of his recording contract. We felt there

had been such a severe schism that it would probably be best for business, and best for George's career, to do so. I knew that David Geffen desperately wanted to sign him. So in a short period of time we worked out all the deal points and George Michael ended up on Geffen Records. From a pure dollar and business standpoint we came out great. Not only did we win the case and collect our legal fees, but we made tens of millions by selling the contract to Geffen while retaining the rights to all of George's catalog—including one of the greatest albums of all time, his *Faith* album. So we had the best of the old George Michael, and the new George Michael got just what he wanted—he was free to live his life and career elsewhere. Personally, though, it was sad to lose a great artist like George.

Years later, there was a similar situation when Michael Jackson would try to get out of his contract with Sony after his album sales declined dramatically, dropping the blame on us for the way we'd promoted it. He even took it a step further, calling me the devil, and in one public protest he held up a poster that included facial pictures of himself and George Michael with Xs over their mouths as if Sony had tried to silence both of them.

That's all total crap. We at Sony were the ones who had to—and did—remain silent in front of the public. Let there be no misunderstanding about that whatsoever. We never did and never would attack an artist in public. Anyone in the music business knows that would be total suicide.

It was our job to find, develop, nurture, and release to the consumer as much great music as we could, and ultimately to sell it to as many people as possible. When artists are on the decline, it's just very hard for them to see it that way.

*   *   *

There was sad irony to me in George Michael's departure. That's because we had completely restructured in order to make ourselves the most artist-friendly company in the world.

Yes, we were a huge corporation that had global manufacturing and distribution. But we were also able to act like a boutique company that catered specifically to each individual need. Gone were the days when the bands of Seattle wouldn't talk to us. Now we had Eddie Vedder of Pearl Jam coming through our doors and even borrowing one of my guitars to do an acoustic show. Bob Dylan was knock, knock, knocking on my office door to say hello. *C'mon, Bob Dylan, one of my heroes, are you kidding me?* This was a 180-degree turn from the days at the old CBS prior to its transformation to Sony Music Entertainment. We welcomed our artists with open arms and tender loving care, and continually tried to help push them into new frontiers.

One of the greatest things we were able to pull off, and that I am still so proud of to this day, was to be able to reposition Tony Bennett. Tony's son and manager, Danny, had come up with a fresh and amazing strategy. Tony was nearing seventy years old in 1994, but his voice was eternally twenty. Danny's concept was that great songs, great singers, and great records will appeal to any generation and live forever. And in his father's case, he couldn't have been more correct.

So together with Danny, we positioned Tony in an *MTV Unplugged* concert to introduce him to a younger audience. It was a historic night. Tony was dedicating songs to Duke Ellington and singing duets with k.d. lang and Elvis Costello. It worked on every level because Tony had never played to a specific demographic. He was authentic, and that sincerity translated across generations.

Tony Bennett and *MTV Unplugged*! Can you believe it? This

concert was accompanied by black-and-white music videos, along with an incredible album. Suddenly, something old became something totally new. Kids were watching the same Tony Bennett whom I listened to with my parents when I was a kid—and loving it. And to think that Michele Anthony, who had grown up with Tony because her father was his manager, was now my senior executive vice president—and that she was also simultaneously signing the hottest alternative and rock bands in the world. Talk about contrasts. This is exactly the kind of stuff that makes a great music company. The ability to do it all and do it authentically—without smelling like a big corporation.

We all had to walk a tricky high wire with Pearl Jam. The group did not seek to be famous. Eddie Vedder did not want to be on the cover of *Time* magazine, and he felt horrified when he saw his picture on that cover after he and Kurt Cobain had promised each other they wouldn't participate in a grunge story. It was distasteful to Eddie when designers started copying his flannel shirts and his brown corduroy jacket and selling them for $750. It was everything he was against. He did not want to put a wall up in front of his home, but he had to, and it saved his life when some stalker got in a car and tried to crash into his house. All Eddie and Pearl Jam wanted to do was make music and play it for their fans at a reasonable price. That was it. Period. So it was always a balancing act when it came to promoting the band. But it always went smoothly because Kelly Curtis, Pearl Jam's manager from day one, and any of the band members could go straight to Michele and the A&R specialist Michele brought in, Michael Goldstone, whom they knew and trusted from the very outset.

Pearl Jam followed *Vs.* with another megahit called *Vitalogy* in 1994. People in the industry saw what was going on.

Aerosmith, which had started out on our Columbia label back in the early seventies but then departed for Geffen Records in the mideighties, would soon come back and re-sign with us in the nineties. Again thanks to Michele Anthony and the team. Further testament to how important it is to have all the *right* people working toward and believing in the same goal.

All of this momentum converged at a very significant time—and, of course, timing is everything. I believe that the passing of Steve Ross in 1992, along with his leadership and style of management, began to weaken the music companies at Warner just as Sony was coming into full bloom. Warner began to get bogged down with people who were brought in for more corporate governance. Suits who knew nothing about the business. We had just climbed over that mountain, and now we were in the lead, and not just in the United States. We began dominating every territory on the globe and we would later hit our ultimate goal: *the* number one company in *profitable* worldwide market share—not just sales alone.

But rest on your laurels in this business for a minute and you're toast. Yes, that fast. We knew that in order to continue as the greatest music company in the world, we needed to compete in places where we hadn't been before. So we were constantly evolving with new ideas, coming up with amazing box sets and digging deep into the history of our company to showcase legends like Robert Johnson, Bessie Smith, and Johnny Cash while feverishly developing new artists. There was always the constant pressure of being able to deliver volume while looking for that big new breakthrough artist whom we could establish on the world stage.

Reinventing our catalog was simply just great business, since we already owned all the masters. There was virtually no expense to produce it other than repackaging the content

and marketing costs. But more than that, it continued to give tremendous credibility and integrity to our history-rich company. Going back to those great legacies was almost as critical as taking leaps and bounds to push it forward. The artists who were signed to Sony, and the artists outside of Sony, all took notice and, as musicians first, truly appreciated what we were doing—not to mention consumers who simply loved music that should live forever.

Tony Bennett's *MTV Unplugged* concert was so successful that it still resounds to this day, nearly twenty years later. Just recently Tony did a duet album with younger artists, like Lady Gaga, that entered *Billboard*'s chart at Number One. And he's currently doing another duet album with all of the top Latino artists singing in English and Spanish—including Thalia. Eighty-seven years old, and still crossing over...

So the fairy tale continued. Mariah and I built a castle in Bedford, New York. It contained just about everything that a person could possibly wish for. Together, we studied Georgian manor houses and the homes in Newport and then built it with my best friend, Ronny Parlato. There was a salon for Mariah to get her hair done, a world-class state-of-the-art recording studio with every new piece of equipment in the universe for her to sing in, and an indoor swimming pool covered by a cloud-painted ceiling for her to swim in. All my best intentions were working against me. Sadly, I just couldn't see it.

In fact, one night she even said to me, "In a few years, let's just run away and escape to an island and buy a little nightclub. I'll be the singer in that club and the rest of the time we can hang out on the island and chill." I was so smitten that

I actually believed it for a second. Not only did I drink the Kool-Aid, I guzzled the whole fucking bucket. After all the hard work we'd put in, what a finish to the fairy tale. Funny, the paths that life will lead us down, even when you think you know it all.

Strangely, the very thing that had brought us together—music—now was starting to cause huge disagreements between us. A little while after the success of *Music Box*, I said to Mariah, "Wouldn't it be a great idea for you to do a Christmas album?"

After all, every great artist, and I mean *every* great artist, who came along when I was growing up put out a Christmas album. It was simply part of their repertoire. Phil Spector made one of the greatest Christmas albums of all time—it still plays in my house year after year. Even Bruce Springsteen did one of the best renditions ever of "Santa Claus Is Coming to Town." Christmas was one of the best times of my childhood, and one of the happiest times of the year for Mariah, so it was only natural to me that she'd jump at the idea. Everybody at Sony was onboard and gung-ho. There was only one person who resisted it: Mariah.

She resisted it, probably thinking that a Christmas album would be very, very uncool to her hip-hop fans. We went back and forth. Finally, she began to open up to the idea, and once she started, she dove into it with Walter A., writing some new songs and also covering the classics. This album ended up, in my opinion, as the single greatest modern Christmas album. And when she finished we even created a homegrown video with images of a sleigh, live reindeer, and the best decorations of Christmas lights ever from the Bronx. And guess who dressed up as Santa? The album cover photo was to be a sleigh

and live reindeer with Mariah in a very sexy Santa suit. That was her idea—and very cool. And the entire Sony team was overwhelmed with enthusiasm when the album cover photo came in. But when Mariah looked at the same photo she turned to me and said, "What are you trying to do, turn me into Connie Francis?"

Rather than fight about it, I just walked away, although I had to hold back my laughter as soon as I got into the next room and thought: *How the hell does she even know who Connie Francis is?*

Her rendition of "All I Want for Christmas Is You" has now become a modern-day classic, played as much these days as any song you know, probably even more than "White Christmas." All the TV news broadcasts use it as their intro and outro. It was also covered recently on albums by Michael Bublé and Justin Bieber. Mariah's gospel rendition of "Joy to the World," which was in a Christmas television special filmed at the Cathedral Church of Saint John the Divine, still stands out to me as one of the greatest live vocal performances of all time. The initial release of *Merry Christmas* sold almost 15 million copies, and today that number is in excess of 20 million. It sold almost three million in Japan alone—and Japan is a Buddhist country. Helloooo!

Other than the success of the album, the only good part of this story for me is a magazine article not long ago in which Mariah told a writer how she thought I was crazy for asking her to do the album and how she initially resisted, but that in retrospect it's become one of her favorites and that she was really happy I made it happen. That same year there was a television special in which she sang Christmas songs with her mother, and it made me feel good to know that she'll be able

to treasure all those Christmas songs and sing them with her children for the rest of her life.

If I'm rambling on about this, it's only because of the unavoidable conflicts that were occurring between us, which musically brought out fear, not only in me but in everyone at Sony who cared about her career, because her heart more and more wanted to go in a different direction. Going down the path she wanted to go could only result in a narrower audience and less airplay formats, and it could possibly alienate the broad spectrum of consumers who loved and bought her music.

Suggestions about what music to record were a very natural discussion between the artist and the business side, and disagreements were common. The artist is the artist. But the business side has many creative people with their own ideas. That's why when you added it up it was called the *music business*. I'd watched these conflicts unfold from as far back as when I was managing Hall & Oates, and initially Celine Dion did not want to sing "My Heart Will Go On." That song only generated a billion dollars in business. So it was nothing new that these disagreements came up with Mariah. In fact, there's another story that comes to mind on this topic that bears telling, and it has to do with Luther Vandross.

Luther was one of the greatest R & B singers of all time. His voice was like a powerful instrument that played velvet. From a pure singing point of view—just his pipes—you'd have to consider him to be at the top of the list.

He always had success, but he was headstrong and he always wanted to do the material that either he had written or that he had personally selected. He was usually never open to much suggestion. And we were perfectly fine with that if

he was perfectly fine with that. But, of course, he wasn't completely okay with it, because he wanted to be selling much more than he was.

We, too, as a company always thought that Luther had the ability to sell not just a million with every release. But we knew he was capable of selling at least five million. We told him the only way he could do that was to cross his R & B success over into Top 40 radio. But in order to achieve that, he would have to be open to working with new producers and songwriters, experiment, and try some new things. We never, *ever* could, or would, force it on him. But we always urged him to try. "If you don't like it," I assured him, "we won't put it out. We'll respect your decision."

Luther finally agreed to try around 1994. And one day after he had agreed, while Mariah and I were driving in my car, I mentioned that Luther was doing an album called *Songs* that paid tribute to some of the classic hits that had inspired him over the years. I asked her for suggestions and she quickly blurted: "Why don't we do 'Endless Love' together? He is one of my favorite singers ever, and I would do it with him if you could get him to do it."

I absolutely loved the idea. "Endless Love" was a classic originally sung by Diana Ross and Lionel Richie. There were only two risks involved—starting with Luther. I would have to tiptoe through the tulips and walk on glass to ask him if he would do the duet—all of which I did do. The second risk was that Sony would be putting its biggest-selling recording artist on the line to front this experiment.

Luther went for it hook, line, and sinker—he absolutely loved and respected Mariah as a singer and was completely surprised that I would suggest it. The team at the company also

jumped on board, making it a collaborative effort between two separate labels. Mariah was on Columbia, and Luther was on Epic. So we put out the album and the single. The single climbed the Top 40 radio charts straight to Number Two, lit up the phones, and ended up selling millions. Luther was a very, very, very happy camper. But the rest of the songs on the album—most of which were Luther's choices—just didn't have the same success. So, of course, no good deed goes unpunished. Luther thought we took the single "Endless Love" that high only because Mariah was singing on it with him.

Mariah was having success after success after success, and each album was becoming sort of a landmark. She threw herself head over heels into her next project, *Daydream*, and the company went out of its way to bring together the elements, producers, songs, and musicians that leaned in the direction that she wanted to go and would make her happy.

We brought in Dave Hall, who was working with Mary J. Blige. I was able to commandeer the hottest group at the time, Boyz II Men, to come in and complement her on "One Sweet Day." And Jermaine Dupri, the youngest and coolest producer out there at that time, came in to work on "Always Be My Baby." The album was so well rounded that it gave her fans everything they wanted while forging ahead.

I will admit that I was not nuts about the idea of inserting Ol' Dirty Bastard as a featured rapper on a remix version of "Fantasy" that Sean Combs (aka Puff Daddy, aka Diddy) ended up producing. This guy, ODB, may his soul rest in peace, had tremendous issues with drugs and alcohol and was certainly a contrast to Mariah's girl-next-door image, and I just didn't see him jumping on a record with the Pop Princess. But in the end you couldn't deny his street poetry. It

was a bold and dangerous move. And Mariah's judgment was completely right—it worked.

The video of "Fantasy" was the first one that Mariah ever directed on her own. So we surrounded her with all the best technical and lighting people so there would be absolutely no potholes to stop her from creating her vision. The song sounded like airy summer breezes, the boardwalk, a Ferris wheel, and all of that. So I suggested shooting it at Rye Playland—my old childhood stomping grounds. You could smell the summer salt air as Mariah Roller-bladed on the boardwalk while singing, then mimed the lyrics on a roller-coaster ride, then stood and danced on a Hummer in the parking lot with the lights of the amusement park behind her. It turned out Ol' Dirty Bastard's appearance was the perfect complement.

As soon as I heard it and saw the video I knew she was 100 percent spot-on. And, of course, the record just blew up. "Fantasy" went straight to Number One. I always applaud things that work, and this didn't just work...it was huge. My feeling about it was simple: *Great! Now we've totally captured the hip-hop audience, too.*

Mariah looked at it in a very different way. She felt like it had broken the dam for her. She thought: *This is what I've wanted to do for a long time. See what happens when I do this? This is the only direction I should be going.*

Which worried all of us at Sony. While she was dead right to add ODB to the remix version of "Fantasy," it was another thing to think about framing her entire career this way. So once again, we were at a fork in the road. She was adamant about the direction that she wanted to pursue. The advice from everyone at Sony was very different. We continued to say: *Yes, do what your heart wants,* but at the same time we were

stressing to her: *You can have it* all. *All markets. All demographics. You can have it all like no other artist who's ever come before you.*

The ever-widening crack between us got much wider. I was the chairman of Sony Music and she was the biggest-selling artist on the label, and we were married, and there was no escaping the friction because we came home to it every night.

VOICES

GLORIA ESTEFAN

Tommy wanted to protect Mariah, to do what was best for her career. Tommy believed in her so much. She went from a background singer to the biggest star in the world. But you can't convey experience. She was just too young.

Fame is very treacherous. It is given, and it can just as easily be taken away. A star that's riding high in a music career is only as good as their biggest hit. The consumer is in control. It's a tough ride if your feet are not firmly planted.

MICHELE ANTHONY

Music executive

It always struck me as odd that Tommy got painted as the bad guy in that relationship, when all he did was take her from nothing, fall in love, and give her everything he possibly could.

Because here's the thing about Tommy. It can be annoying, but if you love him you will find it endearing. Tommy is a 100 percent type of person. That can be all-consuming. We'll be with him for hours and then after one of us leaves he'll call up twenty minutes later. It's not

that he's being controlling to me. He's like, "Did I miss anything? What's going on?"

It's enthusiasm. It's exuberance. He gets obsessed with things. I guess in certain situations that can play out or feel like control. But it's really passion and obsession.

11

The Billion-Dollar Song

At roughly the same time, things were rapidly changing across the ocean at Sony Tokyo. Akio Morita, the founder, had had a stroke while playing tennis, and he'd passed on his position of CEO to Norio Ohga. We were constantly dealing directly with Ohga, but sadly he, too, was ill. He'd had multiple heart attacks. Fortunately, they were mild enough for him to survive, but he looked more and more tired every time he would fly to New York, and it was clear to see that he was growing weaker and weaker.

Both Sony's founder, Morita, and his right hand, Ohga, had created the finest brand of electronics in the world with brilliant thinking that was so far out of the box it extended into other universes. But it was inside the box where their biggest flaw surfaced. They had never groomed and developed one or two executives who could succeed them. There were some good individual managers running individual units like electronics, semiconductors, and PlayStation, as well

as the insurance and finance businesses. But when Ohga was handed the reins from Morita, a lot more attention should have been paid to developing someone who had a parallel vision for Sony. Had Ohga done so, Sony would not be where it is now—which is a far cry from the leading brand that it was when it purchased CBS Records back in 1988.

There was shock and surprise when Ohga, as CEO, hand-picked Nobuyuki Idei to succeed him as president. Idei had not stood out in any way in Sony Corp., and Ohga had chosen him over fourteen more senior executives. No one knew how things would unfold. Certainly, no one had a clue that a decade later Idei would be appropriately named by *Business-Week* as one of the worst managers of 2005. The only thing we hoped for at that time was that Idei would take notice of the giant profits that Sony Music was generating and leave us to do what we knew how to do best. But my antennae were raised, and I had a very strange and uneasy feeling in my gut, because I sensed that changes would be coming.

One of Idei's first targets was Sony Pictures, formerly Columbia Pictures, which had been hemorrhaging money under Peter Guber and Jon Peters. Guber was one of the brightest guys in the movie business, and also one of the greatest talkers and salesmen I've ever encountered, but the company fell into a slump, and he was able to get away with these incredible financial losses only by befriending Mickey Schulhof, who had overriding responsibility for the film company. Mickey was blinded by the Hollywood lights, and he simply stood by as movies tanked and losses mounted. He was able to get away with this because of his longtime friendship with Ohga. But there were too many red flags that Mickey should have acted on. When your film company is bleeding billions of dollars and it becomes cheaper to close the company than

back up the losses, something drastic is bound to happen even when you are good friends with the CEO. I stayed at a distance from it; there was nothing I could do about it, and it certainly was not my problem. But it was definitely a house on fire.

The company had been forced to write off a nearly four-billion-dollar loss in 1994, and it started to implode the year after. Guber forced Peters to walk the plank, then he jumped ship himself. Somebody had to pay for the mess. Unlike Norio Ohga, Idei had no attachment to Schulhof. In fact, knowing full well of Schulhof's loyalty and friendship to Ohga, he quickly forced Mickey to resign at the end of 1995, to Ohga's dismay. Idei knew that Ohga would not go against him, because he was Ohga's new appointee, and any backlash would send the wrong signal to the company in Tokyo.

I was sad about Mickey's departure because Mickey had always been so good and generous to me. But the move was completely justified and understandable. It was a sign that Ohga's power was definitely waning. My eyes, like almost everyone else's in the company, were now wide open.

For as long as I knew Michael Jackson, the concept of working within a budget to create his art did not exist. Michael spent whatever it took on his projects without a thought or a care. Expensive recording costs for another artist might run a million dollars an album. Michael's albums could actually cost up to $40 million to record. The industry standard for a video was roughly $200,000 at the time. Michael's short films—again, he would correct you if you used the word *video*—would easily run to several million. Dave Glew would put a million-dollar cap on these film expenditures, but it didn't faze Michael. He'd take out advances on the overages and be on the hook

for the money himself. His feeling was, *I'll get it back when the CDs sell.*

The ability to maintain a peak over time, whether it's in art, fashion, sports, or music, is for the most part impossible. So it becomes what those next levels and plateaus are going to be and how you're going to hold on to them. You can maintain your superstar status, you can certainly be a bigger celebrity, you can continue to work at a high standard of art, but there will always come a drop-off in sales over enough time.

Not only did Michael Jackson refuse to acknowledge that drop-off, but he challenged it in the most audacious way that he could. After the molestation charges were settled, Michael prepared a comeback album that he hoped would sell a hundred million. It was a two-CD set released in the middle of 1995 called *HIStory: Past, Present and Future, Book I.*

The costs to produce it were astronomical because he'd rent out entire studios when he recorded, and he'd have producers in six recording studios around the world working simultaneously. We did our best to suggest all the hottest new producers to keep his music current. But when things are that diffused, it's always hard to keep the core focused.

There was no question that a lot of the music on *HIStory* reflected the recent turmoil in his life.

His inner voice was speaking. Artists express their inner selves all the time—on pain, love, conflict, life, society—and we were never judgmental about what they were trying to say. We judged the music in two ways: Is that a good song? And will it be commercial?

One of the CDs in the double set contained Michael's handpicked favorite hits. His loyal followers were sure to be happy with this bonus. But it was the new material on

the other CD that would inevitably drive the sales. The new music included a song that he sang with his sister Janet, called "Scream." Maybe the best window into how Michael was feeling at the time is a look back at the "Scream" video—which cost $7 million to produce. The lyrics "Stop pressurin' me! Stop pressurin' me! Stop pressurin' me!" say it all. Along with images of glass roofs crashing down around Michael.

There was also a rendition of the Charlie Chaplin masterpiece, "Smile," included on the new material, which was one of the most beautiful vocal performances I'd ever heard in my career. The song, all about pushing through pain with a smile, is touching and emotional, and I'd go as far as to call what Michael did with it perfection. Amid all the chaos within and around him, you couldn't help but feel for Michael. Especially knowing that underneath everything he went through he was really a good guy.

But he was also one of the most complicated people I ever met, and his need to be adored at this point knew no bounds. The full teaser for the album that ran in movie theaters before films featured what looked like a ten-thousand-man Eastern European military march led by Michael in full regalia with his signature white glove—to the adoring screams of children. It was filmed in Budapest and led to the unveiling of what looked to be a five-hundred-foot statue of Michael. This teaser was wild and spectacular, and must've cost another $5 million. But even with all that grandiosity, if the overall music is not there from top to bottom, then the release is going to have problems.

We did everything we could to promote *HIStory*. We must've put ten times the marketing emphasis into it that went into *Thriller*—something like $30 million. From our view, the

album did good numbers and great business—selling 20 million, making it the top double album ever sold. In the end, though, from Michael's point of view, the numbers were slipping even further away from *Thriller.* His subsequent *HIStory* tour did phenomenal business. There were eighty-two concerts around the world that altogether drew between four and five million people. But, again, the show was so over the top with backup singers, special effects, a massive crew, a convoy of trucks, elaborate stages that needed to be shipped from city to city, and huge statues of Michael that popped up all over the world near concert sites that it had to severely cut into Michael's profits. He was simply addicted to Number One hits and roaring crowds, and he didn't care what he had to pay to get them. Again, no one would say no.

Six months after the release of *HIStory*, Mel Ilberman helped bring about what everyone saw as a great deal. Michael had paid $47.5 million in 1985 for the ATV Music catalog that contained most of the Beatles' music up until the time of the split between John Lennon and Paul McCartney. Sony, as I've already mentioned, had foolishly sold its own catalog just before I'd arrived. We crafted a deal a few months after *HIStory* was released in which Sony paid $90 million to Michael to merge our catalog with Michael's ATV catalog.

It was a great deal for Michael. He basically had given up control of only half the catalog in exchange for twice the money that he'd paid for it. Plus, the way Sony/ATV would market the overall catalog, it would be highly profitable and in Michael's best interests over the long run. Further, Michael as a partner would participate in Sony's publishing interests. If Michael had been only a businessman, it would have been a dynamite win-win for everyone.

The only problem was the deal connected Sony and

Michael at the hip at a time when Michael the artist was in decline and would spend any amount of money to prove that he wasn't.

Mariah and I headed to Los Angeles in February 1996 for the Grammy Awards looking forward to a huge night. She had been nominated in six categories based on the success of her *Daydream* album, which was the most nominations she'd ever received in one year and, of course, you never know how these things will turn out, but we all figured she had a big chance to win at least three, including Album of the Year.

We couldn't have had a better setup strategy. We arranged with Ken Ehrlich, the producer of the Grammys, to have Mariah and Boyz II Men open the show at Shrine Auditorium with "One Sweet Day." A poll in *Rolling Stone* would call their collaboration the best of all time, and it was deeply moving that night, as it always was, because the inspiration, the lyrics, and the "see you in heaven" message were so personal, encapsulating Mariah's feelings following the loss of one of her producers, David Cole, and also what the death of a road manager meant to Boyz II Men. When you pull off an opening to a show like that, all eyes and ears are on you for the rest of the night. "One Sweet Day" had broken Elvis's and the Beatles' records when it remained Number One on the charts for sixteen straight weeks. Of the six nominations, Best Pop Collaboration with Vocals seemed to be a slam dunk.

But when the award came up we didn't hear Mariah or Boyz II Men called to the podium. The award was given to a traditional Irish band that had been playing for more than three decades, the Chieftains, along with Van Morrison, for "Have I Told You Lately That I Love You?"

It was a wonderful song, and let's face it, there's no definitive way to say that one beautiful song deserves an award over another beautiful song in the first place. But it's always kind of a kick in the stomach when you don't win, especially when you're that heavily invested. I stayed cool. "Okay, so you didn't get this one," I told Mariah. "You've got a lot more categories to go."

Mariah was also invested big-time in "Fantasy." In her mind it was the song that firmly established what she wanted more than anything—hip-hop credibility—and it was up for an award in the Pop Vocal category. This time we watched Annie Lennox get called to the stage for "No More I Love You's."

There are times at the Oscars when a big box-office hit is beaten out by a small independent film. People love to get behind the underdog. But it seemed to me that there was something else going on here. I began to wonder if this was a clear signal of what the night was going to become—a backlash to Mariah's success from the same Grammy organization that had lifted her to the podium twice on her first album.

To understand why I felt that way, it's important to know exactly who votes for the Grammys. Ballots are cast by members of NARAS—the National Academy of Recording Arts and Sciences—and that certainly sounds impartial. But the fact is, the voters are anything but objective. It's just the opposite. The voters are artists, producers, songwriters, and A&R execs who are in constant and intense competition with one another. They all want to have their creativity recognized, as well as higher chart positions and bigger sales.

The people who voted for the awards presented that night seemed to be sending a message that said: *We can lift you up, but don't forget, Ms. Pop Princess, when you get too big we also have*

the power to bring you down. We want some of these opportunities back. We're not going to give it all to you. You get everything all the time. We're going to give it to other people now.

Third category: nothing. Fourth category: nothing. Fifth category: nothing. I could feel Mariah bristling beside me. I felt like ducking under my seat each time the winners were announced and the cameras panned on our faces to see our reactions. I was later told that my face looked more concerned with each loss. Deep down I knew that somehow I was going to get blamed for this, even though it had nothing to do with me. How else could Mariah possibly perceive what was happening? In her mind, the result had to be a backlash against the big machine that was propelling her to number one. And who was the face of that big machine? The guy sitting right next to her.

The award for Album of the Year went to Alanis Morissette for *Jagged Little Pill*. That was certainly a great album and anybody could make a case that it deserved the award. Alanis was the newcomer that year and she stole the show with four Grammys. Her success was the headline of the evening—along with MARIAH CAREY SHUT OUT.

Mariah internalized her humiliation and her anger as we returned to the Beverly Hills Hotel. You could hear the crack between us creaking open a little wider on a night that I was hoping would allow us to look back on all the good times that had brought us this far. Fat chance of that!

Instead, we quietly drove to the Sony Grammy after party where the awkwardness continued. Sony had seven winners in all. Our company was soaring and a big celebration was in order. But simultaneously I quietly asked one of the technical guys to remove the replay of the Grammy TV broadcast on the monitors around the party and replace it with videos of our

artists to avoid incensing Mariah. Can you believe this? You can't make this stuff up. But I really did feel terrible for her.

If she had won four or five Grammys, the night might have put a Band-Aid over the deeper issues in our relationship. But getting shut out created a much different dynamic. Tension was inside both of us and things were not good when we arrived home. Even a simple word that I considered a compliment would set her off into fireworks. A Columbia Records executive had been quoted in the media as calling Mariah a "franchise." He said it in the most complimentary context— meaning that she was an enormous star who was loved in every part of the world. But that wasn't the way Mariah took that word. "You guys are not letting me be me," she said. "You're trying to make me into a franchise. What do you think I am, McDonald's?"

She came up with a line that was even better than her Connie Francis crack about the Christmas album and sometimes, when in her circle of friends, she would laugh and call the house in Bedford...Sing Sing. As if the mansion had become a prison, and she'd been forced to *sing...sing...sing...sing...* in the recording studio that *she* herself designed and built with everything *she* wanted in it. She was constantly writing and producing new songs and always loved to record them in that studio. So when I first heard about Sing Sing, I laughed myself. Just as I did when she told me she would be seen like Connie Francis because of the Christmas album.

It was as if all the encouragement and direction that had been given to Mariah by me and everyone around her at Sony and helped create this enormous success made her feel like a bird in a cage. The little girl who was raised with no guidance, direction, or constraints was now feeling totally shackled by the responsibility of her success. Even her assistants took on

an attitude. "We're going on a trip," one said, "and Sony's not coming."

Look, here's the reality. The people in her entourage began to spin stories that Mariah was locked in with security guards all around her when the truth is that so many nights while I was at home sleeping, preparing for my next twenty-hour day, she was hanging out at clubs and coming back at daybreak. Mistrust, and my anxiety, was mounting. There was no winning. No matter how you choose to see it, no matter how many good intentions I had, it was a lose-lose.

It's hard enough to deal with a crumbling relationship, but when it reaches the media it shifts to a whole new level. And, of course, just at this time, *Vanity Fair* magazine requested to do a profile of me. The story was going to be done with or without my cooperation, so I knew going in that it was probably going to be a hatchet job. But there could be no denying the success that Sony Music was having. Six of the top ten singles and albums in the United States came from Sony artists—and I agreed to cooperate and let the writer, Robert Sam Anson, in the door, figuring that no matter how many shots the writer would take at me, at least the truth would resonate in some of my own words. Of course, he twisted everything I said to fit the story he wanted to write.

I was eager to talk about the roll that the company was on, but "Son of Sam" Anson seemed to have a very different agenda. He wanted to dig up dirt about the conflicts Mariah and I were having. And worse, every other question seemed to be filled with ethnic innuendo. My radar realized something was really up when the photographer asked me to pose at my desk with the blinds lowered. He said it would look terrific and have a great

contrast. The photographer was well known, accomplished, and had credibility, so I went along with it. But then I called up the magazine's editor, Graydon Carter, and asked him what exactly was going on. "You're a Runyonesque character," he said. "What are you worried about? It's going to turn out great."

I should have listened to my instincts, because in the end the photograph was designed to make me look like some sinister don, and the story made it sound like I'd make sure that decapitated horse heads would show up in the bedsheets of anyone who'd ever cross me.

Yes, I once spilled a drink on an asshole's head. He deserved it. And to this day I'm still embarrassed about it. But if you want to talk about ethnic slurs, this magazine story was the epitome. And I had no Al Sharpton standing next to me to yell character assassination.

Look, I can take a hit. I took plenty of them. But when the writer misrepresented my father, for supposedly associating with "unusual businessmen," it gave me particular offense. My father was one of the sweetest, kindest family men who ever lived, and all he ever did in his entire life was work to build his business and support that family. The story was pages and pages of flaming dogshit that someone placed on the steps of my front door, just before ringing the doorbell and running away. And I'm not joking when I say "running away," because years later I saw the writer at a supermarket in Sag Harbor and when he saw my face this pathetic pussy broke an Olympic record heading straight out the door.

But one of the most hurtful parts of this story came afterward when Mariah never really commented on it, and it was obvious that her entourage actually participated in it. I ran through walls for Mariah, especially to protect her in so many situations like this. But, hey, if you're not happy...

As I reflect now, I can certainly understand how things must've felt so overwhelming to her, especially coming into this relationship from a place without rules or regulations and entering a world that planted both our feet all the way down on the gas pedal with the needle pinned to one hundred miles-an-hour day in and day out. Navigating through this hurricane of responsibilities—with experienced people in every part of her life constantly making quick-fire decisions, and everyone around her suggesting and telling her what to do—could've been overwhelming and actually made her feel like she'd lost control of her life. If it seemed like I was controlling, let me apologize again. Was I obsessive? Yes. But that was also part of the reason for her success. Her success and my success. If you're not controlling things when you're running a company with four hundred artists and fourteen thousand employees, you're not going to be successful—or on the job very long. The problem was that I was the chairman of Sony and her husband at the same time.

She grew resentful. I was the person there in the morning. I was the person there in the evening. The resentment landed on me. Things got more difficult and tense by the day. One morning, before I left for work, I wrote a little note to her and left it on the night table. It was from the lyrics written by Bernie Taupin for a song by Elton John called "Someone Saved My Life Tonight."

Butterflies are free to fly . . .
Fly away . . .

Weeks later we were separated, and that separation ultimately led to divorce, and the sale of the fairy-tale home. There were so many deep feelings involved on both of our

parts. But in the end, the fairy tale ended like no other fairy tale before it. Years after it was sold, the home literally caught fire and burned to the ground.

I tried to never let the difficulties in my personal life affect my work. But it certainly was not an easy time. The newspaper was a daily reminder, the gossip pages filled with reports of Mariah out clubbing till 5 a.m. around town and hanging with some ballplayers. I threw myself into my work more intensely than ever before. I don't know if it was irony or coincidence, but it was around this time that a song came to my attention that I knew would have a huge impact: "My Heart Will Go On."

We had gotten a call about a movie about to be released six months down the road. It was called *Titanic* and starred a young Leonardo DiCaprio and Kate Winslet. There was a lot of buzz going around about it. It was directed by James Cameron, and James Horner had composed the sound track. There were no songs in the movie. It was all orchestration. But Horner thought that it was really important to have a theme song.

Cameron disagreed. He didn't want to be criticized for going too commercial. But he was also eager to make the studio heads happy, and he knew that a hit song from the movie would only help guarantee its box-office appeal. So he was reluctantly open to it.

We had launched Celine Dion's career with a movie— *Beauty and the Beast.* Now she was one of the biggest recording artists in the world, and Horner wanted Celine—and only Celine—to sing the theme to this movie. So I went with some Sony execs to see a screening without the music. Hey, if they

wanted to use one of our biggest assets to help their film, then we needed to see what it was going to look like.

I was vibrating with enthusiasm as I walked out of that screening. But I quickly realized that most of the people from the company who'd come along had mixed feelings. A lot of them thought that it was too over the top, and others simply didn't like it. I could hear a group in a little coffee klatch knocking it down.

I burst straight in. "You guys are all nuts," I said. "You don't get it. This is Romeo and Juliet on a boat that sinks. Are you kidding me? It's a smash. It's a monster!"

When James Horner played Celine the song for the first time she didn't really like it. So you've got a director who really didn't want a song in his movie and a singer who didn't like the song composed for it and didn't want to sing it. René and I had to persuade Celine to at least do a demo.

I have a clear memory of the night Celine flew in for that demo. We all entered the big Studio A at the Hit Factory— Horner, René, Celine, and myself. Celine walked into the vocal booth, ran through the song quickly, and then said: "Okay, I'm ready to sing it. Let's go." She put on her headphones and the playback of the track started. Celine opened her mouth and started singing, and goose bumps filled my body. When you know it, you know it. I was listening to one of the classic vocals of all time being recorded. She stopped singing, and that was it. One take. One take! No fixes. Nothing. That demo recording became the recording that you heard in every country around the world and will hear for the rest of time.

My only concern was the placement. We went back to James Cameron and asked where the song would be set in the movie. "If I do this at all," Cameron said, "it will be at the end of the movie when the credits are rolling."

I came back at him sharply. "Nobody will give a shit," I said, "everyone's going to be walking out of the theater."

We went back and forth but, long story short, we folded. After all, it was James Cameron's film, and he easily won the battle because it was his way or no way. So I took the opportunity because it was crystal clear to me how big this was going to be. And looking back on it, I have to say James Cameron's decision was 100 percent right. Placing it anywhere else in the film would have been wrong. The song provokes tears, and I walked out of the completed film knowing that the song was going to be even bigger than I'd originally thought.

We decided to put all the chips on the table.

Celine was recording a new studio album that was due to be released at the same time as *Titanic*'s sound-track album. It was called *Let's Talk about Love*. We brought in Walter A. to rerecord "My Heart Will Go On" with the same orchestrations that Horner had composed along with Celine's original vocal. We put that track on her studio album, so it would be released on each of the albums. The idea was to release both albums on the same day: November 18, 1997.

Most people in the company were approaching me as if I were crazy. "Tommy, why would you do something like that? The two albums are going to cannibalize each other!"

"No way," I said. "This movie will be huge, and those records will have two different audiences."

There was something else that I knew. It had been four years now since I had been named chairman of Sony Worldwide and taken over all the international operations. All of the fiefdoms had been destroyed in that time. The whole company was being run differently. It was no longer: *Let's break England, France, or Germany individually, and then let's break Belgium and Holland. Let's see how it goes in Asia and . . .* No more

of that. There was one unified operation, one global company that could strategize and market a worldwide mandate. When we wanted to break some music all over the world there were no longer any hesitations or internal obstacles. We were set up to unleash a marketing tsunami. And we had the amazing Polly Anthony, who would work her way up from secretary to president of the Epic label, totally focused on helping Celine succeed. Competitors would wonder, *Why is it that when we have a biggest hit in the world we sell five million, while Sony's biggest hits sell twenty?* It was not by magic. It was all by deliberate design, and *Titanic* is one of the best examples.

Within a twelve-month period, *Let's Talk about Love* sold more than 30 million copies and went to Number One all over the world. Simultaneously, the sound track also sold more than 30 million albums. On top of that, "My Heart Will Go On" won an Academy Award the following year, and the song took away four Grammys. Let me explain what this meant financially. Selling more than 60 million copies meant almost a billion dollars in sales for Sony Music—and just from one artist. Today, given the state of the music industry, it's easy to predict that this will never be done again.

Our last half of '97 was like watching quick cuts of a sizzle reel. Sales of both Celine's albums just kept soaring. And Bob Dylan's *Time out of Mind* was like a Picasso. In fact, it was one of those Picassos that remind the world just how startling a Picasso can be. At the next Grammy party I was happy to replay the telecast of Dylan receiving his award for best album. But there was no time to stand around and watch our company's highlight reels. If we weren't moving forward, we were going backward.

Record companies have success in cycles. So what the public saw and heard in '93 could've been signed and developed since '90. And what happened at the end of '97 generally had started incubating in '94. Every few years, a huge burst of creativity and hits tends to be followed by a transitional lull. By no means does this signify the company has gone cold. It's simply a transition. It is part of the process of this beautiful business that we call music. Once you understand this, you know that this lull has to be confronted head-on with a new period of lots of artists in development.

We were totally prepared for 1998. Not only had we placed a huge emphasis on the discovery of young talent, but we were also focused on every genre of music. This allowed us to meet this transitional period with hit after hit.

We had set up a regional A&R scouting system, interviewing dozens and dozens of college kids and young music lovers across the country, and hiring the best to scour campuses and clubs to provide monthly reports on new acts. These scouts were in addition to the A&R scouts that each of our labels employed. It was our scout in Texas, Teresa LaBarbera Whites, who found Jessica Simpson and, even more stunningly, a young girl group called Destiny's Child.

Of course, back then Beyoncé Knowles was the lead singer and star of the group. But there were four members of Destiny's Child when the group recorded its first album in 1998. Some important dots were connected when we brought in Cory Rooney, the amazing producer who had worked with Mariah, and Wyclef Jean from the Fugees, to help execute their debut album. The single "No, No, No" shot to Number One and the album sold three million worldwide.

There was a lot of legal wrangling and shifting of performers in the act, and by the third album the group had consoli-

dated into Beyoncé, Kelly Rowland, and Michelle Williams. We continued to connect the dots and wisely placed their song "Independent Women Part I" into the movie *Charlie's Angels*. That helped shoot the album *Survivor* into the stratosphere.

It was clear through all of this that someday Beyoncé could and would emerge as the solo superstar that she is today, not unlike how clear it was for Diana Ross when she left the Supremes. It took a little more time for another amazing solo act, Lauryn Hill, to emerge from the Fugees. Lauryn was one of the most unique artists I've ever encountered, but everyone in the office was a little nervous when we heard that she wanted to do a solo album.

The Fugees were extremely successful and had sold nearly 15 million copies of their last album. There just seemed to be no reason to rock the boat and to possibly and prematurely break up the group and end its career if she emerged and became successful. So we met with the group to see if Lauryn would hold back and do one more album with the Fugees first. But a few months later, Lauryn called and said, "Why don't you come by and listen to the solo project that I'm working on?"

A group of us went to the studio, sat down, and listened to quite a few songs that she had recorded. We were completely blown away. Each track was better than the last. The album had it all—R & B, soul, hip-hop, and reggae. We were sitting there thinking, *Oh, my God, here we go. She will definitely be our next big worldwide superstar.*

The album that grew out of those songs came to be called *The Miseducation of Lauryn Hill.* It came out in 1998 and subsequently won five Grammy awards—including Album of the Year and Best New Artist. When you walk off that stage with five Grammys for your first solo album, the force can be like

stepping on the gas of an eighteen-wheeler—or getting hit by one. It affects every aspect and detail of your life. The positives are obvious. You get a bigger career, make a lot more money, and become famous—either for the rest of your life or just for fifteen minutes. The negatives can be the enormous pressures that come along with that. You get followed everywhere. The press will write about anything and everything that you do, even if you didn't do it. Photographers will come to your home and take pictures of your children through the windows. They will follow you to the point where you will ask yourself, *Is all this worth it?* Bottom line: your life is no longer your own.

There's just no way to tell who can handle the pressure of that kind of success, even though it starts out as the dream of a lifetime. You can only tell after the dream becomes an insane reality. If you win a bunch of Grammys as a member of a group and there are a lot of people around you who can function as shock absorbers, you might have a chance. Unfortunately, I'm sure Lauryn did not feel that whatever support she had around her was enough to protect her from the avalanche of attention that hit.

What's more, she was sued by a couple of writer-producers she'd worked with who claimed that they should have received credit on the album. We advised her to make a relatively modest settlement, but she refused, and when the case went to court she broke down on the witness stand and ultimately had to pay millions. Shortly afterward, she seemed to shut down emotionally. She just wanted to get away from everything, and she did. I think she made a very conscious decision to save her own personal life. All I can tell you is that for a while, we were totally unable to reach her. She just disappeared. So sometimes even when you are fortunate enough to develop and break a great talent, when planning out your business and

your budgets, you never know if you can count on the artist going forward in the way you might think. What most business-people don't know is this is an extremely fragile and delicate process, which is why continued and constant artist development on a daily basis was an imperative mandate for all of us.

A contrast was taking a great talent like Will Smith, who was already a star when we signed him—he had started as a rapper in Philly, then as an actor had a big hit with *The Fresh Prince of Bel-Air*, and he was exploding on the movie scene—so there was no concern about him being tripped up by success. *Big Willie Style* was an amazing blend of pop and hip-hop that was released at the tail end of 1997 and set him up to sell more than 14 million. The music was fun, cool, and street. In his case, celebrity and notoriety only helped.

Simultaneously, one of the biggest artist development stories for us in 1998 was in country music. The Dixie Chicks were like a breath of fresh air and so distinctly different from anything you had ever heard. All you had to do was listen to Natalie Maines and her lead vocals and the way the group blended their harmonies, lyrics, and melodies in "Wide Open Spaces" in order to understand how exceptional they were. Individually they were incredible musicians. But it was more than that. They had huge personalities, and really intelligent points of view, and their physical presence was alert, alive, and in your face.

We brought them to the forefront of awareness in our company at one of our global music conventions. There were thousands of employees from all around the world at our conventions, plus retailers, radio programmers, and vendors. Any act that had a great new album and was able to nail a performance at our convention was guaranteed that a top priority spot would be mandated to the whole company.

The Dixie Chicks' performance was so amazing that nobody could resist them. They became one of the biggest breakthroughs in the history of country music, morphing their style into pop music and opening the door for what was to come more than a decade later for some of my favorite artists now, like Taylor Swift and Lady Antebellum, who are completely different musically but are seen as major pop stars as opposed to just country stars.

The hits were coming out fast and furious in this transition and pushing our company into the future. We felt like kids in a candy store. And just when you think you don't have room for one more chocolate, there's that extra special treat that you can't turn away from. That was a stunning Spanish-language album by Shakira called *Dónde Están los Ladrones?*

She was not more than sixteen when I first met her. She barely spoke English and *seemed* to be very shy. Her vocals and her musicianship were stunning. Later on, I would come to find out that she was not shy at all. In fact, she is extremely intelligent, completely articulate, and, I will endearingly say, somewhat demanding.

After a couple of years of convincing her to cross over and sing in English, I remember the day she brought me her new album. I sat back and read the lyrics and was mesmerized by the amazing poetry that she had created. It made me sense we were on to something so special and once again so different that the feeling of being able to establish another super-star was in the air all around us. Because anyone who could create these words, compose them into beautiful songs, and sing them was compelling enough to get the attention of millions of people all over the planet. It felt like an explosion was coming.

So much for a transitional period.

VOICES

CELINE DION

René and Tommy had to talk me into singing "My Heart Will Go On," and when I look back on it I'm so happy that they did. Singers should always be involved in important choices like these, but you also have to trust people who know the business.

I remember going to record it. It was supposed to be a demo. I flew into New York, and I wasn't really ready to record—not vocally, not emotionally, not physically. But, hey, it was a demo. At that point, the track was still not done. I figured I'd do a couple of takes to see if the key and the rhythm was right.

So I decided to go for a black coffee, with sugar, which I would never do when I record for real. The coffee might change the vibrato a little bit, and caffeine can just bring you to the roof, and not in a good way—for me, anyway.

So I had a coffee on the plane and after landing I had another coffee. What the heck, it's only a demo, right?

I went to the recording studio, met with everybody, and started to sing.

The song I recorded that day is the one that you still hear on the radio to this day—with black coffee and sugar all over it.

RENÉ ANGÉLIL

Sometimes a singer comes out with a great song, but the record company doesn't know when to launch it, how to market it, where to show it. That's where Tommy's the greatest.

MICHELE ANTHONY

Yes, I was at that screening. I admit it, a few of us didn't like it [*Titanic*]. We thought it was too long and kind of cheesy. Then Tommy came over and was saying, "This is gonna be the biggest movie of the decade," and a few of us kind of rolled our eyes. But he was right.

Selling tens of millions of Celine records was really important for Tommy, too, because it showed that here was another female vocalist whose career he helped develop and broke who was now outselling Mariah. To be able to replicate what he'd done with Mariah was really important to him.

He proved he could do it again. And then again with Shakira. And then, yet again, with the whole Latin Explosion.

ROBERT DE NIRO

Tommy's story is one of those great American success stories. The kid coming out of one of those neighborhoods, getting some street smarts, and making it out to become somebody.

Then comes some hard times. But the real test of a man is how you get through those hard times and how you come out of it.

306

JOE PESCI

Tommy was deeply hurt by the breakup with Mariah. A lot of people don't realize that. But we all go through those kind of things. He was hurt before with his first wife and children. He loved his children so much—and they're such great kids.

You don't get used to going through situations like that. That stuff hurts you every time it happens in your life. People think you just hate the other person. No, it's not that. You hate what happened. It's not about blaming the other person. He was just very hurt. I know because we spoke about it a lot.

But then he came back stronger than ever—and a lot of that comes from the neighborhood, you know, the background, because you get knocked down a lot. You gotta get up, or you just back up. But Tommy never backed up. He just kept going forward. Because to become a Tommy Mottola, that's what you have to do.

Column 1

e U Been Gone" • Kelly Clarkson

Digger" • Kanye West featuring Jamie Foxx

ndy Shop" • 50 Cent featuring Olivia

hake It Off" • Mariah Carey

Mr. Brightside" • The Killers

er" • Destiny's Child featuring T.I. and Lil Wayne

"Switch" • Will Smith

Humps" • The Black Eyed Peas

"Feel Good Inc." • Gorillaz

"Collide" • Howie Day

a Tortura" • Shakira featuring Alejandro Sanz

Cater 2 U" • Destiny's Child

"1 Thing" • Amerie

t's Like That" • Mariah Carey

cause of You" • Kelly Clarkson

e Words" • Natasha Bedingfield

"Get Right" • Jennifer Lopez

"Daughters" • John Mayer

rdinary People" • John Legend

derful" • Ja Rule featuring R. Kelly and Ashanti

Mississippi Girl" • Faith Hill

"Don't Bother" • Shakira

ou're Beautiful" • James Blunt

s Is How a Heart Breaks" • Rob Thomas

"Fix You" • Coldplay

Hard out Here for a Pimp" • Three 6 Mafia

e Breakthrough • Mary J. Blige

written • Natasha Bedingfield

vils & Dust • Bruce Springsteen

"Me & U" • Cassie

en the Sun Goes Down" • Arctic Monkeys

"SOS" • Rihanna

One" • Mary J. Blige and U2

"Smile" • Lily Allen

Suddenly I See" • KT Tunstall

ergalicious" • Fergie featuring will.i.am

"London Bridge" • Fergie

"Steady, As She Goes" • The Racounteurs

"Irreplaceable" • Beyoncé

"Crazy" • Gnarls Barkley

t Your Records On" • Corinne

Column 2

Don't Forget about Us • Mariah Carey

"Bad Day" • Daniel Powter

"Hips Don't Lie" • Shakira featuring Wyclef Jean

"The One That Got Away" • Natasha Bedingfield

"I Wasn't Kidding" • Angie Stone

"Ooh La La" • Goldfrapp

"The Long Way Around" • The Dixie Chicks

"What Hurts the Most" • Rascal Flatts

Back to Black • Amy Winehouse

FutureSex/LoveSounds • Justin Timberlake

Dreams: The Ultimate Corrs Collection • The Corrs

"Bleeding Love" • Leona Lewis

"Beautiful Liar" • Beyoncé and Shakira

"Give It to Me" • Timbaland featuring Nelly Furtado and Justin Timberlake

"Love Like This" • Natasha Bedingfield and Sean Kingston

"Do It Well" • Jennifer Lopez

"Apologize" • Timbaland featuring OneRepublic

"Home" • Daughtry

"Taking Chances" • Celine Dion

"The Sweet Escape" • Gwen Stefani featuring Akon

"Big Girls Don't Cry" • Fergie

"Glamorous" • Fergie featuring Ludacris

"The Way I Are" • Timbaland featuring Keri Hilson

"Crank That (Soulja Boy)" • Soulja Boy

"Cupid's Chokehold" / "Breakfast in America" • Gym Class Heroes featuring Patrick Stump

"Stronger" • Kanye West

"Runaway Love" • Ludacris featuring Mary J. Blige

"Lost without U" • Robin Thicke

"Shut Up and Drive" • Rihanna

"No One" • Alicia Keys

We Were Dead before the Ship Even Sank • Modest Mouse

Undiscovered • James Morrison

Life in Cartoon Motion • Mika

Call Me Irresponsible • Michael Bublé

"We Belong Together" • Mariah Carey

Column 3

Gold Digger" • Kanye West featuring Jamie Foxx

"Candy Shop" • 50 Cent featuring Olivia

"Shake It Off" • Mariah Carey

"Mr. Brightside" • The Killers

"Soldier" • Destiny's Child featuring T.I. and Lil Wayne

"Switch" • Will Smith

"My Humps" • The Black Eyed Peas

"Feel Good Inc." • Gorillaz

"Collide" • Howie Day

"La Tortura" • Shakira featuring Alejandro Sanz

"Cater 2 U" • Destiny's Child

"1 Thing" • Amerie

"It's Like That" • Mariah Carey

"Because of You" • Kelly Clarkson

"These Words" • Natasha Bedingfield

"Get Right" • Jennifer Lopez

"Daughters" • John Mayer

"Ordinary People" • John Legend

"Wonderful" • Ja Rule featuring R. Kelly and Ashanti

"Mississippi Girl" • Faith Hill

"Don't Bother" • Shakira

"You're Beautiful" • James Blunt

"This Is How a Heart Breaks" • Rob Thomas

"Fix You" • Coldplay

"It's Hard out Here for a Pimp" • Three 6 Mafia

The Breakthrough • Mary J. Blige

Unwritten • Natasha Bedingfield

Devils & Dust • Bruce Springsteen

"Me & U" • Cassie

"When the Sun Goes Down" • Arctic Monkeys

"SOS" • Rihanna

"One" • Mary J. Blige and U2

"Smile" • Lily Allen

"Suddenly I See" • KT Tunstall

"Fergalicious" • Fergie featuring will.i.am

"London Bridge" • Fergie

"Steady, As She Goes" • The Racounteurs

"Irreplaceable" • Beyoncé

"Crazy" • Gnarls Barkley

"Put Your Records On" • Corinne Bailey Ray

12

The Latin Explosion

It had become clear that the new president, Nobuyuki Idei, had no knowledge or practical experience operating the huge Sony company. He most certainly had no understanding of the music, movie, or television divisions. And he definitely had no grasp or even a desire to understand how to manage and treat employees—particularly the executives who were making money for him.

Ohga and Idei came from two different schools of thought, as different as night and day. Even though Norio Ohga lived six thousand miles across the ocean and was culturally different from Steve Ross, there were so many similarities in their styles of developing executives into entrepreneurs. Ohga came from the school of building, developing, and rewarding. He would sit back and smile at success and think: *I helped plant this seed, and now it has developed into a flower.* It made his garden only more beautiful.

The contrast in Idei was that he had come up through

the ranks and was involved in communications, which I guess was a fancy way of saying he was in charge of public relations. Interesting, because he had such a hard time communicating. He came from a Japanese cultural philosophy very much different from that of Morita and Ohga, which was that any successful manager of a particular unit—let's say, electronics or insurance—could be mixed and matched to go run the music company in Japan or its movie division. He had no sensitivity toward understanding all the intricate and delicate matters that go into managing a highly specialized creative business. And he began to make moves along those lines.

The guy Idei chose to replace Mickey Schulhof, Howard Stringer, also had little knowledge of the music business or the movie business or the electronics business or any real hands-on operational experience running any entertainment businesses. He'd been the head of CBS News—a unit of journalists—before talking his way up to the head of CBS, which he then left to join a faltering television start-up called Tele-TV. But that was very different from signing talent, marketing, merchandising, and turning that talent into global superstars or creating the next piece of hardware that would dominate the world stage. Sir Howard was a very cordial gent, though, the ideal guest at your next cocktail party, because he loved to bloviate. Instead of knighting him in 1999, Queen Elizabeth should have appointed him the Empire's Toastmaster General. Anyway, I did like him.

Stringer was born and grew up in Wales, immigrated to the United States, was drafted into the Army, and served in Vietnam. The Welshman got into communications and ended up as an executive producer for *CBS Evening News with Dan Rather*, then talked his way up to the office of CBS News president. He had great stories and could make you feel like he

really knew what was going on in show business. If you didn't know the real deal, you would think Howie was one of the smartest people in the room. Actually, he was perfectly suited for the news division. *Sir* Howard gave no reason for anyone to question what he really knew, because everybody liked him, so friendly and jovial was he. After moving to the tech television company, he was handpicked by Idei. So now we had two guys at the top of the company who knew nothing about what they were doing, and certainly not the music business. Even worse, they kept getting more power.

As Ohga grew physically weaker and weaker, he became overwhelmed with taking care of his health, and he transferred more and more authority to Idei. In 1998, Idei was named co-CEO. But you could tell Idei was insecure by the way he constantly belittled Stringer in public. Howard would just smile. I remember one important management conference where he introduced Stringer on the dais by saying something like: "And, of course, tonight I brought along my wine steward, Howard Stringer." It almost seemed like when the boss is not really sure of what he's doing, the one thing he is sure of is to let the guy underneath him know who is boss.

I just kept a simple view of it all. Do what you know how to do. Try to stay out of the line of fire. And if direction is coming down from the top, do what you are told. I figured the guy who keeps hitting the ball out of the park never gets taken out of the game. Right? And with everything we had in development, I knew there were lots of home runs coming.

Aside from the normal business phone calls I got from Emilio Estefan, he kept calling me to tell me that there was a woman he and Gloria wanted me to meet. I was still caught

up in the Mariah fallout, and they were both always there to watch over my emotions.

"Who is she?" I asked the first time he told me.

He said, "She's a singer and an actress that Gloria and I know from Mexico. Her name is Thalia."

Thalia was a huge superstar from Mexico City also known across all of Latin America for her *telenovela* performances and as a singing sensation for all her hit records, and by that point was even the biggest star as far off as the Philippines.

"Oh, no," I told him. "I'm not going *there* again. I already did that movie."

But Emilio just kept insisting. "Look, I think you're going to like her. Just have a drink with her," he said. "That's all. Just a drink."

Gloria and Emilio were trying to convince Thalia the same way for about a year and a half. "You're like two drops of water," Emilio would tell her. "You have the same composition." But every time they mentioned my name to her, Thalia responded in pretty much the same fashion that I did to Emilio. *No, not interested. He's coming off a celebrity marriage. Divorced. Kids. Don't want any part of that.*

Thalia was in New York for a few days toward the tail end of 1998, and finally, Gloria and Emilio convinced both of us to get together for a drink. So we arranged to meet at one of my favorite restaurants, Scalinatella, which has a dining room set underground, on East Sixty-First Street. I really wasn't sure that I wanted to have a blind date, and so I had three of my Sony cronies sitting around the table with me just in case it wasn't comfortable for either Thalia or me right off the bat. Of course, if things were going well, I could ask my friends to leave.

So I was sitting at my table having a martini, and here comes Thalia, walking down the steps, in a white cashmere

coat with long, beautiful, curly brownish-blonde hair. I don't want to go Hollywood on you, but for me it was like an angel coming out of a cloud and walking down the steps. I was sitting there in a black cashmere sweater—what else?—and it was as if the darkness in the restaurant all around me was suddenly filling up with light.

I stood and reached out to her with my hand, but she leaned over and gave me a kiss on the cheek, the customary greeting in Mexico. "Please sit down," I said. "Let me take your coat." But I was almost fumbling. *Wow.* I quickly nodded for the guys to hit the road.

Thalia and I started speaking, but it wasn't really a conversation because she spoke very little English and my Spanish was barely basic. She was just finishing up acting in a movie in New York that week and had memorized lines phonetically in English without completely understanding what they meant, and she tried to comically insert those lines in what she thought were the right places in our dialogue. But, mostly, the conversation was a lot of facial expressions, hand motions, and broken phrases. We had to use every physical way of communicating that we could think of to try to make ourselves understood. It was beautiful, just beautiful. We may not have had the clearest understanding about the actual words we were hearing, but it was the most passionate, sensual, captivating, and mesmerizing conversation that I ever participated in. The distance between us was a gift from God.

Thalia said she had to go to a wrap party on the film she had just finished. It was her last night in New York.

"Okay," I said, "so when can I see you again?"

"Well, I have to do a *'novela*," she said.

"What does that mean?"

"I'll be filming in Mexico City for six to eight months."

"What? You mean I'm not going to see you for maybe eight months?"

"We'll communicate," she said. "We'll figure out a way."

At least I think that was what she said. So I dropped her off, and sat stunned in my car, thinking, *I can't believe this just happened to me.* I immediately dialed Emilio and said, "What's wrong with you? Why didn't you tell me about this woman sooner?"

"You jerk," he said. "I've been trying to tell you for a year, and you've been saying, 'I don't want to meet anybody. I don't want to meet an actress or a singer.' Whenever I told you about her, you told me, 'Shut up, forget about it!'"

"She's the greatest woman I've ever met," I said.

"I told you! I told you!"

Talk about a Latin Explosion...

That was the first week of December, and Christmas was right around the corner. So I made a quick run down the street to FAO Schwarz. I searched for a big teddy bear and sent it to her home in Mexico City. You could never go wrong with a teddy bear, right? Even if she doesn't like *you*, she's gonna like the *teddy bear.*

I sent it with a note that told her I was going to take a Christmas vacation on a yacht I had chartered, that I would be in Saint Barths with my son and daughter, and that I'd call her when I returned to New York. Within a few days, just before I left, a package arrived and I could see it was from Mexico. I got really excited. I opened it and found two gifts: a pair of sunglasses and a terry cloth robe that had my name stitched on the front and into the little loop on the back of the collar. Details, details—something I'm always aware of and take great pride in. There was also a card, and I paused over the note Thalia had written in English. It said, "These glasses are

to protect your eyes from the sun and this robe will keep you warm when you get out of the sea."

Wow! Who would ever think of saying that? Or saying it in that way? It had so much heart and soul, so much caring. Some other chick would have written: "Hey, here's some stuff to wear on the boat. Merry Christmas." But that's the Latin culture, warm and embracing. The words in that note told me a lot. It told me that Thalia's first instinct was to protect me. And how the hell did she get the monogram and my name on the loop done so quickly?

When I got back to New York, the daily phone calls started. Sometimes we'd fall asleep at the end of our eighteen-hour days while talking to each other. We took photos during our workdays and mailed them back and forth as if we were high school pen pals. The distance, and the language barrier, only intensified our feelings.

Throughout this period of time another Latin Explosion was about to erupt—the musical one. It had been building for a few years and we were working night and day on it, but it really was ignited on one special night: February 24, 1999. That was the night that Ricky Martin appeared onstage at the 41st Grammy Awards.

Ricky had been a performer ever since he was a young boy. He joined a Puerto Rican boy band back in 1984 called Menudo, which was so successful and organized at that point it had its own private plane to tour the world, and it rotated members out when they reached sixteen and their voices changed. Ricky became the group's most famous member, and after he graduated from the group he moved to Mexico City and began to act in soap operas and plays. Between his raw talent, incredible dance moves, and looks to kill, he had every ingredient to become the Latin Elvis Presley. At the height of his singing

career on his Spanish-language albums we started discussions with him about crossing over and making an album in English.

He'd been asked to put together a song for the World Cup, and with help from Desmond Child he came up with "La Copa de la Vida" for the 1998 tournament hosted by France. The song was an instant success all over the world, and the Spanish-language album it appeared on, *Vuelve*, went straight through the roof everywhere except the United States. That put Ricky's crossover potential on our radar. Everybody who'd watched the World Cup was already swooning over Ricky. We all began to envision what could happen if Ricky were correctly guided and developed to cross over into English.

There were no apparent obstacles. Ricky had been working in show business since the age of nine, and he was focused and disciplined, especially from the schooling he encountered while in Menudo. He spoke flawless English and was certainly no stranger to success. *Vuelve* sold ten million albums and was up for a Grammy. We had the idea to break him, then and there, by turning his World Cup theme into the biggest crossover event ever.

We leveraged all of our Sony muscle to get him that slot on the Grammys that year and onto the stage that night. The competition for those slots is intense, and sometimes it can even become bloody. When I think back on that night it strikes me just how much talent Sony Music had in the room. There was Lauryn Hill, who as I mentioned would take home five awards. The Dixie Chicks won two Grammys that evening, creating a tremendous spark and helping *Wide Open Spaces* sell more CDs in the year after it was released than all the other country groups combined. And, of course, Celine took home two Grammys with her hit song from *Titanic*, while her albums were honored with two more awards, as well. So we felt entitled

to ask the Grammys to showcase a guy who had never put out an album in English. It was a ballsy move, but I was certainly not shy and we knew what it would mean to Ricky's career.

Ken Ehrlich, the producer of the show, knew how great Ricky was and how great he would be for his show, but he had to get the approval of his obstinate boss, Mike Greene, who liked to say no to everybody just so he could get them to call and beg him to do it. Nice guy. And then there was the rest of the CBS television management and sponsors to contend with. The fact remained that no matter how good Ricky Martin really was, he was still virtually unknown to the American television audience.

So I picked up the phone and called CBS president Les Moonves, as I had done so many times before on behalf of people we believed in, and told him how confident I was that Ricky's performance would lift the show. Les knew that when I made those calls we would have an army behind them to back them up. He agreed. Ken Ehrlich agreed. Mike Greene capitulated. And we prevailed.

A lot of people think Ricky sang "La Vida Loca" that night. He didn't. "La Vida Loca" came out on his new English cross-over album after this show. The song he sang that night was the one that had given him international notoriety, "La Copa de la Vida." As a performance piece, it was a lot more dynamic than "La Vida Loca," and it allowed Ricky to seamlessly alternate between English and Spanish. He knew the power of it. We knew the power of it. Everybody who'd seen it in rehearsal knew the power of it. The unknown, of course, was we didn't know how strongly the public would react to it.

I was anxious and nervous until the moment Ricky started. But instantly he turned the song into an extravaganza, and a conga line of musicians beating tambourines and drums came down the aisles, making the entire audience feel like it

was in the middle of a gigantic fiesta. Ricky absolutely tore the house down. People simply could not believe what they were seeing and hearing. This had not happened on the Grammys or any music variety television show in many years.

Madonna, sitting in the first row, rushed the stage and stood there clapping, yelling and screaming like Ricky's biggest fan. And then, immediately following his performance, she raced backstage just to meet Ricky. Right on the spot I made a deal for her to sing a duet with him on his upcoming album. That made it official. The explosion had begun.

When *Time* magazine put Ricky Martin on its cover, we could suddenly make an argument that we could do the same with any one of our great Latin stars. It wasn't even an argument anymore. The Latin Explosion was already in full bloom. Within the next six months we released albums by Jennifer Lopez and Marc Anthony that sold millions of copies. The explosion was so sudden that few people really understood just how long the fuse had been burning.

Latin sounds had been in my ears and consciousness as a kid walking by the record shops and hearing the rhythms of Tito Puente coming out of apartments in the Bronx. When I was an eight-year-old trumpet player, one of my solo pieces in the band orchestrations at Iona Grammar School was a song called "Cherry Pink and Apple Blossom White," which was made famous by Perez Prado. As a guitar player at fifteen, I would slap my guitar on the neck and then play chords for that Latin touch. I was nineteen when Frank Sinatra released an entire album of Brazilian rhythms with Antonio Carlos Jobim. Songs like "Tequila" and groups like Sergio Mendes & Brasil '66 also had their moments. And before my arrival at Sony, Julio

Iglesias and Willie Nelson released a song called "To All The Girls I've Loved Before." What I was never really conscious of was how all of this was subliminally rolling around in my ears, mind, and senses, and just how much influence it would all have on my future. But the stars were aligned.

We had the foundation and support of the most successful and powerful Latin division in the world—Sony Latin in Miami. And coincidentally, one of the first people I met in 1988 when I entered the company was the man who was doing a brilliant job heading that division, Frank Welzer. After that meeting I embraced that division without the slightest idea that the culture would be such a big part of my life.

We continued to keep Julio Iglesias as a major cornerstone artist after I arrived. Then came Gloria mixing Afro-Cuban rhythms and sounds, and singing amazing lyrics in English to pave the way for all Latinos to cross over. We came up with special packages and CDs for the Latin market, and we would have our biggest superstars like Mariah and Celine record one or two songs in Spanish so we could market and develop them across Latin America and Spain, and allow those audiences to enjoy them in their native language. The crossover was now going both ways, establishing Latino stars in English and having some of our great superstars now singing in Spanish. And it resulted in the sales of millions and millions of albums.

We also forged major corporate alliances around the world, especially one with Pepsi, which in tandem with Sony worked to market music for the World Cup. Obviously this worked out great for Pepsi, which is served in Latino households much more than Coke. People inside our company got motivated and were constantly coming up with new ideas, always pushing, pushing, pushing, for techniques that were outside the box. Our vice president of promotion at the Columbia label, Jerry Blair, sparked

many of the strategies early on for Ricky Martin. So many years of effort and a lit fuse seemed to converge all at once.

That slow fuse led to the Latin Explosion, but what I didn't know was that I would eventually find my soul mate in a woman from Mexico.

The fuse to Thalia didn't burn quite as long and slowly, even though the distance between us gave it a drawn-out feeling. Thalia occasionally got weekends off while shooting her *telenovela, Rosalinda,* and she would come to Miami where we would spend a couple of glorious days together. It was a beautiful way to fall in love and build a bond that would last forever.

Thalia was twenty-eight at the time. Her mother and all four of her sisters married men who were a generation older. And she had grown up in an area of Mexico City that had a feel of the Bronx. Emilio was absolutely right. There were so many similarities.

After months of eighteen-hour workdays on the set, Thalia was at the point of exhaustion, and as soon as the *telenovela* was done she came to visit me in New York for "a couple of weeks." I was putting the finishing touches on the renovation of an old barn in Sag Harbor that Billy Joel had taken me to and told me would make an incredible house. I went to JFK Airport to pick up Thalia and saw her enter customs with nine suitcases and her dog.

The guy who cleared her through customs whispered to me, "Listen, my wife is from out of the country. She showed up one day like this and never went back home." He said it to me as if he was trying to warn me, but it was music to my ears. I had a big smile on my face, because that was exactly what I was hoping for.

The barn became a beautiful home and it was quite special. It overlooked the harbor and the marina and reminded

me a little of south France, especially at sunrise and sunset when the light hit the water.

Thalia walked through the front door, put her suitcases down, and took a deep breath. All of a sudden she had this relaxed look on her face that said: *I feel like I'm home.* She had worked so hard for so many years, starting at the age of seven. When I say she was on the brink of exhaustion, I'm not kidding—her doctor in Mexico had ordered her to take off one whole year.

On the third day after she arrived I was up before 5 a.m. I went out to a sitting room in my office at the top of the house and had a spectacular 360-degree view of the harbor. Shortly after, Thalia came in to find me staring out at the sunrise. There was a stunning purple light that I'd never seen on any color palette. What a gift. We couldn't believe it. We felt like it had been made just for us. The greatest painter in the world would never have been able to capture this scene on canvas. In that moment, I was no longer moving at a thousand miles an hour. I felt very still and calm, and we held each other closely in that stillness.

I really began to feel that this was where God intended me to be—together with her. Our relationship just kept getting closer and closer, and we began to think and talk more seriously about our future.

One day in the middle of work I decided to skip lunch to meet a guy who was not bringing me a new recording artist but instead bringing me beautiful diamond engagement rings that I would consider for Thalia. I found the exact one that I thought she'd love. But I knew I had to wait for just the right time to give it to her. In fact, it took me three months to sense that the right moment had arrived.

The moment came one weekend when we were visiting Miami and staying in Emilio and Gloria's guesthouse on Star

Island. Thalia's mother and sister had also flown in. We were getting ready to go out to dinner with family and friends.

There was a beautiful Miami sunset over the water, so Thalia and I walked to the dock to watch it. We kissed, and then Thalia said, "This is such a beautiful moment." Of course, I tried to stay focused, but my mind was on fast-forward, screaming: *This is it! This is it!*

"Wait here," I said. "Wait here."

"What's wrong?" she asked. She looked at me in dismay, but I was already gone.

I ran inside at full speed, up the steps to our room, pulled the black ring box from its hiding place, ran back down the stairs, and sprinted back outside to the dock. I was out of breath when I arrived. I looked at her ears and touched them gently.

"You always wanted beautiful earrings," I said. "So I wanted to get you these." It worked. She had no idea what was to come.

She opened the box and saw this beautiful diamond engagement ring and started crying, hugging and screaming so loud that her mother and sister came running out of the house, and then everybody was around us, hugging and yelling and screaming.

Another fiesta had begun.

For the first time in my life I began to think everything was coming together. My personal life could not have been better at home, and Sony Music was delivering record profits each year. But there were smoke signals and warning signs on the horizon.

Allen Grubman, my daily dose of reality, sent up the first red flag. Allen had gotten a call from Sir Howard Stringer, and he repeated exactly what Sir Howard had told him. "You know, I went to the Grammys this weekend and I didn't feel

like I was taken care of the right way by the music company," Stringer complained to him. "I went to the after party and I didn't feel like I was part of it."

"Allen," I said, "what are you talking about? He was there. We got him the right seats. What's the problem?"

What Stringer was really trying to say was he wanted even better seats at the event, and he wanted to be sitting next to me at the after party while I was conversing with the artists.

Looking back on it, it certainly would've been easy to make him feel more comfortable. So I have to take full responsibility for that. But after Idei had forced Mickey to leave, all of us at Sony Music had an uneasy feeling about getting too close to the corporate people. And so it seemed wiser to keep Stringer at a cordial distance. Sony's film company, on the other hand, was trying to recover from its devastating debacle, and Stringer's newly appointed executives in Hollywood went out of their way to roll out the red carpet for their new boss. So Sir Howard had a very stark comparison.

I also began to feel that when I went out of my way to make Sir Howard feel comfortable my hospitality turned against me. I remember inviting him to my home in Westchester for a Christmas party one year along with a lot of friends, some of the biggest stars on the label and some very well-known actors. Mind you, it was a Christmas party, but this was work for me. Part of my job was continuing to nurture the relationships we had with the artists and the entertainment community. It was part of how I did business day-to-day, part of how I got things done. The following Monday morning, Grubman got a call from Sir Howard, who was saying, "Wow, Allen, Tommy's *really* living it up."

Of course, it was not meant to be a compliment. Underneath the comment was a reference to many disparities. Perhaps it was uncomfortable for him to see me so close to all the celebrities

in my house, when he was supposed to be the corporate king. And, of course, with him being new to the job, there was a disparity in our compensations. I was compensated and incentivized based on the company's sales and results, and Sony Music had grown from one billion dollars in 1988 to almost seven billion in 1997. When Celine Dion alone sold a billion dollars' worth of music, everybody on the team who was responsible for the planning and marketing was justifiably rewarded. That was the way Norio Ohga managed, and that was the way Steve Ross took care of Ahmet, Mo, and Geffen.

But Stringer was certainly no Steve Ross, nor was he a visionary like Norio Ohga. I believe my success, the success of Sony Music, and my personal lifestyle created tremendous resentment. What's more, I believe that even if I were serving him high tea and scones at 4 p.m. in his office, he still would have had that resentment. But make no mistake about it, I take full responsibility for this. I certainly could have and should have done a much better job of puckering up. But my Sony team was even more wary of corporate intervention than I was. So we politely tried to protect our turf. After all, we were pouring billions of dollars of profits into the corporate coffers of Sony Tokyo. And I had taken Sony Music into the number one spot worldwide. That should count for something, right?

Separately, sparks were starting on the Internet that would eventually lead to a bonfire, and warnings to all of us at Sony and the industry were coming from Al Smith, who was the director of our new technologies group and had been instrumental in the construction and operation of Sony Studios. Smith had been alongside me from the early years at Champion, and I had complete faith in him—although his message was hard to fathom.

Al had a son who, at the time, was a student at Carnegie Mellon, and so he was not only on the cutting edge of technol-

ogy, but he knew how kids were using it. He'd tell me that students were downloading graphics and sharing them with each other from one college to the next. And that wasn't all—they were sharing their music, too.

This was well before the file-sharing site Napster became popular. While jumping around bulletin boards at the corners of the Web, Al noticed a connection between porn—which has traditionally been at the cutting edge of technology—and music. A lot of times sites advertising porn would offer music. And, oddly, some sites advertising free music were offering porn. In either case, all anyone had to do was simply download the music. The bottom line was that there was no bottom line in this for us. Music was being offered for free over the Internet, and Smith immediately sensed where this could lead. It seemed like he was overreacting, though. He would go so far as to tell me that we were in the buggy-whip business and could soon be obsolete. This was hard for anyone in the entire music industry to comprehend. I was looking at sales numbers skyrocketing, and at the same time he's telling me the company is soon going to be obsolete?

All of us, the entire industry, viewed this as a mosquito at first, just a mosquito buzzing around our ears. We all thought it was just another form of counterfeiting. There was another pirate on deck. Okay, I said, let's figure out a way to get rid of the pirate. But it's hard to shoot an invisible pirate. We might as well have been aiming at a ghost.

None of us could believe that at the end of the day, consumers wouldn't want to buy music the way they had for the last fifty years. The experience of pulling a freshly pressed piece of vinyl out of a record jacket—which transitioned to looking at a beautiful jewel box and CD—and browsing in the record stores was culturally part of the whole experience.

Sony Music was enjoying some of its most successful sales when a revolutionary peer-to-peer file-sharing site appeared next. As soon as Al Smith saw Napster, he knew it wasn't a mosquito buzzing around anybody's ear anymore. He saw it as an elephant about to put its foot on our chest. We all picked our heads up and started to pay attention.

Napster was founded by Shawn Fanning, John Fanning, and Sean Parker. When Parker was seven, his father had taught him how to program an Atari. As a teenager, he hacked into a Fortune 500 company and attracted the attention of the FBI. Now, he had helped create a system that basically offered an ever-expanding library of songs that anybody could easily download. Of course, it was not legal. It was done without paying any royalties to the artists or the composers. But the people doing the downloading didn't seem to care. They were just sitting in their rooms. Napster was still in its infancy, and it didn't make much of a dent in our numbers at first. So we took what seemed like the right approach. We instructed Al Smith and his new technologies group to deal with it, and to reach out to all the other record companies in the industry to see if there were some joint solutions that could be helpful and productive. We also asked him to check with Sony Tokyo and their R & D division to see if we could create a new technology that protected our product and could become a source of income for us.

This, we would come to find out, was much easier said than done.

From early on, Thalia's childhood dream was to be married in Saint Patrick's Cathedral. So when the discussion of our wedding came up, she told me that was where she had hoped to one day be wed.

I just looked into her eyes and said, "Okay, no problem."

I wasn't sure how to infiltrate the archdiocese, so I enlisted the help of two friends to make some introductions. One was New York City Police Commissioner Howard Safir, and the other was John O'Neill, who was in charge of the FBI's New York office and one of its top experts in counterterrorism. Both of them had an excellent relationship with the cardinal, and they set up a meeting for me with Msgr. Anthony Dalla Villa, another Italian from 187th Street in the Bronx. As soon as I sat down with the monsignor I felt like I was back home again. What an amazing and beautiful man. I told him how I'd once been an altar boy, and he loved it. Not that there was any kind of halo over my head, but he was happy that I wanted to come back to the church. I discussed with him my strong feelings for Thalia, and how she had left her home and family in Mexico City to be married and start a family with me, and I told him I wanted to be able to give her the wedding of her dreams at Saint Patrick's.

Dalla Villa looked me in the eye and said: "Tommy, we've got one very, very, very, very big problem. You've already been married in a Jewish ceremony and your second wedding was at an Episcopal church. Under Catholic law, we can't marry you, and you can't be married here, unless your previous two marriages are annulled."

"Okay," I said, "no problem. So let's get them annulled."

Which led to the famous David Geffen wisecrack: "Every time Tommy gets married, he converts."

Now I had come full circle. There were several clandestine meetings and a couple of ceremonies at the church—you know how mysterious the Catholic Church is. And then a message was sent to me that it would be appropriate to make a serious contribution. So I took care of all the business at hand, and there I was, back where I'd started.

Thalia and I began to make all of our wedding plans and focus on logistics. The administration office at Saint Patrick's Cathedral had only one date available before the end of the year 2000—and that was December 2. My mind started reeling. Oh, boy, I thought, Christmastime, on a Saturday night, lots of crazy traffic but also freezing cold. But my brain quickly switched to the thought of how festive and beautiful it would be, taking place almost directly across the street from the majestic Christmas tree at Rockefeller Center. It would almost feel like it had been lit that night for us. So, with Thalia's approval, I took the date with the church, and we began searching for the ultimate location for our reception. There was a beautiful building that was an old bank downtown, and it was just about to open. Back then it was called the Regent Wall Street. We took a tour, and we both felt that it was very, very special. Done. And then I knew I had to pull another rabbit out of my hat when it came to the entertainment.

We couldn't have just another lame wedding band, right? So I made a call to one of Thalia's favorite artists, and my longtime friend, Donna Summer.

"Donna," I said, "Thalia loves you. She loves every one of your songs. You're the only person I would ask to do this because you're the only person I know who can turn this reception into a party. You gotta do me this favor. Would you please come and sing at my wedding?"

Of course, I offered to pay her, but before I could get those words out of my mouth, Donna stopped me and said, "This will be my pleasure, and it'll be my gift to you and Thalia." I kept it a secret. Just as Thalia kept her wedding gown a secret from me. She worked for months on it with the famous Latin designer Mitzi, and I was not allowed to know anything about it until the moment she walked down the aisle.

The night before our wedding, I went to visit Thalia in her suite at the Mark Hotel. I was so nervous. I wanted everything to be perfect. As I anxiously began talking about the day to come, Thalia grabbed my hand and said, "Stop. Why don't we pray? It will be good for us."

So we knelt down on the bedroom floor and held hands, and there was so much intensity and clarity in that moment that tears filled my eyes, and hers, too. My freight-train brain finally stopped. Cold. That room was filled with the understanding of everything that I had to be grateful for with this beautiful woman who was holding my hand. Together we simply asked for God's blessing as we were about to begin our new journey together. There were no guests, no custom-made outfits, no musicians, no worries about traffic in front of the cathedral, no concerns about the press and how everything would read; it was just a very pure moment in which the two of us asked a greater power to help us find our way together for the rest of our lives. To this day, Thalia will tell you that was the moment when she felt that we were married.

Everything else was icing on the cake.

Sadly, my parents were getting on in years, and they had moved into an assisted-living facility. Getting them out of their living quarters in the facility and to dinner was a stressful event in itself, and it most certainly would have been overwhelmingly difficult to get them to Saint Patrick's, and then to the reception. Finally, finally, I had gotten it right. And now, the two people whom I loved more than anyone and had raised me so wonderfully could not get to the event. The good news was they had met Thalia quite a few times, and I could see in their expressions how happy they were for me. And my two children, Michael and Sarah, filled in for my parents and were at my side as I walked into the church that day.

It's usually the parent who gives the children as many chances as they need in life to find the right path. But now I was asking my children for yet another chance. They'd been so hurt and bruised by my divorce with their mother, and negatively impacted by my marriage to Mariah. I'll carry that pain with me for the rest of my life. But they, too, had gotten a chance to spend time with Thalia and to see how caring, warm, and welcoming she was. Thalia loved family, and they were my family, so she loved them. I will never be able to describe how proud and happy I was when Michael and Sarah accompanied me into that church that day.

Maybe it was because they were with me, but I felt very comfortable from the moment I came through the doors. I was completely relaxed in the grandiosity of Saint Patrick's Cathedral. Perhaps it was also because everything was really right this time. I even had a momentary chuckle when I got word that one of our guests, Ozzy Osbourne, had been freaking out because he didn't have a suit for the wedding.

He was in his suite at the Plaza with his wife, Sharon, who kept assuring him that she'd ordered his suit and it would be delivered soon. But twenty minutes before they were supposed to leave for the ceremony it still had not arrived.

Ozzy screamed at Sharon: "Where is my suit? I need my bloody suit! I can't go to this wedding in my banana hammock."

Soon afterward, there was a knock on the door. A delivery guy stood in the doorway with a big box. When Ozzy opened it, he found three suits.

"Sharon," Ozzy called out, "how many women is Tommy marrying today?"

As I walked down the aisle, I spotted Ozzy seated near the aisle and reached out to touch the material on his elbow.

"Hey, Ozzy," I said. "Nice suit." Funny, the things you remember.

I got to the altar. Emilio was standing there with a big smile on his face. He was the Cupid and the matchmaker, so of course he was entitled. My best man.

Then the organ started playing, and I began to get very nervous. I looked down. I didn't want to look up at anyone. When I finally looked up, what I saw was better than any movie I could ever imagine. All the way at the back of the church was Thalia, as beautiful and radiant as I'd ever seen her, walking down the aisle in her gown with a fifty-foot train. As she approached the end of her walk, her mother joined her, raised her veil, and kissed her before passing her on to me.

I was pulsing. I held Thalia's arm, and we walked up to the altar together. But I almost had to pull her because her dress must've weighed nearly half as much as she did. I'll never forget how perfect and articulate Thalia's English was as she repeated Monsignor Dalla Villa's words to me. It was as if that oath was pouring out of her heart and soul.

The ceremony was everything we wanted. We walked back down the aisle, smiling at all of our guests and family, finally reaching the two gigantic doors that opened to the street. Just then, a gust hit us, and Thalia's veil was blowing in the wind. There were ten thousand of Thalia's fans standing on Fifth Avenue—the entire street had been shut down—and they all screamed at once when she appeared, and then we kissed.

We got through the crowd and paparazzi and into our car, and people followed us all the way downtown. Finally, we arrived at the Regent Wall Street, where I had another surprise waiting. After we relaxed for a half hour and were about to walk into the reception, a large mariachi band in full regalia played the traditional Mexican music when the bride

and groom enter the room. I wanted to make sure that Thalia knew that although she was leaving her home, her family, and her culture, I wanted in every way to be part of what she was and have her feel comfortable in her new home, as well.

When the mariachis finished, we sat down at our table and the festivities began. The food couldn't have been better, and the band started playing. About an hour into the event, the bandleader stopped and said, "Thalia, tonight your husband wanted to give you a very special gift." He didn't say anything more. The band hit the downbeat and the music began. Out onto the stage walked Donna Summer.

The whole room went crazy when Donna began singing "MacArthur Park." Every single guest in that room—every single one—stood up and headed to the dance floor. It was surreal to see so many artists that I had worked alongside, and whom we all associate with standing out front onstage. I mean, c'mon, Bruce and Michael in the middle of a crowded dance floor? But that tells you how deeply Donna's music was hooked into everyone.

At one point, Marc Anthony, Gloria, and Thalia went up to sing backgrounds for Donna. And then Emilio, who created the Miami Sound Machine and was also its percussion player, pulled me with him as he jumped onstage. We had the time of our lives. The evening became one gigantic party.

Finally, when the moment was right, I stepped up to do something that I had secretly arranged with the band. I picked up the microphone, looked into my bride's eyes, and sang one of my all-time favorite Sinatra songs: "I've Got You Under My Skin." I did my best version of Frank and Count Basie at the Sands. And for that moment, I was the singer I had always wanted to be.

VOICES FROM THE LATIN EXPLOSION

JENNIFER LOPEZ

When I went to Tommy's office for the first time, I was nervous. He sat me down and said: "What do you want?"

I was speechless.

"What do you want to do with your career?" he said.

I didn't know what to say, so I said: "I want an A-list deal."

Tommy said: "Okay, you got it. But I want to sign you right now."

I said: "Wait a minute. I don't have my manager here."

He said: "Let's call him. Get him on the phone. We're making the deal right now."

Tommy always knew what to do. That kind of record company executive doesn't exist anymore.

RODNEY JERKINS

Producer

Tommy said: "Listen, I got an artist I want you to work with. She's a movie star. Her name is Jennifer Lopez."

This was the first deal that Tommy and I did together.

At that time, Jennifer Lopez had no music credibility outside of doing the movie *Selena*.

I had other people in my ear telling me, "Don't work with Jennifer Lopez, because she's not a singer."

Tommy said: "If you deliver the song, I'm telling you, it will be a smash hit."

I had this great idea for a song and I brought the track into Tommy's office, confident that I had something special. Tommy listened to it and said: "What if the melody went: 'Da-da-da-da-da-da, da-da-da-da-da...'"

That blew me away, because that's really A&R to me, creative A&R, which we're missing now in this generation of music men. We're missing the guys that really have those ears. Tommy understood melody, and he understood where a song should go. He did the melody.

I pulled out my Dictaphone and said, "Do it again, Tommy!" And he sang that melody and I went right back to the studio and it became "If You Had My Love." That song was Number One for five weeks. Millions of albums sold.

JENNIFER LOPEZ

All these amazing artists with such great catalogs, it all has to do with Tommy.

If one of my records was not performing well in a certain area, Tommy would go to that city and make sure it got heard. My second album with Tommy was a huge success. I said, "Where do we go from here?"

I'll never forget his answer. He said, "There are no limits—except the ones you create."

Years later, when he left Sony, I felt orphaned.

MARC ANTHONY

I remember one night I was in the Sony studio recording. It was around one or two in the morning and I was just leaving. I met Tommy on his way in. He was rolling up his sleeves. I said: "Tommy, what are you doing?"

He said: "I'm going to mix your record."

I said: "But it's two o'clock in the morning."

When you see the general doing it himself, you have to step up.

SHAKIRA

It is very rare to find people who really understand music, who can see beyond prejudices, and who can see the dreams that are boiling inside someone, the way he saw the dreams inside me.

You can imagine how hard it is for someone like me, coming from Barranquilla. There were many battles. So when I got to Tommy Mottola's office, my career in the Spanish world had already arrived at a certain point. I was ready to take the next step. I had high hopes. But I spoke very poor English.

I had a feeling that I could learn how to write songs in English. Finding Tommy was an injection of optimism.

I started to think, *Hey, I can do this because he's got faith in me.* And sometimes that's all it takes. You just need a person who deposits the amount of faith that you need to really take off with your dreams.

THALIA

When we met, both of our hearts had Band-Aids on them.

In my case, it was always kind of difficult. I had been performing for so many years. People who wanted to take me out were seeing me as the character they saw on television, the person that they thought I was. I never knew if they wanted to be with me or just wanted to be in a photograph with me. And there was this whole matter of impressing me. The whole restaurant would be closed with a table just for me. One time, a guy tried to send me a Rolls-Royce with the keys. They weren't seeing the real me.

And from a distance, a lot of people don't see the real Tommy. When people meet him they expect to meet this character—like this strong bull or something. But once you meet him, you see that he's a very friendly guy, very happy, with funny stories. He has very strong points of view, yet he hears what other people have to say. You come to understand: behind that strong persona is a very sensitive person. When he commits to something, to a friendship, to a love, it's from his core.

So when we met, it was two hurt souls that just needed the authentic in this crazy world of show business. I'd felt rushed my whole life. If it was not to a soap opera, it was to a tour, or a promotion in Barcelona, and if it was not Barcelona it was Buenos Aires. I was ready to get out of the Ferrari of that crazy, frenetic life and take a bike ride in the country.

That was what it was like when we met. One of the blessings for us was the language barrier. The language

barrier made everything slow down for both of us. And then we got to know each other through the telephone.

I think the magic of getting to know one another through the telephone is it's not how you look or what you're wearing. It's not about putting up the best pose or what you're putting on your lips. It's just about you. I thank God for that.

We came to find that we had so many similarities. I was born eleven years behind my sisters. Almost the same for Tommy. The neighborhood where I grew up in Mexico City had food stands and markets. In some ways, it was like the Bronx.

Also, Tommy and I met at a great point in our lives. Tommy was already successful. I was already successful. So we came together as equals.

But it's kind of funny, because as perfect a soul mate as he is, there are always those moments that seem unreal. I remember at the wedding, the moment of the cake, when everybody started singing: "The bride eats the cake, the bride eats the cake...."

And it really hit me: "Whoa! I married a gringo?"

EMILIO ESTEFAN

You could see it in Tommy's eyes that night. Every time you looked at him, it was the happiest moment in his life.

Kissed a Girl" • *Katy Perry*

ketful of Sunshine" • *Natasha Bedingfield*

"So What" • *Pink*

"I'm Yours" • *Jason Mraz*

"Paper Planes" • *M.I.A.*

"Hot n Cold" • *Katy Perry*

erican Boy" • *Estelle featuring Kanye West*

Money" • *Lil Wayne featuring T-Pain*

etter in Time" • *Leona Lewis*

the Ayer" • *Flo Rida featuring will.i.am*

"Say" • *John Mayer*

te That I Love You" • *Rihanna featuring Ne-Yo*

erstar" • *Lupe Fiasco featuring Matthew Santos*

"Love Story" • *Taylor Swift*

"Just Fine" • *Mary J. Blige*

All Summer Long" • *Kid Rock*

rd Comma" • *Vampire Weekend*

"Jai Ho" • *A. R. Rahman*

ken Fried" • *The Zac Brown Band*

"Low" • *Flo Rida*

19 • *Adele*

"Warwick Avenue" • *Duffy*

"Just Breathe" • *Pearl Jam*

se Somebody" • *Kings of Leon*

ngle Ladies (Put a Ring on It)" • *Beyoncé*

ook to You" • *Whitney Houston*

It Up to Me" • *Shakira featuring Lil Wayne*

's Not My Name" • *The Ting Tings*

"Tik Tok" • *Ke$ha*

ta Feeling" • *The Black Eyed Peas*

om Boom Pow" • *The Black Eyed Peas*

Hotel Room Service" • *Pitbull*

"We Made You" • *Eminem*

ght Round" • *Flo Rida featuring Ke$ha*

 You Like Me Now?" • *The Heavy*

"Blood" • *The Middle East*

"Hey, Soul Sister" • *Train*

st Dance" • *Lady Gaga featuring Colby O'Donis*

u Belong with Me" • *Taylor Swift*

"LoveGame" • *Lady Gaga*

"If I Were a Boy" • *Beyoncé*

"Fireflies" • *Owl City*

"Sweet Dreams" • *Beyoncé*

"Diva" • *Beyoncé*

"I Run to You" • *Lady Antebellum*

"Green Light" • *John Legend featuring Andre 3000*

"Already Gone" • *Kelly Clarkson*

"Pretty Wings" • *Maxwell*

"Out Last Night" • *Kenny Chesney*

The Blueprint 3 • *Jay-Z*

Wolfgang Amadeus Phoenix • *Phoenix*

Lady Antebellum • *Lady Antebellum*

Quiet Nights • *Diana Krall*

The Fame • *Lady Gaga*

Crazy Love • *Michael Bublé*

"Love the Way You Lie" • *Eminem featuring Rihanna*

"Dynamite" • *Taio Cruz*

"Teenage Dream" • *Katy Perry*

"Not Afraid" • *Eminem*

"Alejandro" • *Lady Gaga*

"Good Intentions Paving Co." • *Joanna Newsom*

"Dog Days Are Over" • *Florence and the Machine*

"Only Girl (In the World)" • *Rihanna*

"American Honey" • *Lady Antebellum*

"Need You Now" • *Lady Antebellum*

"We Are Young" • *Fun. featuring Janelle Monáe*

"I Believe" • *Nikki Yanofsky*

"California Gurls" • *Katy Perry featuring Snoop Dogg*

"Bad Romance" • *Lady Gaga*

"Break Your Heart" • *Taio Cruz featuring Ludacris*

"Nothin' On You" • *B.o.B. featuring Bruno Mars*

"I Like It" • *Enrique Iglesias featuring Pitbull*

"Just the Way You Are" • *Bruno Mars*

"Empire State of Mind" • *Jay-Z featuring Alicia Keys*

"DJ Got Us Fallin' in Love" • *Usher featuring Pitbull*

"Billionaire" • *Travie McCoy featuring Bruno Mars*

"Sexy Chick" • *David Guetta featuring Akon*

eaturing the Cataracs and Dev

"Carry Out" • *Timbaland featuring Justin Timberlake*

"Haven't Met You Yet" • *Michael Bublé*

"Club Can't Handle Me" • *Flo Rida featuring David Guetta*

"Live Like We're Dying" • *Kris Allen*

"Hard" • *Rihanna featuring Jeezy*

"Magic" • *B.o.B. featuring Rivers Cuomo*

"Paparazzi" • *Lady Gaga*

"Forever" • *Drake featuring Kanye West, Lil Wayne, and Eminem*

"Stuck Like Glue" • *Sugarland*

"The Cave" • *Mumford & Sons*

Doo-Wops & Hooligans • *Bruno Mars*

The Suburbs • *Arcade Fire*

Contra • *Vampire Weekend*

How I Got Over • *The Roots*

The Promise • *Bruce Springsteen*

Brothers • *The Black Keys*

"Take a Bow" • *Rihanna*

"I Kissed a Girl" • *Katy Perry*

"Pocketful of Sunshine" • *Natasha Bedingfield*

"So What" • *Pink*

"I'm Yours" • *Jason Mraz*

"Paper Planes" • *M.I.A.*

"Hot n Cold" • *Katy Perry*

"American Boy" • *Estelle featuring Kanye West*

"Got Money" • *Lil Wayne featuring T-Pain*

"Better in Time" • *Leona Lewis*

"In the Ayer" • *Flo Rida featuring will.i.am*

"Say" • *John Mayer*

"Hate That I Love You" • *Rihanna featuring Ne-Yo*

"Superstar" • *Lupe Fiasco featuring Matthew Santos*

"Love Story" • *Taylor Swift*

"Just Fine" • *Mary J. Blige*

"All Summer Long" • *Kid Rock*

"Oxford Comma" • *Vampire Weekend*

"Jai Ho" • *A. R. Rahman*

"Chicken Fried" • *The Zac Brown Band*

"Low" • *Flo Rida*

19 • *Adele*

13

The Trojan Horse

Just as all the pieces of the complex puzzle of life were finally coming together for me, as I was beginning to feel grounded and right for the first time, and as the Latin Explosion reached its pinnacle, we began feeling seismic shifts underneath our feet throughout the entire music industry. It was sort of like hearing an avalanche miles and miles away, but also thinking that this would never hit any of us.

Sony Music was operating at peak performance, and everybody on the team was doing what they did best—and better than ever. It was happening in all sixty of our companies around the world. It was at the same time that we had encouraged Shakira to work on her first bilingual album, entitled *Laundry Service.* One particular song stood out for me in such a strong and powerful way. It was called "Whenever, Wherever," and it was one of the most infectious pieces of music I've ever heard. It had Latin rhythms, instrumentation and sounds from the Andes integrated with a masterfully constructed pop

melody, killer lyrics, and a vocal to die for, and it was crystal clear to me that this song was the first single that was going to propel the album into a global smash.

But Shakira felt differently. She did not think it was the first single, and by this time she had a good grasp of the English language and by no means came off as a shy little girl anymore. She began to show up at meetings with a yellow legal pad filled with fifty questions and details that she wanted addressed—which really earned my respect and admiration. But she played another song for us that she insisted was the right first single. After having seen this movie hundreds of times, I tried to explain to her that if we made a mistake and came out with the wrong first single there was a possibility that this album and its launch could get off to a very shaky start.

She continued to persist, so I called our friends at Z100, the top radio station in the country, and asked them to do me a favor. We slipped them "Whenever, Wherever" and had them spike it—just spot-play it once or twice. The next day it went on the radio and the phones rang off the hook. Shakira grudgingly smiled when she heard about the response, and consented to release the song as the first single. It went straight to the top of the charts all over the world, took the album with it, and sold 15 million copies.

Shakira's success was the cherry on top of the cake. Our Latin Explosion was in full bloom. Starting with a cornerstone like Julio Iglesias and then moving on to Gloria Estefan and the Miami Sound Machine, then to Ricky Martin, Jennifer Lopez, and Marc Anthony, and now Shakira, we helped create a movement that had never happened before. Developing artists and having them sing in their native language, then crossing them over to English and back to Spanish was a windfall of success for the company.

It was hard to imagine at this point that we would have to compete not only with the other companies in the industry but also with our consumers, who could now download for free the music that we were selling.

Music file transfers were swamping the Internet networks at colleges. Napster had 25 million users, and it wasn't like these people were passing around a couple of songs. They were sharing and downloading entire libraries.

Somebody actually wrote an op-ed in one of the major newspapers wondering why record companies didn't just do what Napster was doing.

Well, first of all, it was illegal. Napster wasn't clearing the songs or paying royalties to the artists or the record companies. It was stealing our music and allowing it to be shared for free. And second, there was no technology that actually existed for us to legally license, collect, account, and pay royalties for the record company's music. Third, there were concerns from the Justice Department about antitrust violations in the event that the record companies would band together and try to create their own infrastructure. The point is, anybody who thinks that we at the record companies just sat on our hands and did nothing about the free downloading of music is totally misinformed. We were all handcuffed.

You've got to remember, we were not selling to people individually. We distributed to huge accounts like Walmart and Tower Records. And these retailers were resistant to Internet sales, figuring that it would be a flash in the pan. I'll say it for the hundredth time: rest on your laurels for a minute in this business and you are toast. Only a few years later, the iconic Tower Records, the retailer that we teamed up with to break and develop so many stars, went bankrupt and belly-up.

It would have been so much easier if accounts like Tower

had added a digital component. But their inaction created a void. No single music company could ever deliver the wide array of content that Tower Records offered. Sony, the industry leader, had only 18 percent of the total market share, which meant that all of the music companies would need to get on the same page to sell digitally, and track and account for royalties. What we got was—and excuse me for saying it this way, but it's the most genteel way of putting it—a total clusterfuck. Every company had its own ideas and agendas to get the most out of the market. We held lots of meetings, but there was little cooperation, because so many of the competing music companies had competing parent companies and nobody had the right user-friendly technology.

For instance, Sony Tokyo wanted all of its technology to dominate the market just as it had with the CD nearly twenty years earlier. Don't forget, Sony corporate viewed itself as a hardware and manufacturing company. With the exception of Morita and Ohga, none of the Japanese brass were ever comfortable being in the entertainment business—and I mean ever. Time Warner wanted to muscle AOL into the picture in a big-time way. Microsoft was trying to figure out a way to get music into its software, while Steve Jobs had a vision of music as a portal to devices that had not yet been released but would operate as telephones, miniature jukeboxes, and bookshelves.

Microsoft reached out to Sony with a proposal for a partnership that sounded like this: *You show us your technology and we'll show you ours.* When a Sony Tokyo exec heard of this he told our New Technologies guru, Al Smith, "That's crazy! We can't do that. And we won't do that!" I guess you could say it was understandable. At the same time, the two companies were in a sales war over Xbox and PlayStation. Apple, on the other hand, needed our content. So Sony Tokyo met with

Apple. But, again, Sony Tokyo's vision of total domination shut those talks down because unless it could control proprietary technology there was absolutely no interest in an Apple partnership. You can't make this stuff up. Sony Electronics in Japan had such success with the Walkman and the CD, and it was looking to have that success with music on the Internet. It wanted to be able to have the technology behind anything we did. Just imagine what could have happened if a partnership between Sony and Apple had evolved.

Idei and his technology team had their heads in the sand. The sad truth is that if Norio Ohga had been well, functioning, and on top of his game the way he was when I first joined the company, I'm sure that he would have been motivated to join forces to create the Internet successors to the transistor radio, the cassette tape, the Walkman, and the CD. Ohga got it, and was always focused on the big picture, and he would've grasped that the Internet was all about sharing. But now he was semiretired and had relinquished nearly all of his power.

Sony ultimately created an online store in conjunction with Universal that was called Pressplay. It was criticized for not having enough content—of course, nobody had the full store the way Napster illegally did—and crazier still, even with only two companies involved in the venture we had to deal with a formal inquiry from the Department of Justice about whether this combination was creating antitrust issues. We were still making great profits, but slowly there was slippage. I knew, and we all knew, the music industry needed to be completely rethought and reconfigured. So I began to formulate a new model based on what I had seen while working with Jennifer Lopez and Celine Dion.

When Al Smith first told me about music being downloaded on the Internet, I had pointed out to him the huge

numbers that Celine's albums were selling after the movie *Titanic*.

"You may sell 60 million this year," Al said. "But next time it'll be 40 million. The time after that it will be 20. Then 5…"

Al was right. We all assumed that the fan wanted the quality recording. It didn't matter if you had these lesser-quality bootlegs out there, because a serious fan would want the better quality recording.

Even when Napster hit and Internet piracy started, those of us from a different generation were thinking, *Oh, well that's okay. It's not really going to impact sales because kids are going to want to hold the CD booklet. They're going to want the better version of the recording.* We thought that they were going to want what we wanted when we were kids. Well, guess what? It turned out they didn't care.

These kids were happy to listen to a crappy MP3 version for free rather than buying it. Once downloading started, it became a part of the culture. It was the start of generations growing up to believe that music should be free, and not believing in the value of intellectual property. It was really a whole cultural revolution, because it was not only the ease with which you could obtain the music and share it with your friends, but also the belief that you shouldn't have to pay for it.

Even though the sales numbers were shrinking because of free downloads, that didn't mean there was any less love or demand for Celine's music. This became quite apparent when we teamed up with her husband and manager, René Angélil, to create a breakthrough for Celine in Las Vegas. Celine was going to appear for a five-year run at Caesars Palace, at a theater the hotel was renovating just for her. We helped arrange

new alliances with Chrysler, and I got the company to commit to being a $10 million sponsorship partner. I also worked along with René to bring in funding from billionaire entrepreneur Phil Anschutz. René worked tirelessly to get the deal done, and it was a tremendous success.

Even though the geniuses behind Cirque du Soleil helped create the theatrical spectacle, there were people in the industry who questioned how all this would turn out. Flash-forward: Celine sold out every single night for five consecutive years.

The retail store placed directly next door to the theater to sell Celine's memorabilia and merchandise turned out record numbers. It became a huge windfall for Caesars, a magnet and a destination, drawing guests into the casino, and it was a win-win for all of us, and mostly for Celine and René, who shared in the revenue of the whole entity.

Watching what was happening all around us, I began to have many discussions with my senior execs about turning Sony Music into a total entertainment company. The idea was to sign artists and develop them and their intellectual property, and then form a management team inside our own company. This way our company could form alliances with venues all over the world (exactly like the one hosting Celine in Las Vegas), manage and book the talent, sell the tickets, and manufacture and sell the merchandise. We could also have extended agreements with those artists to own and share in all of their ancillary revenues, as we were the ones funding and financing their development and success, anyway.

Let me give you an example of what I'm talking about. We signed Jennifer Lopez and spent millions of dollars on marketing and developing her. She sold millions of albums and evolved. After her success had peaked in record sales and was on the decline, J.Lo became a billion-dollar brand.

Fragrances. Clothing. Cosmetics. Hair care. You name it. This new concept would mean we'd have a share in all of this, and our newly forged alliances with all the venues would turn us into what Live Nation is now, only we would have had it even better, because every artist that the company developed would be an investment and annuity in the company's future.

Managing music and musicians like this would have been a radical concept—but one so familiar to me. Don't forget my roots coming up in the business were tied to exactly what I'm talking about here. It would not have compromised our day-to-day core business whatsoever. It would have been meant to be an adjunct, a parallel business to enhance what we were already doing, and we had plenty of experience going down this road. For instance, one of the first acquisitions we made when I arrived at Sony was a deal with Pace Entertainment to buy amphitheaters. That was our entry into owning venues, and a very successful one. Then we acquired Signatures, and expanded it into a merchandising company that sold products at concerts and retail outlets. This was prospering, as well. The idea of corporate sponsorship was so familiar to me from my past that it was a natural. And we knew that we easily could have attracted outside investors, so this could all be done off the balance sheet with no capital investment to hit our bottom line.

If only I could've looked into Norio Ohga's eyes and explained the concept to him, surely we would've gotten the nod. But I was now proposing this idea to Sir Howard and his Tokyo boss, *BusinessWeek*'s worst manager of the year. Enough said.

Meanwhile, back at the ranch, Michael Jackson was preparing his first major album in six years since *Dangerous*. Michael

would generally write and look at 120 songs before he edited them and selected the songs that would end up on his new album. But recording costs on *Invincible* were beginning to spiral out of control.

One weekend while Thalia and I were in Miami, Michael asked me to come to see him. He was doing some recording at the Hit Factory in Miami. This studio had five or six recording rooms, and Michael had booked every single one of them around the clock.

Thalia and I arrived at the studio and went inside to find Michael. But the studio was empty. Nobody. No producers. No engineers. Nothing. It was like a scene out of *The Shining*. Normally, there are people working in every one of those rooms that were costing around five thousand dollars per day. One of the studio managers came walking down the hall. "Where's Michael?" I asked him. He pointed back to the parking lot, and out in the lot I saw a remote recording truck, which is an actual studio built inside the truck. So Thalia and I walked out to the parking lot and knocked on the door. Michael was sitting very quietly, all alone, inside.

I couldn't believe that he was sitting in a remote truck outside an empty recording studio that we were paying for, while there must have been six more studios inside that he had booked and that we were paying for simultaneously. As Thalia and I stepped through the darkness, there was a blue light, just enough to see Michael.

"Hi, Michael," I said. "How come you're not in the studio?"

"I like it here," Michael said. "It's quiet. It's peaceful. It's private, and I can think."

The only thing going on in my mind right then was that we had already exceeded costs of $30 million on this album and I hadn't even heard one single recording yet.

Michael turned to me. "This is going to be a great album," he said. "We're going to sell more than a hundred million. This is gonna be the biggest album of all time."

I know that was how he justified all of this in his own mind. To him, it didn't matter how much he spent—or borrowed—to create his art. He thought he would make it back as soon as the album was released and became a megahit. And all of his handlers—and I mean all of them, every single one, allowed this to happen. No one said no. Ever. You only said yes to Michael Jackson or else you were history.

Michael was so welcoming that day, and he treated Thalia and me as special guests. Thalia told him a story about when she was a young teenage girl, back in the days when she was Mexico's next rising star, how she had gotten up onstage at one of his concerts and danced with him. Michael remembered. For some reason, the image of Thalia as a young girl opened the door to Michael telling her a story about his childhood, and how hard it was for him, and what he had to endure at the hands of his father through the daily rehearsals. I'm not going to go into any of the details that he told us, but they would make any parent or child shiver. My point is, you would never mention details like those to anyone you saw as an enemy or the devil. It was so sad to hear arguably the biggest star in entertainment sitting in the back of a dimly lit recording truck telling these stories. Thalia and I almost had tears in our eyes. You wanted to just put your arms around Michael and hug him. There never was any question in my mind, then or now, that all of Michael's intentions were loving and good, and that he was a kind soul. Which was why we were all in shock when eight months after *Invincible* was released, the poor sales flipped Michael into becoming another person.

We were advancing Michael tens of millions of dollars

to rent all this studio space, pay an army of producers and writers and directors to create his short films. And then on top of that he went to the banks to borrow huge amounts of money, loans that we cosigned at Sony, using half of his ownership of the Sony/ATV catalog as collateral. This put him in a very compromising and vulnerable position. *Invincible* needed to be hugely successful to wipe those debts off the ledger. Everyone in the company was shocked that he was not advised against making all these business decisions. We are still shocked to this day.

One day, the album was done. And Michael, the ultimate perfectionist, finally handed it over to us. Everyone in the company thought that it was good, but by no means Michael's best work. After years of recording and close to $40 million in the red, we were not about to ask him to go back and cut some new tracks. For all we knew, that might take another two or three years.

We were all hoping that the work was good enough to get the legions of Michael Jackson fans to rush out and buy it. Simultaneously, we helped arrange with CBS to do a television celebration of his career at Madison Square Garden. We were hoping that it would tie in as a huge promotional vehicle for *Invincible.* The concept was to film two special-event concerts. We all looked at this as a very encouraging sign. We had hoped that it would propel a concert tour that would help shore up more album sales after *Invincible* was released.

It was called the thirtieth-anniversary special because various artists came to celebrate Michael's three decades in show business. Usher, Gloria Estefan, Ray Charles, and Whitney Houston were among the artists on hand to perform Michael's music over the years. Michael's family was there to sing with him and reenact the success of the Jackson 5. Marlon

Brando and Elizabeth Taylor showed up to make speeches. Ticket prices were among the highest ever for a concert. The best seats went for $2,500 and included dinner with Michael. Within five hours of being placed on sale, the entire Garden had been sold out for both dates. I can't say for sure, but it has been reported that Michael made more than $7 million for those two performances. Seems like the right number to me. It would have been a complete success and a beautiful stepping-stone toward the release of his new album if not for one thing. The date of the second of these two concerts was September 10, 2001.

Obviously, nobody was talking about Michael Jackson on the following day.

Right after the first night of Michael's Madison Square Garden concert, Thalia and I had left for L.A. She was to perform in the Latin Grammys. We were at the Beverly Hills Hotel when the phone rang just before 6 a.m. local time on September 11. I had a bad feeling when I heard the phone ringing that early. I was told to turn on the television because an airplane had hit one of the World Trade Center towers.

I dialed my office while I was fumbling with the television remote control. My office in Manhattan was on the thirty-second floor and had a perfect view of the towers. My two assistants were talking to me, trying to describe what was going on over the phone, when I could hear them scream, "Oh, my God! Oh, my God!" Then I looked at my television screen and saw the second plane hit the other tower. And that's when we all knew that something terribly, terribly wrong was happening.

My first thought was my children: Michael and Sarah. I

knew that Sarah was going downtown that morning to the DMV. I began to feverishly make calls to them, but I couldn't reach them. I kept trying as reports came in of the plane crashing into the Pentagon and another crashing in a field in Pennsylvania. The full impact of this was beginning to set in. We were under attack. We were all in total shock and scared to death, not knowing what was next. And then, no telephone service to New York at all.

All the airports had shut down. Marc Anthony, who was staying at the same hotel with us, had a tour bus. We all packed and were moments from jumping on it to get back home, if that was our only way. Finally, when we were able to get some telephone service, I found out that both of my children were safe and uptown. Not knowing what was to come, I tried to get them out of Manhattan as soon as possible.

As soon as the flight ban was lifted, we were able to secure an airplane that enabled all of us who had come to L.A. from Sony to rush back to New York. I just wanted to go home and hug my kids.

On the plane, I had flashbacks of stories being told to me by my friend John O'Neill, who had so generously helped make the introductions for me at Saint Patrick's Cathedral. John had been a special agent for the FBI in New York in charge of counterterrorism. When we'd all be out sitting in a restaurant, after a couple of drinks, he'd go off on a tangent, and go on about a guy named Osama bin Laden—who, quite frankly, none of us had ever heard of. We'd all turn to him and say, "John, calm down, this is the United States of America. Nothing is going to happen to us."

But he would rant and continue on about how dangerous this guy really was. And the saddest and sickest thing was that when he left the FBI, he had become the director of security

for the World Trade Center. He was so happy and proud when he got that position.

I never was able to reach John on 9/11. The next year, while I was watching a documentary on PBS, I saw him, running around the burning lobby with bodies falling all around him. The sad irony is that *The Man Who Knew* died at the hands of the man he tried to warn everybody about.

Thinking about it now makes me feel nauseous. None of us on that airplane knew what to expect as we flew in, but as we were circling Manhattan we got a bird's-eye view of what had happened. There was dead silence on that airplane until we landed and long afterward.

We all knew that everything in life would be different going forward.

Walking into my office the next day, I was full of emotions. My assistant's first instinct after having witnessed this tragedy was to get up and hug me. We all hugged each other, and we all thanked God that we were safe.

Nobody who lived in New York felt comfortable. There is an uneasiness to this day that something could happen. And we were a target during that period of anthrax threats to the entertainment companies. But through any and all tragedies life always seems to go forward and that's what we did, putting on a concert at Madison Square Garden to provide relief for the families of the victims.

Business everywhere was affected by the tragedy, and we were certainly not immune as we all went back to our day-to-day jobs. In fact, it took months for any of us to begin to feel like we were in full operation again. It was a trying time,

having to restrategize, deal with lots of emotions and sensitive feelings surrounding so many people who'd been affected.

A month later, we released Michael Jackson's *Invincible* album, and the good news is that it immediately shot straight to Number One.

But it opened to mixed reviews along with lots of publicity and speculation about Michael's personal life as opposed to focusing on the music. Within a month, it was out of the Top 10.

Invincible sold only eight million copies worldwide. We were all disappointed. Michael's perception was that it was not acceptable and that we had failed him. It was certainly nowhere near the sales that we needed to recoup more than $40 million in expenses. Michael began to call Dave Glew in the middle of the night and ask us to hire independent promoters, to try to manipulate chart numbers, and to do anything to get the album back up to Number One.

Glew and I had constant conversations with Michael and his entire management and legal entourage, explaining how all the controversy surrounding his career certainly had not helped. Although the music on *Invincible* was really good, there was something missing.

When you are used to hearing "Yes, Michael, yes, Michael, yes, Michael, yes," from everybody who is around you, it must be unbearable to hear, "No, Michael, we cannot and will not put millions more into the promotion of this album." Sales had completely stalled, and that was after we had already spent a global marketing budget of more than $25 million.

Artists always react when the success they expect is not achieved. The first thing Michael did was tell his lawyers that he would not sign a new contract with us—and that

his intention was to fulfill the remaining obligations on the existing deal and then become a free agent. Then something snapped in his mind and he decided to lash out at me publicly.

I was on a weeklong vacation that summer with Thalia when I heard her yell to me to come quickly. She was on the other side of the room, watching the news.

I ran over to see Michael Jackson standing at a podium next to Al Sharpton at an organized rally to discuss racial inequality in the music business. Michael was launching an all-out attack on Sony and on me personally, calling me mean, a racist, and very devilish. Can you believe his desperation?

I didn't know whether to laugh hysterically, because it was really kind of comical, or to be violently offended and pissed off. But when it was over I sat there in shock and disbelief about what I had just seen.

So I quickly picked up the phone and called Al Sharpton and asked him what the hell all of this bullshit was about. I had worked for years with Reverend Al—he'd come to see us every three months—and guys like Russell Simmons, supporting their initiatives and projects in the community, and we had great working relationships. I was totally confused why Al would stand next to Michael while Michael said those things.

Reverend Al was profusely apologetic. "Tommy," he said, "I had no idea that he was gonna do that. This conference was supposed to be about black artists and inequality. I had no idea that Michael was going to use it as his personal soapbox. I would never have been there if I knew what was going to happen."

It all became clear to me, and clearer still when Michael got on an open bus and had it driven to Sony headquarters carrying signs of me with devil's horns on my head. Michael was trying to turn this into an escape hatch. He was singling

me out in order to get a release from Sony. But it actually back-fired on him. Did he really think he would embarrass Sony enough to walk away from approximately $50 million in debts or from our joint venture in the Beatles catalog? Michael even tried to bring Mariah into it, knowing that she had just left Sony. But quickly a spokesperson for Mariah defended me and pointed out that Mariah was very unhappy that Michael had dragged her into it. Meanwhile, Reverend Al and Russell Simmons were quoted in newspapers speaking out on my behalf, as well as Sony's.

"There are two things I know," Simmons told the *New York Post*. "Tommy Mottola is not a racist, and, in black music especially, you don't need $30 million to make an album successful. Michael Jackson's album didn't sell because of a lack of quality. If it's a hit record, it'll stick on its own."

I remained quiet at the time and took the high road, which as chairman was the road to take, because it made no sense to respond to such outrageous and ridiculous accusations. But here's the bottom line on this: we were in the business of selling music. Sony had spent more than $30 million in recording costs and another $25 million in marketing costs, and put the full force of the company in motion to promote that album. But despite all of that, people just didn't want to buy it.

VOICES

THALIA

I can remember the moment very well, because I was having breakfast and the orange juice I was drinking kind of got stuck in my throat.

Tommy and I were in Sag Harbor on a boat in the marina. It was the first day of vacation. I was sitting in front of the TV eating breakfast, and Tommy was reading the newspapers on the other side of the living room, having his coffee and making calls.

All of a sudden I see Michael Jackson on TV holding a poster of Tommy with horns on his head. So I was swallowing the juice while I was trying to call Tommy to come over fast. It was a big shock. It just didn't make any sense at all to me.

Michael had been so nice to us in the past. He had come to a Christmas party that Tommy threw at the house—it was the first Christmas that Tommy and I were together. I had just flown in from Mexico with my mother, my sister, and her children and I didn't know many of the people at the party. I only could recognize the very famous ones. At that time, I had no idea who Howard Stringer was. I was on one side of the room with my family, looking at an eight-meter Christmas tree that filled up the living room. Robert De Niro was in another corner and Michael Jackson was coming through the door.

It was a little odd when Michael came in, because he came in with his entourage, they were smiley and quiet, and they went straight to a room that was my husband's den and didn't come out. But all my nephews and nieces had seen Michael come in and they were screaming, "Oh, my God! It's Michael Jackson! Please, Tía, can we have a picture with him?"

With all of that, I went to Michael and said, "I'm so sorry, would you please take a picture with my family?"

He said, "Of course, of course." And he couldn't have been nicer.

After that Tommy and I met him in Miami and he was very intimate and open with us about his childhood, and he and I shared stories about being kids and stars so young. The stories that he told were the kind that you only tell to people you're very comfortable with.

And now I'm on a boat looking at a TV and Michael's holding up a picture of the guy I just married wearing devil's horns? It's hard to describe how I felt in that moment. I'm looking over at the most loving, caring man in the world, and I'm thinking, *First, it's Mariah saying he locked her in a gold cage. And now this! What is going on?*

Tommy immediately jumped on the phone to talk to his friends to try to understand and digest why Michael was doing this. What corner of Michael's brain did this picture come out of, and what was the reason for it? I knew Tommy was going to be on the phone for a while. So I told him: "I'm going into town to see a friend. I'm on the cell if you need me."

When I got back he had calmed down and figured out everything.

REVEREND AL SHARPTON

I'll never forget when Michael came to the National Action Network, and without warning attacked Tommy. Tommy called me right after the rally and said, "What was that all about?"

And I could understand where he was coming from, because Tommy had done more than most record company executives and company presidents in his time to push the boundaries for artists, including Michael, who were black. Tommy had been extremely progressive on these issues. And on top of that, you always knew exactly where you were with Tommy. His yes was a yes. His no was a no. He never promised me something that he didn't deliver.

I told him, "Michael feels that Sony is not being fair to him, and he feels that everyone is trying to take the catalog from him."

Tommy said, "I will answer any question you want. But I cannot make numbers and sales that are not there. His own people are not giving him the right information."

Tommy laid out the whole picture and showed me a lot of things that Michael didn't know: people on his side who were double-dipping, and people telling him things that weren't there. I told Michael, and I told Johnnie Cochran, who was representing Michael.

Tommy was genuinely hurt that Michael didn't understand that Tommy was doing everything he could do for that album based on the business and the circumstances. He genuinely wanted Michael to understand where he was with it all. It was beyond an executive being attacked in the press. He wanted Michael to know that he really cared about him.

CORY ROONEY

I remember one time, Tommy had this amazing Christmas party at his house. This was a new house that he had just built, and I'm telling you, it was the most impressive party I had ever been to in my life.

One of the reasons I say that is because every major superstar was there. You've got Robert De Niro and Julio Iglesias and Cameron Diaz and the New York City police commissioner. I can keep naming names forever. It was weird, 'cause this wasn't the Oscars. This wasn't the Grammys. This was Tommy's Christmas party at his house.

I have two crazy memories from that night that I'll never forget. In walked Michael Jackson—and the room went silent, like it was in slow motion. Because Michael wasn't big on showing up at people's parties. But, you know, at that point in Michael's life he kind of extended himself to Tommy.

The second was that Howard Stringer was at this party. I looked over at him, and he was just kind of in his own world. Here's a guy who is Tommy's boss sitting off in the corner like he was a nobody. My wife noticed Howard Stringer like that, too. And I said to her, "For some reason, something just doesn't feel right about this. I don't think that Howard Stringer's really enjoying this night."

I could feel it even then: This is not gonna be good. Somehow, some way, Howard Stringer's gonna try to get revenge.

Lotus Flower" • *Radiohead*

rton Hollow" • *The Civil Wars*

"Do I Wait" • *Ryan Adams*

arty Rock Anthem" • *LMFAO eaturing Lauren Bennett and GoonRock*

"Firework" • *Katy Perry*

" • *Katy Perry, featuring Kanye West*

ive Me Everything" • *Pitbull aturing Ne-Yo, Afrojack, and Nayer*

"Grenade" • *Bruno Mars*

k You" (aka "Forget You") • *Cee Lo Green*

oves Like Jagger" • *Maroon 5 featuring Christina Aguilera*

Can't Get Enough" • *The Black Eyed Peas*

n the Floor" • *Jennifer Lopez, featuring Pitbull*

st Friday Night (T.G.I.F.)" • *Katy Perry*

Born This Way" • *Lady Gaga*

What's My Name?" • *Rihanna featuring Drake*

"Someone Like You" • *Adele*

"Good Life" • *OneRepublic*

he Lazy Song" • *Bruno Mars*

he World Ends" • *Britney Spears*

e Show Goes On" • *Lupe Fiasco*

e Edge of Glory" • *Lady Gaga*

"We R Who We R" • *Ke$ha*

ters" • *Bad Meets Evil featuring Bruno Mars*

reo Hearts" • *Gym Class Heroes featuring Adam Levine*

Time (Dirty Bit)" • *The Black Eyed Pears*

ot 7 Foot" • *Lil Wayne featuring Cory Gunz*

ust a Kiss" • *Lady Antebellum*

o Hands" • *Waka Flocka Flame aturing Roscoe Dash and Wale*

Sexy And I Know It" • *LMFAO*

tten in the Stars" • *Tinie Tempah featuring Eric Turner*

Found Love" • *Rihanna featuring Calvin Harris*

"You and I" • *Lady Gaga*

st Thing I Never Had" • *Beyoncé*

re Them Girls At" • *David Guetta aturing Flo Rida and Nicki Minaj*

featuring Grace Potter

"Body and Soul" • *Tony Bennett and Amy Winehouse*

"Knee Deep" • *The Zac Brown Band featuring Jimmy Buffett*

21 • *Adele*

"Set Fire to the Rain" • *Adele*

"Part of Me" • *Katy Perry*

"What Makes You Beautiful" • *One Direction*

"Young, Wild and Free" • *Snoop Dogg and Wiz Khalifa featuring Bruno Mars*

"We Take Care of Our Own" • *Bruce Springsteen*

"Thinkin Bout You" • *Frank Ocean*

"I Will Wait" • *Mumford & Sons*

Area 52 • *Rodrigo y Gabriela*

Tempest • *Bob Dylan*

"Rolling in the Deep" • *Adele*

"Lotus Flower" • *Radiohead*

"Barton Hollow" • *The Civil Wars*

"Do I Wait" • *Ryan Adams*

"Party Rock Anthem" • *LMFAO featuring Lauren Bennett and GoonRock*

"Firework" • *Katy Perry*

"E.T." • *Katy Perry featuring Kanye West*

"Give Me Everything" • *Pitbull featuring Ne-Yo, Afrojack, and Nayer*

"Grenade" • *Bruno Mars*

"Fuck You" (aka "Forget You") • *Cee Lo Green*

"Moves Like Jagger" • *Maroon 5 featuring Christina Aguilera*

"Just Can't Get Enough" • *The Black Eyed Peas*

"On the Floor" • *Jennifer Lopez, featuring Pitbull*

"Last Friday Night (T.G.I.F.)" • *Katy Perry*

"Born This Way" • *Lady Gaga*

"What's My Name?" • *Rihanna featuring Drake*

"Someone Like You" • *Adele*

"Good Life" • *OneRepublic*

"The Lazy Song" • *Bruno Mars*

"Till the World Ends" • *Britney Spears*

"The Show Goes On" • *Lupe Fiasco*

"The Edge of Glory" • *Lady Gaga*

"We R Who We R" • *Ke$ha*

"Stereo Hearts" • *Gym Class Heroes featuring Adam Levine*

"The Time (Dirty Bit)" • *The Black Eyed Pears*

"6 Foot 7 Foot" • *Lil Wayne featuring Cory Gunz*

"Just a Kiss" • *Lady Antebellum*

"No Hands" • *Waka Flocka Flame featuring Roscoe Dash and Wale*

"Sexy And I Know It" • *LMFAO*

"Written in the Stars" • *Tinie Tempah featuring Eric Turner*

"We Found Love" • *Rihanna featuring Calvin Harris*

"You and I" • *Lady Gaga*

"Best Thing I Never Had" • *Beyoncé*

"Where Them Girls At" • *David Guetta featuring Flo Rida and Nicki Minaj*

"Price Tag" • *Jessie J featuring B.o.B.*

"You and Tequila" • *Kenny Chesney featuring Grace Potter*

"Body and Soul" • *Tony Bennett and Amy Winehouse*

"Knee Deep" • *The Zac Brown Band featuring Jimmy Buffett*

21 • *Adele*

"Set Fire to the Rain" • *Adele*

"Part of Me" • *Katy Perry*

"What Makes You Beautiful" • *One Direction*

"Young, Wild and Free" • *Snoop Dogg and Wiz Khalifa featuring Bruno Mars*

"We Take Care of Our Own" • *Bruce Springsteen*

"Thinkin Bout You" • *Frank Ocean*

"I Will Wait" • *Mumford & Sons*

Area 52 • *Rodrigo y Gabriela*

Tempest • *Bob Dylan*

"Rolling in the Deep" • *Adele*

"Lotus Flower" • *Radiohead*

"Barton Hollow" • *The Civil Wars*

"Do I Wait" • *Ryan Adams*

"Party Rock Anthem" • *LMFAO featuring Lauren Bennett and GoonRock*

"Firework" • *Katy Perry*

"E.T." • *Katy Perry featuring Kanye West*

"Give Me Everything" • *Pitbull featuring Ne-Yo, Afrojack, and Nayer*

14

Round 3

While we were trying to support the release of *Invinci-ble*, a much more powerful force of nature was being released and unleashed upon the public. I had gotten a delivery from Steve Jobs's office. So I opened the box, and staring at me was a new and elegant device that could play music in a digital format and that had the potential to store thousands of songs. I wanted to hold the iPod and embrace it in that moment, in the same way that we all had embraced the Walkman. But I knew this was different. When I took it out of the box I felt like I was holding kryptonite in my hands—but certainly not being Superman, I'll need a better metaphor. It was like looking at the Trojan horse.

There was no denying that it was a brilliant device with revolutionary technology. But I understood full well that it was a full-fledged attack on the entire music industry as we knew it.

I looked closer and closer at the device, and all I could

think was: why couldn't the new Sony Tokyo have had the vision to partner with Apple in the same way that Ohga had done when he was in full command and introduced the compact disc in partnership with Philips-Siemens? The new Sony Tokyo simply walked away from the discussions with Apple on the insistence that it had to be their proprietary device.

At one point after the iPod was in full bloom, Steve Jobs even toyed with the idea of buying Sony or Universal Music. When he stepped back, he very wisely looked at the broad picture. He did not need to burden himself with the acquisition of a content provider when he could get the content for almost nothing—and everybody had to give it to him. The entire music industry tried to resist at first. But in the end, everyone folded and capitulated. Everyone thought, *Better to get* something *for the content than nothing.*

There was a paradigm shift. Kids were now able to choose the singles they wanted instead of having to buy whole albums. In advertising parlance, the music industry went from a push environment to a pull environment. Kids were empowered, and their attitude was: *You can't tell me what to listen to. Here's what I'm going to choose.*

It was totally clear to all of us, after the release of the iPod, that Sony Music needed to turn on a dime and make serious changes as quickly as possible. If there was any time to transform our company into more of a total entertainment company rather than sticking to selling CDs, it was right then and there. The business plan had already been devised and drawn up.

Idei had a trip scheduled to New York. Perfect. I asked for a private meeting with him, and he arranged to meet with me. So we were one-on-one. It was one of the most important

conversations I would ever have with him, so I got up from my chair, which was across from him, and sat down beside him on the sofa. I wanted to look him directly in the eyes. I began to explain how we could evolve our company into this total entertainment unit and participate in all revenue streams from the artists. We were already spending all the money on signing them, developing them, marketing them, and making them into huge superstars. We were creating their brand. Now it was time to be their partner in the ancillary businesses that we had helped develop. As I intensely explained this to him, he listened, and he nodded his head up and down as if he was saying yes, but he wasn't saying yes. What he was saying was: *Yes, I hear you.* But looking into his eyes, I knew his nod was completely empty.

That same week, Norio Ohga had also visited New York. He still held the title of chairman even though he had relinquished all of his power to Idei. So I scheduled a meeting and went to his office to try to get some answers. I wanted to find out what was going on with the new management that he had put in place.

"Norio," I said, "the way that you allowed us and supported us to build this company is not going to work anymore. I know that, and you know that. There is a technology revolution happening all around us. Of course, we need to protect and keep our core business strong, but we've got to evolve Sony Music into a new direction—because a decline in sales is inevitable."

Ohga picked up his head, and looked at me sadly. His eyes were like a fading light.

"To be totally honest," I said, "we're all confused about our direction from the top. There is no real direction from the top."

The look on his face told me everything. Then the words came out of his mouth. "It was not the best choice," he said, "but it was the only choice I had."

In Japan, developing or picking successors from internal executives was a very important part of their culture. But it did not mean that you would always end up with the best choice or the best manager. Can you possibly imagine what incredible talent would have been available out there in the world to take the top position at Sony Corp—the way it is for most normal corporations? But those were not the cards on the table. The culture demanded that the company choose from within.

By 2002, downloading songs was already a part of pop culture. While all of this was going on, Stringer had positioned himself so close to Idei that he was awarded a new five-year contract. Talks of evolving our company had fallen upon deaf ears. And my antennae were up big-time.

Illegal downloading was already taking its toll and profits were down. The volume of digital sales was nowhere near enough to offset the decline of physical sales—and the tidal wave was coming. At that time we were making huge internal plans to redefine the company and deal with any cutbacks that were necessary worldwide. There was more and more corporate governance coming from Tokyo and now from Stringer. Idei and Stringer were now aligned. Stringer had his new contract, and Idei was no longer introducing him as his wine steward. Stringer was now emboldened, and with all these seismic changes upon us, he now had the perfect opening.

Grubman again reminded me that I wasn't managing up to Stringer properly. And, for me, a person who so acutely pays attention to details like those, it might have seemed like a critical error. All of us knew we needed to be respectful of Stringer because he was the corporate boss, but we tried our best to

keep the music company away from the dangerous wake of Sony corporate governance. It was hard to trust and respect these people who had absolutely no experience in managing an entertainment and electronics giant. They definitely were not Norio Ohga or Akio Morita.

Grubman was handling my new contract negotiations with Stringer, and those discussions went on for about six months. But early one morning, in January 2003, Allen called me. I thought he was calling for our usual 7:30 a.m. chat. But he said he was with Mel Ilberman. Odd, for them to be together at that time. Allen said they both wanted to come over and see me.

"What's going on?" I asked.

"We'll be right there," Grubman said. When he said that, I knew it was going to be either very good or very bad.

"Okay," I said, looking into their eyes when they arrived. "Give me the bad news first."

Even though I still had a year and a half to go on my current contract, Mel said Stringer had decided not to renew. The change would be effective immediately.

Allen quickly jumped in. "The good news is that Stringer has agreed to fund a new joint-venture music company for you. The funding would have an initial commitment of $60 million."

It was a lot to take in. So we talked it through for a while, as I tried to digest all of this. But I always believe in hearing news directly from the source, so I went to meet with Stringer in his office that afternoon.

"This will be great for you," Stringer said. "You will own your own company in a joint venture with us and operate independently of Sony. We will totally fund the company, and all marketing and distribution will be handled by the people you've hired and have worked with all these years."

As he was talking, my mind was clicking into fast-forward about the great possibilities that could come out of this.

That daydream was broken when Stringer then made a joke, telling me that based on the remaining time in my contract, with bonus pools and et cetera, I would now get more money than he could make if he stayed with the company for the next ten years. Great line from the Toastmaster General. But certainly not the best choice of words to someone who had given every drop of blood and sweat to build this company over the last fifteen years into the global powerhouse that it had become, developing the biggest superstars in the industry who were recognizable by their first names alone.

There was a sense of bittersweet relief as I left that meeting, but shortly after that I found out that Stringer's plan was to hire his longtime crony, Andy Lack, who was being squeezed out of NBC by Bob Wright. Andy Lack. Another news guy with absolutely no experience operating a music company.

As soon as Lack's hiring was announced, Grubman and my close associates inside the company began to warn me. "I know we're making this new deal with the company for you, but it may be foolish in the end," Grubman said. "Andy Lack will never feel comfortable in the Sony building knowing how close you are to all the executives and the artists. He would feel undermined by your relationships, and it may become impossible for you to have success."

And how right he and everyone else was. It was a wise choice to not go forward—and Lack was beginning to put the brakes on the deal anyway. Simultaneously, a constant source of support and encouragement came to me daily from my longtime competitor and good friend Doug Morris, the chairman at Universal Music. Doug had gone through the same experience of what had just happened to me when he

was at Atlantic Records, about to become chairman of the whole group of Warner music companies, when he was summoned to the corporate office to meet with the chairman and CEO, Michael Fuchs. Doug even called me that morning. He was excited, and I was excited for him. He walked into Fuchs's office feeling like it was his day to be made. Instead, Michael Fuchs fired him on the spot for *absolutely no reason*. Here was one of the greatest record executives building that company up toward becoming the next world music power, and suddenly he walks into this guy's office and just gets whacked. It's amazing what ego and fear can provoke. All of us in the entire industry were in shock. But that's how it goes sometimes. "Listen," he told me every day, "if this new deal does not take shape then you and I will finally get a chance to work together. Tommy, I will make that same deal with you at Universal."

No one was as good a friend to me as Doug was at that time—and I'll never forget that. After about a month of negotiations with Sony, I signed a new deal with Doug and Universal Music. I kept hearing my mother's favorite expression: *When one door closes, another one opens.*

It seemed like a line of demarcation had begun to be drawn at that time. iTunes became the most popular digital retailer, and enter *American Idol* as the new platform for making more impressions than radio. Now, a decade later, with five music competition shows being televised on the major networks nearly every night of the week, it's not far-fetched to say that for some people the public perception of the music industry *is American Idol.*

I can remember tuning in for the first time and loving Simon Cowell's brash, occasionally rude, and always

straightforward comments, and how well his attitude rubbed against Paula Abdul's dizzy, zany advice. He is the ultimate A&R man and usually spot-on. Watching Randy Jackson on that panel also made me very happy, since he had worked for us at Sony for eight years, and it gave me great pride to see his brilliance shine. As time passed, it seemed that everyone on that panel was in one way or another part of my life. Aerosmith's Steven Tyler was signed to our Columbia label and, of course, I had spent years developing and working with Jennifer Lopez.

The ironic thing about these music competition shows is that the roles have flipped. Now, the judges have become the stars and the talent has become fungible, almost disposable, entertainment. Of course, there were a few exceptions and breakthroughs like Carrie Underwood and Kelly Clarkson, but it's really not much different on *X Factor* or *The Voice*. I'll bet you can't name one singer who was on any of those shows the year before last. The singers are now just a momentary distraction for the audience as opposed to being compelling artists with great bodies of work, engaging album art, lyrics that could change your life, and music that inspired and motivated you to do great things. But you certainly wanted to watch to see what J.Lo was gonna wear that night, or what antics Tyler would pull on the next show. Or how Simon was going to put Britney down. These shows are built around the judges as stars and they pull it off. It's simply great TV.

This shift is now part of the reason why you hear:

"Oh, I like the sound of that song. I'm going to download it."

"Great. Who's the singer?"

"I don't know. I just like the song."

Our ever-changing culture now instantly gets the one

thing that it may want to hear by touching a screen and having the sound shoot straight into their ears. The industry was going through a whirlwind of these very changes throughout the time of my joint venture with Universal, which was called Casablanca Records. We had successes, but the digital landscape was turning the music industry into a different place. There was no clarity yet, and the only people making huge profits at this time were the people who weren't making music—Steve Jobs and Apple. And if it seemed like the industry was navigating through a sandstorm to me, I can't even imagine what it was like for Stringer and Lack, who had no idea of the terrain they were stepping into in the first place.

Apple had flipped the economics of the industry upside down. As singles began to be downloaded for 99 cents, the industry was thrown into a tailspin. Record companies accustomed to making profits of between three or four dollars on a CD were now bringing in nickels and pennies for a single. Without the usual profits, the record companies no longer had large reserves of money to devote time and manpower to nurture new talent and support the artist development process by meticulous recording and rerecording, detailed care with imaging, going the extra mile on videos, and providing rigorous backup on tour. All of which is exactly what the artist needs to have a chance to emerge as one of the world's next great superstars. And—whether it was on the first, second, or third album—would enable them to present a body of work that is so compelling that it sells millions of copies. We had the luxury of time to do this right. Success didn't have to happen on the first album. But diminishing revenues in this new environment created a *one strike and you're out* mentality, and many companies began to shy away from taking risks. The economics simply could not support it anymore. A circle of

creative destruction was under way. Artists who didn't obviously fit into a formula or format were not being signed and developed because the companies became risk averse, which only accelerated the shift to social media and other digital platforms where artists could be discovered.

Digital technology and emerging social media platforms offered amazing opportunities and freedom to artists and fans. All the barriers were knocked down. No longer would an artist have to send in a demo or knock on the record company's doors to ask for an audition. Anyone from anywhere on the globe could instantly upload his or her music, become a YouTube sensation, and have fifteen minutes of fame. But what happens after that fifteen minutes are up? Overlooked in this changing landscape was what was being lost—the invaluable experiences that an artist receives when he or she is allowed to perform in clubs, make albums, perfect their craft, and galvanize their image while trying to become the next Bruce, Billy, Bono, or Mariah.

Of course, Stringer and Lack had no experience creating iconic superstars. Within a short period of time, Lack failed miserably at trying to run Sony Music, confronting artists head-on instead of nurturing them, and having confrontations with people outside the company from Grubman to Jon Landau to Steve Jobs. All you have to do is turn to page 401 of Jobs's biography by Walter Isaacson to understand what happened when Lack and Jobs met to negotiate selling music on the iPod. "With Andy, it was mostly about his big ego," Jobs said. "He never really understood the music business, and he could never really deliver. I thought he was sometimes a dick."

Lack and Stringer then engineered and negotiated a terrible merger with BMG, allowing the execs from the German-based company to seize authority, until Sony was embarrassingly

pushed into a corner and had to purchase the other half of BMG to regain control of itself. Shortly after that, Stringer was forced to push out his handpicked man. To save face, and to avoid his crony's social embarrassment, Stringer kicked Lack upstairs.

Sadly, it was only the beginning of what was happening to the great Sony Corporation—which became a global electronics giant starting with the transistor radio back in the fifties and then kept producing state-of-the-art products over the decades—which should have, and could have, been where Apple is today, or at the very least, might have had an alliance in all of the cutting-edge music technology and devices with Apple.

Clearly Stringer and Idei had absolutely no finesse or experience like their predecessor, Norio Ohga, at making a partnership work the way Ohga did with Sony's introduction of the compact disc alongside Philips-Siemens. In Jobs's biography, Idei calls trying to work with Steve Jobs "a nightmare." And Stringer added, "Trying to get together would frankly be a waste of time."

Stringer, who never seemed to understand this revolution, succeeded Idei, and media accounts paint a sad portrait of what happened when the same parochial decisions mounted.

It had to be a huge embarrassment to the Japanese corporation that Microsoft's Xbox triumphed over Sony's PlayStation, for PlayStation had it all, even as a home entertainment device, not just as a conveyer of video games. With incredible holiday sales one year the company simply had fallen extremely short of product demand, and that opportunity to get a grip on the market slipped away. The company that invented the renowned Trinitron, the global brand leader of the television industry for so many years, handed over the entire flatscreen business to Panasonic and Samsung, and then was left in the dust. Sony Corp recently wrote off $6.4 billion in losses on Stringer's watch. These accounts, which have

appeared in every major newspaper around the globe, suggest that only a few men without foresight turned one of the greatest companies in the world into a mere shadow of what it once was. And to nobody's surprise, now Stringer, too, has been cast aside. The only one bright spot is that before Howard's demise—and only because timing was on his side—he hired my dear friend Doug Morris to run Sony Music.

Fear and panic might have gripped many in the music industry at the height of what initially felt like a sandstorm. But the sky has cleared and we can all see the astonishing advantages that technology has given the world of music. In ten years we've gone from the iPod to iTunes to Facebook to iPhone to YouTube to iPad to nine hundred channels on TV to social games on mobile devices to streaming, subscription services, digital radio, Twitter, Instagram, and Spotify. In the time it took me to drive over to a party and be handed a demo tape containing Mariah Carey's voice, I can now listen to hundreds of artists living in every inch of the world. And any manager can now tell you exactly how many followers his or her artists have on Facebook and Twitter and reach them all directly in an instant. The monetization of music is also showing signs of working out. New models like YouTube and Internet radio are bringing revenue to record companies. They are streams of income now, but as Doug Morris points out, they will merge into a river that will become the future of the music business. Most people don't realize this because they're looking at the tumbling sales of albums. But a million things are happening right now that will always take us back to the same starting point.

That is this: Greatness and great music will *always* rise to the top. Look what happens when the new paradigm works. After a friend of Adele's posted her demo on Myspace in 2006, the English singer attracted the attention of XL Recordings.

Put together Adele's incredible voice, great songs, lyrics that resonate, fantastic arrangements, horns and a great rhythm section, some savvy marketing, and guess what? There are 20 million CDs sold. Serious talents like Adele and Lady Gaga will fill venues, even stadiums, just as the void and the demand for a new teen idol will never go away, and why a really talented artist like Justin Bieber, who was discovered on YouTube, was able to step up and hit it out of the park. Anybody can put his or her music up on the Internet. But Justin Bieber's talent wasn't harnessed until he signed with Usher and had a record company putting the wind at his back.

So on reflection, I must say, it's amusing to me. It's not like the old game ended when the iPod came out and then a new game began. In fact, there really was no line of demarcation. The A & R process is still the same game for the record companies. You find a spark, whether it's on YouTube, iTunes, Instagram, or Facebook, and you fan it until it becomes a global fire. Content and great artists are still king and queen—just as they've always been, and just as they always will be. But now that the pool is open to everyone there is so much more content. In this landscape, the world more than ever needs filters like the record companies that also know how to expertly fan that precious spark once it's discovered.

The fashions will continue to evolve, just as Elton John's large glasses and feathers and the vogue spectacles created by Cher and Madonna have given way to the stunning abstract visuals conceived by Lady Gaga. The music will go in new directions, just as hip-hop has now become pop music and the DJs and electronic dance music have superstars with names that rival all of the greats. Not long ago, disco beats turned into new forms of music, and the beats coming from the current DJs will also evolve into something incredible.

Just as consumers get to pick the songs they like with the touch of a finger, I'm now blessed to be able to handpick the projects that I am working on.

All the mistakes, all the lessons learned, all the relationships and alliances formed, all the consumer behavior that I've dissected and studied over the years, have now become all of the positives in my day-to-day business life: whether it's applying those skills in private equity, where billions of dollars are at stake, and many of the deals have even greater consequences and financial rewards than the ones I did in the music industry, or in the Broadway shows we're now developing and producing, or in the launching of television shows and other new ventures, or while sitting on different boards of directors.

My business life and my personal life have come together in exactly the place that I want them to be. Like I've always said, if you're not moving forward, you're moving backward. And my family has moved forward, too. Thalia and I both had our hands on the scissors that cut the umbilical cords of our daughter, Sabrina, and our son, Matthew. And spending more time with Michael and Sarah, after living through the hurricane of the eighties and nineties, has made me realize the precious value in the moments there are for us now. I am so blessed to be with Thalia, who understands me so well, and who makes me realize every day just how grateful and appreciative I am to have gone through so many challenges to get to the ground on which I now stand.

And, yes, I'm still always looking for that next great beat, that next great song, that next great artist, that gives me chills.

Round 3...

Acknowledgments

I never thought I would write a book. I've always believed that the work I've done should speak for itself. To me, at the end of the day, the only thing that really matters is to have accomplished a goal and achieved a result.

But a good friend of mine, Dan Klores, who'd watched a lot of the work unfold during the Sony years, kept pushing me to tell the story. "You've gotta do a book," he'd say. "So much has happened. You have to document it!"

That was to be expected. Dan is a filmmaker and documentarian. He arranged some meetings with agents and writers. I met with them, but didn't go forward.

A few years passed, and then I came across a newspaper story about a guy who went into one of the last remaining music stores that was open at that time. He asked the clerk behind the counter what section the Frank Sinatra CDs would be in.

The kid behind the counter was of college age. "Frank Sinatra...Frank Sinatra..." the kid repeated, as if he were searching the back alleys of his mind. "You know, I think I've heard of that guy. I think my father used to listen to him."

That became one of the motivating factors for me to tell my story. Otherwise, I thought, the years would pass and all the work would eventually turn to vapor.

This book has allowed me to tell the story about some of the things I did right, or tried to do right, as well as my mistakes and what was going on behind closed doors when I made certain decisions.

Now that I have finished, I have to say, I feel pretty good about it. But the thing that I feel best about is that years from now my children, Sarah and Michael and Sabrina and Matthew, will be able to pass this book on to their children, and say, "This was my father. This is what he did."

For this, I owe much gratitude, because it took so many people to help me through this long process.

So I'd like to sincerely thank everyone who made this book possible, whether they're acknowledged on these pages or not, but especially:

Elvis. You lit the fuse.

Daryl Hall and John Oates. You guys started the fire. We had the ride of a lifetime, and I'll always treasure every minute of it.

Allen Grubman. Your friendship and your daily reality check have kept me on track through all the years.

Norio Ohga and Akio Morita. My Sony godfathers. You fully supported me through this journey and were the unrelenting visionaries, inventors, and world leaders in technology.

Jeb Brien. You've been through nearly every minute of the hurricane with me and have always come up with the best ideas—all the while watching my back.

Al Smith, Randy Hoffman, Brian Doyle, and the rest of my family at Champion Entertainment. You are the definition of the word *trust*.

Joanne Oriti. You've dealt with fourteen thousand people every day at Sony, not to mention my insanity, and still man-

aged to masterfully and politely handle all the details perfectly and always, always, make me look good to all.

Dave Glew. My buddy. You were always there with your steady and unrelenting positive energy to make things better, along with that yellow legal pad filled with details, and it was the details that took us to the head of the pack. I'm proud to say you're my friend.

Ann Glew. The energizer. You should've been running Sony. On top of that, you are the best event planner the world has ever known and now you are Tía Ann to my children. We love you.

Michele Anthony. You've been my right hand and sometimes my left hand, too. You put up with me night and day and helped me through every single dilemma—including trying to document this, make sense of it, shape it, and then layer in the richness of this amazing period of music. There's no way we could've stayed ahead of the pack without you.

Mel Ilberman. Hyman Roth. Yoda. You provided my college education and PhD in music "business" on a daily basis, and I learned more every time you chewed me out.

Ronny Parlato. You've been through it all with me since riding our bikes when I was two years old in the Bronx. You are in the spine of this book in the same way your spirit has been in the too many homes that we've built together.

Doug Morris. A great friend. A fierce competitor. I will never forget you calling me every single day after Sony, which finally led to us to work together after thirty years. Your friendship means everything to me.

David Vigliano. The agent. You connected the dots and now here we are. How much did I pay you?

Ben Greenberg. The editor. You were the first to dive in, never wavered in your commitment, and came through with

some incredibly creative ideas, constantly pushing me and pushing me.

Cal Fussman. The writer. Your dedication and patience guided me through a project that at times seemed overwhelming. You have masterfully helped organize my words and stories. Now you, too, will always be at home on Arthur Avenue.

Frankie Thomas. The transcriber. Your speed was essential and your readings were absolutely first rate. You'll be in my new movie.

Michael Chu. You came through with an amazing critique. Your meticulous attention to detail lifted the book in so many unexpected ways.

Chazz Palminteri. You, the ultimate storyteller, helped me tell my story.

Dan Klores. You offered just the right encouragement and incredibly astute advice on this book and in so many other situations.

Everybody who so kindly and generously gave their voices to help tell this story: Walter Afanasieff, René Angélil, Babyface, Marc Anthony, Charlie Calello, Sean Combs, August Darnell, Robert De Niro, Celine Dion, Emilio Estefan, Gloria Estefan, David Foster, Jimmy Iovine, Rodney Jerkins, Randy Jackson, Billy Joel, Jon Landau, Jennifer Lopez, Dave Marsh, Sharon Osbourne, Joe Pesci, Cory Rooney, Shakira, Al Sharpton, Steve Stoute, Harvey Weinstein, and Frank Welzer.

My teachers. Ahmet Ertegun, Mo Ostin, Clive Davis, David Geffen, Jerry Wexler, Arif Mardin, Phil Spector, Steve Ross, Jerry Moss, and Quincy Jones. You are the greats whom I watched, listened to, and learned from.

Every songwriter and producer who ever filled my head with dreams and aspirations.

And the beat goes on . . . and on . . . and on . . .

Index

Note: Album and song titles are followed by name of recording artist in parentheses.

2/13